D0940688

Alexis de Tocqueville
and American Intellectuals

American Intellectual Culture

Series Editors: Jean Bethke Elshtain, Ted V. McAllister,
and Wilfred M. McClay

When All the Gods Trembled: Darwinism, Scopes, and American Intellectuals
by Paul K. Conkin

Heterophobia: Sexual Harassment and the Future of Feminism
by Daphne Patai

Postmodernism Rightly Understood: The Return to Realism in American Thought
by Peter Augustine Lawler

A Requiem for the American Village
by Paul K. Conkin

A Pragmatist's Progress? Richard Rorty and American Intellectual History
by John Pettegrew

The Next Religious Establishment
by Eldon J. Eisenach

A World Made Safe for Differences: Cold War Intellectuals and the Politics of Identity
by Christopher Shannon

Ralph Waldo Emerson: The Making of a Democratic Intellectual
by Peter S. Field

Intellectuals and the American Presidency: Philosophers, Jesters, or Technicians?
by Tevi Troy

*American Feminism and the Birth of New Age Spirituality: Searching for the Higher Self,
1875–1915*
by Catherine Tumber

The Lost Soul of American Protestantism
by D. G. Hart

Transnational America: Cultural Pluralist Thought in the Twentieth Century
by Everett Helmut Akam

Creating the American Mind: Intellect and Politics in the Colonial Colleges
by J. David Hoeveler

Species of Origins: America's Search for a Creation Story
by Karl W. Giberson and Donald A. Yerxa

Apostle of Human Progress: Lester Frank Ward and American Political Thought, 1841–1913
by Edward C. Rafferty

Brahmin Prophet: Phillips Brooks and the Path of Liberal Protestantism
by Gillis J. Harp

Culture's Vanities: The Paradox of Cultural Diversity in a Globalized World
by David Steigerwald

Woodrow Wilson and the Roots of Modern Liberalism
by Ronald J. Pestritto

From Nature to Experience: The American Search for Cultural Authority
by Roger Lundin

The Constant Dialogue: Reinhold Niebuhr and American Intellectual Culture
by Martin Halliwell

Alexis de Tocqueville and American Intellectuals: From His Times to Ours
by Matthew Mancini

Alexis de Tocqueville and American Intellectuals

From His Times to Ours

Matthew Mancini

ROWMAN & LITTLEFIELD PUBLISHERS, INC.
Lanham • Boulder • New York • Toronto • Oxford

"The Scientific Clover Leaf": triple portrait of Lieber, Bluntschli, and Laboulaye is repro-duced in chapter 4 from the Daniel C. Gilman Papers Ms. 1, Special Collections, The Sheridan Libraries of the Johns Hopkins University. Reprinted with permission from the Johns Hopkins University.

ROWMAN & LITTLEFIELD PUBLISHERS, INC.

Published in the United States of America
by Rowman & Littlefield Publishers, Inc.
A wholly owned subsidiary of The Rowman & Littlefield Publishing Group, Inc.
4501 Forbes Boulevard, Suite 200, Lanham, Maryland 20706
www.rowmanlittlefield.com

PO Box 317
Oxford
OX2 9RU, UK

Copyright © 2006 by Rowman & Littlefield Publishers, Inc.

All rights reserved. No part of this publication may be reproduced, stored in a retrieval system, or transmitted in any form or by any means, electronic, mechanical, photocopying, recording, or otherwise, without the prior permission of the publisher.

British Library Cataloguing in Publication Information Available

Library of Congress Cataloging-in-Publication Data

Mancini, Matthew J.
   Alexis de Tocqueville and American intellectuals: from his times to ours /
Matthew Mancini.
      p.   cm. — (American intellectual culture)
   Includes bibliographical references and index.
   ISBN 0-7425-2343-8 (cloth : alk. paper)—ISBN 0-7425-2344-6 (pbk. : alk. paper)
1. United States—Intellectual life.   2. Tocqueville, Alexis de, 1805–1859—Influence.
3. Tocqueville, Alexis de, 1805–1859. De la démocratie en Amérique. English.   I. Title.
II. Series.
E169.1.M247   2006
973.5'6—dc22   2005018870

Printed in the United States of America

⊗ ™ The paper used in this publication meets the minimum requirements of American National Standard for Information Sciences—Permanence of Paper for Printed Library Materials, ANSI/NISO Z39.48–1992.

In Memoriam

ROBERT EARLE GRAHAM
Townsman of a stiller town.

But of books one can say what Machiavelli said of men, that they are confronted by Fortune with an irreducible element of opposition, described by him as chaos, fatality, necessity, and ignorance. And while men can resist Fortune with some hope of success by the exercise of Virtue, books and mere *objets de vertu*, lacking the *virtù* of men, are in themselves wholly vulnerable to loss and decay, neglect, and iconoclasm.

—Frank Kermode, *Forms of Attention*

Contents

Preface

Alexis de Tocqueville (1805–1859) was a French aristocrat, politician, diplomat, foreign minister, and author of the classics *Democracy in America* (1835, 1840) and *The Old Regime and the Revolution* (1856). Tocqueville enjoys a status matched by few political philosophers since the time of the French Revolution. His name is now routinely placed at or near the top of the select company that comprises the very greatest political thinkers of the modern era. This prestige is especially evident in the United States. The fact that, especially since the 1930s, the best work done by some of America's most talented historians, sociologists, and political scientists has been on the subject of Tocqueville constitutes in itself a significant point of contrast between European, especially French, and American intellectual history of the twentieth century. In spite of a French government-sponsored edition of the complete works, which is now fifty years in the making and still not complete, a pervasive distaste for the putative shortcomings and failures of political liberalism on the Continent, as well as the prevalence of Marxist and *marxisant* approaches to the study of society and politics, meant that—for Europeans—Tocqueville was securely lodged in the second rank of political theorists for much of the twentieth century. It is a remarkable fact that the very first French state thesis on Tocqueville, Jean-Claude Lamberti's *Tocqueville et les deux démocraties*, was not published until 1983.[1] The alteration in Tocqueville's status among European political philosophers and historians since the 1980s was therefore a dramatic event, and indeed constituted one of the most striking phenomena in European political thought at the end of the past century.

The conventional understanding of the history of Tocqueville's reception by American intellectuals is that it describes an inverted bell curve. According to this neatly geometric narrative, Tocqueville was venerated as a sage and as an inquirer of uncommon impartiality from the moment that *Democracy in America* appeared in 1835 until the beginning of the Civil War, an event that roughly coincided with his death in 1859. After that, however, interest in him fell into a precipitous decline. From the time of the Civil War until World War II Tocqueville was almost completely forgotten, his works lay unused on dusty library shelves, and in university classrooms throughout the land his name was never uttered. His fate was to have been consigned to oblivion and totally neglected by American intellectuals. As historians Lynn L. Marshall and Seymour Drescher expressed it in 1968, prior to 1938, "only an occasional seminal European political scientist or sociologist" paid any attention at all to Tocqueville's *Democracy*.[2] Then in 1938 a great work of scholarship about Tocqueville and Gustave de Beaumont's journey to the United States awakened American intellectuals from their undogmatic slumbers. This was George Wilson Pierson's *Tocqueville and Beaumont in America*, a work whose enormous length did little to deter an enthusiastic readership from traveling back in time to the age of Jackson in the company of those two brilliant and amiable French aristocrats.[3] The appearance of that celebrated book, however, was but the prelude to an even more significant publishing event, the Phillips Bradley edition of *Democracy in America*, published to universal acclaim just as World War II came to an end in Europe. After 1945, the narrative continues, Tocqueville's reputation soared into an ascent that was every bit as steep as the previous plunge had been. The esteem that Tocqueville enjoyed by both the right and left endowed him with an iconic status. It just goes to show that history is full of surprises, for, as Drescher put it at a 1994 conference, referring to the fact that Tocqueville's name had taken on an adjectival form, "In 1894, Tocqueville was hardly an adjective, much less an intellectual perspective."[4]

This book is an attempt to level out that U-curve. After years of engagement with the contemporary evidence, I have found that almost every element of the story related above is erroneous. Tocqueville was indeed not an adjective late in the nineteenth century as Drescher rightly said, but he was an intellectual perspective and a respected author who exercised a continuing influence on a broad range of American intellectuals: historians, political scientists, sociologists, hard-driving journalists, university presidents, students of industrial and labor relations, Catholic liberals, Jewish refugee intellectuals, Progressive reformers. And, by contrast, at the turn of the twenty-first century, although Tocqueville's name was ubiquitous, it was certainly debatable whether what he actually did and said was more widely known or accurately understood than it had been a century earlier. Much was written but, in fulfillment of an inexorable law of intellectual history, the publication of superb scholarship proceeded apace with the appearance of the trivial and the misinformed. The reception of Tocqueville, like that of other standard or "canonical" thinkers, is punctuated by happenstance and accident, while also being the fruit of real merit. There is, in other words, a dialectic of accident and merit, luck and ability, or, as Machiavelli taught us to say, *virtù* and *fortuna,* in the story of Tocqueville's American career. The unmistakable aura of solemnity that surrounds and infuses so much of the Tocqueville discourse is of a piece with its amnesiac quality—the ignoring of scholarship more than a generation old.

On September 9, 1996, Senator Jesse Helms (R-NC) took the floor during the debate over the Defense of Marriage Act, which defines marriage as between a man and a woman. After reminding his colleagues in his faux-avuncular fashion that "God made Adam and Eve, not Adam and Steve," Helms made an erudite reference to Tocqueville: "Mr. President, at the heart of this debate is the moral and spiritual survival of this Nation. Alexis de Tocqueville said a century and a half ago that America had grown great because America was good. Mr. de Tocqueville also warned that if America made the mistake of ceasing to be good, America would cease to be great." This quote about America being great because America is good has a long oratorical pedigree stretching back from President Reagan and up to President Clinton. Senator John Ashcroft used it three times in April 1997 alone, twice in the same speech. In 1998, in Congress the line surfaced twelve times on issues ranging from the budget to sexual abstinence and the space station. Unfortunately, the quotation is nowhere to be found in the works of Tocqueville. "Someone made it up and they've been quoting each other ever since," said Seymour Drescher. Reporter Guy Gugliotta of the *Washington Post,* who dug out the quotes and discovered their provenance, wrote, "It survives because it's much too good to check."[5] On a higher intellectual plane than the United States Senate, an analogous survival of a bad idea took place regarding Tocqueville's reputation, as scholars quoted each other about a belief that was too good to check: the belief that Tocqueville's elevated reputation was the product of postwar anxieties and that it emerged out of nowhere during the fight against totalitarianism.

Tocqueville tells us more about the experience of modernity and its relation to societies based on the principle of equality than any other political theorist of the nineteenth or twentieth centuries with the possible exception of Max Weber. His stature, I believe, emerges directly from his understanding that *démocratie* was a new social formation, a new "regime," in the language of many political theorists. He wrote about democracy as a providential development, meaning that it was inevitable, something that could be modified but not turned back. The most successful interpreters of Tocqueville have understood and built upon this insight. American intellectuals after the 1830s lauded what they called Tocqueville's impartiality, but in doing so they were really, in many instances, just coming to a recognition of the *newness* of the phenomenon that Tocqueville had analyzed. As John Lukacs has said, "We are only at the very beginning of the democratic age."[6] They needed to have this newness pointed out to them because, as Tocqueville had shown, theirs was the first society to base itself on the idea (of course not always the practice) of equality, rather than having equality forcibly established upon the smoldering ruins of a preceding social system that had existed for centuries and been violently overthrown.

In this book I try to present the thoughts of many intellectuals, some of them nearly forgotten writers of considerable insight and ability, who shaped the ways in which we have come to know Tocqueville and his work and who, in some cases, knew Tocqueville personally. I do so because I hope to explicate, specifically and in detail, one of the major themes in American intellectual history, namely the idea of Tocqueville himself. This book is an effort to weave from separate threads that are in quite a few instances already known to specialists, a tapestry that displays a portrait of Tocqueville as nineteenth- and twentieth-century Americans knew him. This means the recovery or reinterpretation of such figures as Prussian immigrant Francis Lieber, a friend and translator of Tocqueville and Beaumont and the founder of the discipline of political science in America; Harvard University's crusty Francis Bowen, "the Old Roman" who at the commencement of the putative era of Tocqueville's oblivion produced an edition of the *Democracy* that was standard for more than a century; Daniel Coit Gilman, the founding president of the Johns Hopkins University; Herbert Baxter Adams, who presided over the diaspora of young Ph.D.s establishing history departments in universities throughout the land; the Progressive Era reformer John Graham Brooks, who compared Tocqueville to James Bryce; Paul Lambert White, dead of appendicitis at the age of thirty-two, who discovered and arranged to have copied large portions of the Tocqueville archive at the family's château near Cherbourg just after World War I; and many others, up through the present period, including such outstanding scholars as James T. Schleifer, Roger Boesche, Seymour Drescher, John Lukacs, Michael Kammen, Harvey C.

Mansfield, Delba Winthrop, and the late John Higham, all of whom I inter-viewed for this study.

Throughout the book I attempt to present my evidence as fairly and objectively as possible. But, as the intellectual historian Thomas Haskell reminds us, objectivity is not neutrality.[7] In the course of many years of research and obsessive thinking about this subject, I have indeed reached a number of firm opinions about it, which are in turn firmly stated.

An old-fashioned study, this book relies on very extensive reading in the secondary sources, archival research, and interviews. In a history of this nature, secondary sources are treated not as elements helping to establish a definitive picture of Tocqueville's work, but as primary sources that must be critically analyzed with respect to their contemporary uses, biases, and corre-spondence with known facts.

In 1966, Norman Mailer received from William F. Buckley an auto-graphed copy of Buckley's memoir of the madcap New York City mayoral race of 1965, in which Buckley and Mailer had been rival candidates. Of course, Mailer opened the book to the index right away and looked up his name, there to find, in Buckley's handwriting, the salutation, "Hi, Nor-man."[8] One danger in writing a book about Tocqueville and American intel-lectuals is that so many people will turn to the index straightaway and look for their own names. In fact, not a few of the readers of this particular page have already done so. Some will have been disappointed. This is not the book to peruse for a mention of every study on the myriad of specialized Tocque-villean topics in a truly mountainous literature. It is an examination of main trends in the American reception of Tocqueville. Many outstanding works and writers are barely mentioned; some, not at all. Their absence is not a judgment on their scholarly merit but rather on the light they shed on my restricted topic.

To add a further clarification, this is also not a work wherein I accord a prominent place to my own interpretations of Tocqueville's works. At times it has proven necessary to clarify or explicate Tocqueville's writings as a tac-tic for helping the reader to understand the perspective of one of his com-mentators, and such explications are often remedial. When, for example, a writer like E. L. Godkin maintained that there were no significant differences between Tocqueville and Edmund Burke; or a furious Forty-Eighter claimed Tocqueville hated liberty; or a prominent historian identified Tocqueville's idea of individualism as a form of philosophical idealism: on such occasions I do intervene with simple elucidations, as hermeneutical acrobatics are not called for. I state my views on Tocqueville plainly, but such views are directed in a spirit of debate toward the commentators much more than they are intended as vehicles of Tocqueville interpretation per se. Given the thesis of the book as I have described it in the preceding pages, I devote the most attention to the period during which Tocqueville was supposed to have been suffering from neglect and when American intellectuals were suddenly seized by an inexplicable spell of amnesia.

Book writing, as many have observed, is both excruciatingly private and, for all but a few exceptional cases, a necessarily social form of labor. Writers need the emotional, physical, and financial support of intimates, acquaintances, and institutions to get the words out. Now I take pleasure in the opportunity to acknowledge the personal and institutional support I received during the years when this book changed its character from a foray into a field in which I thought I was well grounded to a long and fascinating journey into unknown terrain. When I was serving as the chair of the History Department at Southwest Missouri State (now Missouri State) University, I began to amass large intellectual debts from colleagues and to receive lesser, but certainly ample and strategically timed, financial assistance from the university. Two summer research grants from SMSU financed interviews with leading scholars and travel to libraries from Baltimore to Pasadena. My deepest and most long-standing debt there is to the superb historian Dominic J. Capeci Jr., with whom I have discussed every phase of this and my previous projects for the last dozen years.

From Saint Louis University, I received a Mellon Faculty Development Grant for travel, research, and interviews in New England. I am grateful for the professional labors of my graduate assistants, Nancy Thompson, Alexis Azar, and especially Alicja Aftyka. My colleagues in the American Studies Department, Elizabeth Kolmer, Shawn Michelle Smith, Wynne Moskop, Joseph Heathcott, Jonathan Smith, and Candy Gunther Brown, have put up with my neglect of department business, stepped in to help with amazing generosity, and listened to my ramblings on Tocqueville's reception with attentive patience. Their support and, indeed, as I hope they know, their very presence, have been vital to my intellectual and affective equilibrium.

In addition to colleagues at work, friends elsewhere proved to be constant in their support. I incurred immense obligations to a number of scholars who agreed to interviews and, at times, to follow-up conversations by phone or in person. My deepest debt is to Seymour Drescher, arguably the finest Tocqueville scholar writing in English. Even though I take issue with him on a number of points with regard to Tocqueville's reputation, his studies of

Tocqueville's life and work—and, it should be noted, Beaumont's as well—are indispensable contributions. I also derived great benefit from the cordial encouragement of John Higham and Michael Kammen. Wilfred McClay has been a model of grace and discernment in both his writing and his support for this book. I am most grateful for his vigorous, long-standing encouragement. In a curious development, my work benefited immensely from four profound conversations with four different people, none of whom is a Tocqueville expert and none of whom knows any of the other three. They are Dominic Capeci, Michael Maas, Sophie Tomlinson, and Eric Will. My son, Philip, grew suddenly into manhood while I was writing about Tocqueville. He was my most reliable source of perspective, knowing automatically when either humor or empathy was called for in the difficult task of dealing with me. Carolyn Williams and Michael McKeon, my beloved in-laws, read and discussed portions of the book many times over the years. My beloved wife, Nancy Williams, always expressed admiration for my work ethic, even though, as it seemed to me, she was working twice as hard as I was. Thanks to her, I have been able to enter into a normal life.

All deep learning emerges from a clear spring source of great teaching somewhere in a writer's past. This book's dedication acknowledges one such source with a prayer of thanks.

Notes

1. Jean-Claude Lamberti, *Tocqueville et les deux démocraties* (Paris: Presses universitaires de France, 1983); Jean-Claude Lamberti, *Tocqueville and the Two Democracies*, trans. Arthur Goldhammer (Cambridge, Mass.: Harvard University Press, 1989).

2. Lynn L. Marshall and Seymour Drescher, "American Historians and Tocqueville's *Democracy*," *Journal of American History* 50, no. 3 (December 1968): 514.

3. George Wilson Pierson, *Tocqueville and Beaumont in America* (New York: Oxford University Press, 1938), reprinted as *Tocqueville in America* (Baltimore, Md.: Johns Hopkins University Press, 1997).

4. Seymour Drescher, "Worlds Together, Worlds Apart: Tocqueville and the Franco-American Exchange," in *The French-American Connection: 200 Years of Cultural and Intellectual Interaction*, ed. Lloyd S. Kramer (Chapel Hill, N.C.: Institut Français de Washington, 1994), 24.

5. "Defense of Marriage Act," *Congressional Record*, Senate, September 9, 1996, 10067; Guy Gugliotta, "The Tyranny of the Misquote," *Washington Post*, September 6, 1998, W4; John J. Pitney Jr., "The Tocqueville Fraud," *Weekly Standard* 1 (November 13, 1995): 44–45. For an earlier generation's version of the same trickery but with a different quote, see

Odom Fanning, "As Tocqueville (Almost) Said . . ." *Washington Post*, September 27, 1978, D7.

6. Lukacs interview.

7. See, especially, Thomas L. Haskell, "Objectivity Is Not Neutrality: Rhetoric versus Practice in Peter Novick's *That Noble Dream*," in *Objectivity Is Not Neutrality: Explanatory Schemes in History* (Baltimore, Md.: Johns Hopkins University Press, 1998), 145–73.

8. Martin Peretz, "Cape Cod Diarist: I Am a Footnote," *The New Republic* 215, no. 5 (July 29, 1996): 42.

Abbreviations

DIA	Alexis de Tocqueville, *Democracy in America*, ed. Olivier Zunz, trans. Arthur Goldhammer (New York: Library of America, 2004).
Letters	Alexis de Tocqueville, *Selected Letters on Politics and Society*, ed. Roger Boesche, trans. James Toupin and Roger Boesche (Berkeley: University of California Press, 1985).
OC	Alexis de Tocqueville, *Oeuvres Complètes*, 16 vols. to date (Paris: Gallimard, 1951–present).
OR	Alexis de Tocqueville, *The Old Regime and the Revolution*, ed. François Furet and Françoise Mélonio, trans. Alan S. Kahan, 2 vols. (Chicago: University of Chicago Press, 1998, 2001).
R	Alexis de Tocqueville, *Recollections*, ed. J. P. Mayer and A. P. Kerr, trans. George Lawrence (Garden City, N.Y.: Doubleday Anchor, 1971).
TBA	George Wilson Pierson, *Tocqueville and Beaumont in America* (New York: Oxford University Press, 1938), reprinted as *Tocqueville in America* (Baltimore, Md.: Johns Hopkins University Press, 1996).
TBSR	Seymour Drescher, ed. and trans., *Tocqueville and Beaumont on Social Reform* (Pittsburgh, Pa.: University of Pittsburgh Press, 1968).
Gilman Collection	Daniel Coit Gilman Collection, Special Collections, Milton S. Eisenhower Library, Johns Hopkins University, Baltimore, Maryland.

Lieber Papers (H)	Francis Lieber Papers, Huntington Library, San Marino, California.
Lieber Papers (JHU)	Francis Lieber Correspondence and Manuscripts, Daniel Coit Gilman Collection, Special Collections, Milton S. Eisenhower Library, Johns Hopkins University, Baltimore, Maryland.
Boesche interview	Roger Boesche, interview with the author, Los Angeles, California, December 7, 1998.
Drescher interview	Seymour Drescher, interview with the author, Pittsburgh, Pennsylvania, July 14, 1998.
Higham interview	John Higham, interview with the author, Baltimore, Maryland, September 9, 1998.
Johnson interview	Dick Johnson, interview with the author, Los Angeles, California, December 7, 1998.
Kammen interview	Michael Kammen, interview with the author, Ithaca, New York, July 16, 1999.
Lukacs interview	John Lukacs, interview with the author, Phoenixville, Pennsylvania, July 15, 1998.
Mansfield interview	Harvey C. Mansfield, interview with the author, Cambridge, Massachusetts, August 7, 2002.
Schleifer interview	James T. Schleifer, interview with the author, New Rochelle, New York, July 20, 1998.
Winthrop interview	Delba Winthrop, interview with the author, Cambridge, Massachusetts, August 7, 2002.

CHAPTER ONE

Reception and Renown

Soon after the great revolution in Paris of July 1830, which abolished for the second time the right of the Bourbons to occupy the throne of France, a young, restless Frenchman obtained a commission from the new government of King Louis Philippe to visit the United States. Deeply stirred by the July Revolution and the seemingly ineluctable progress of equality that it represented, and also immensely curious and ambitious, the young commissioner—he was only twenty-four years of age when the revolution broke out—desired both to contemplate and to experience the future state of his native land by means of these travels in the United States. For there, across the Atlantic, he was sure, the future course of the leading nations of the West could be discerned.

And so it was that during the raucous, confident, heroic, and shameful era that we have since named after the Indian-fighting president whose personality and policies so thoroughly dominated it—during the age of Jackson—that the young man first stepped onto the pier in New York harbor, and thence, somewhat gingerly, on to the dizzying streets of New York City. They were the first steps in a long and difficult physical and intellectual journey that would eventually result in one of the most remarkable books ever produced on the purpose and direction of democratic and commercial institutions in America. It is indeed one of the most insightful works about American culture ever penned by a person from a different culture.

This remarkable volume is packed with incisive analysis and replete with bold prophecy. A century after its publication, the great Yale historian George Wilson Pierson called it "an economic study and a factual survey of America as valuable and as prophetic" as any that has ever appeared. And it is easy to see why. In the mind of the young Frenchman, the democratic

1

future could be witnessed and evaluated most accurately not in France but here in the United States—for "no people," he judged, "is so peculiarly fitted by its intrinsic character, as well as by the circumstances of its territory and the condition of its population, for democratic institutions. The Americans possess, therefore, in the highest degree, the better features of democracy, and they have also its inseparable defects."

The youthful commissioner astutely foresaw the complex dangers to freedom presented by the apparent tyranny exercised by majority opinion. He predicted the threat to social stability posed by an excessive stress on individual rights. He underscored the need for religious belief and devotion in order to offset the self-regarding, acquisitive individualism that equality seemed to engender: "Religion alone," he warned, "can counterbalance human passions and confine them within the limits in which they serve the progress of society." And most presciently, he anticipated a not too-distant future in which two colossi, the United States and Russia, "these youthful Titans who are watching each other across the Atlantic and already touch hands on the Pacific," might "divide the empire of the world."

The book, in short, was altogether an extraordinary study. It richly rewards careful reading even today. Indeed, no modern reader can help but marvel at the seeming contemporaneity of its descriptions of American institutions and culture. Published in the mid-1830s by Paris's leading publisher, Gosselin, and almost immediately translated into English for an eager American audience, the book bore the title (in English) of *Society, Manners, and Politics in the United States: Letters on North America.* The author was a young government mining engineer and Saint-Simonian publicist by the name of Michel Chevalier.[1]

Few people today have heard of Chevalier; far fewer still have read him. But in the age of Jackson and of the July Monarchy (which were almost exactly contemporaneous), his was a familiar name to the educated public of two nations. His book, too—an effort to describe, assess, and, as it were, translate the manners and institutions of the United States to a foreign audience—was a substantial contribution to a well-established, familiar literary genre.

By 1836, when his book was published, Chevalier had already undergone a colorful, if bizarre, series of experiences, though perhaps bizarre only to those unfamiliar with the intricacies of the Saint-Simonian religion. In August 1832, he had been arrested for conducting meetings in which the abolition of marriage and private property were advocated. He then spent ten months in prison, but even before his sentence was completed, he was appointed to a position on the influential *Journal des débats*, and shortly after his release the government sent him to the United States to study that nation's systems of transportation and communication. After the success of his book (first published in 1836, with a second edition in 1840), Chevalier received the prestigious appointment to the chair of political economy at the Collège de France, from which position he became the nation's foremost champion of free trade and eventually the author, with his far better-known British counterpart, Richard Cobden, of the Anglo-French Treaty of Commerce of 1860.[2]

In 1845, the voters in the Department of Aveyron elected Chevalier to the Chamber of Deputies, but once in the chamber his vigorous advocacy of free trade earned him little more than the wrath of his protectionist constituency and defeat in his reelection attempt. For a brief two years, then, he served in the same chamber as another, more illustrious student of America, democracy, and economics—Alexis de Tocqueville.

Both the extent and the gravity of the differences between the two young deputies would be revealed a few years later, when Chevalier, who all his life had advocated that the state should control the distribution of the labor force, had no difficulty embracing the despotism of Napoleon III after the latter's coup d'état of December 2, 1851, while Tocqueville was thrown into prison for his opposition to it. Indeed, Tocqueville composed a derisive account of the coup and arranged for it to be smuggled out of France by his friend Harriet Lewin Grote. She, in turn, pressed it upon Tocqueville's friend and translator Henry Reeve, who saw to its publication in the *London Times*.[3]

When Chevalier's *Society, Manners, and Politics in the United States* rolled off the same presses that, just one year earlier, had produced the first volume of his own study, entitled *Democracy in America*, Tocqueville refused to read it. After all, he had his own project to complete, and he did not want to be distracted. He feared that exposure to the ideas of others might draw him away from the purpose that, Ahab-like, he had fixed on iron rails. But it is obvious from his correspondence that he felt deeply apprehensive about the appearance of Chevalier's book. "Have you glanced at it and, in that case, what did you think of it?" he asked his trusted friend Gustave de Beaumont, who had accompanied him on his own journey to America some five years earlier. (Five years! How time had sped by! And the world was expecting a second volume from him on the institutions and mores of the United States, a volume that was proceeding at an excruciatingly slow pace.) "What is its spirit?" Tocqueville persisted. "What is its direction? Also, what impression [*bruit*] is it making in the world?"[4]

What impression is it making in the world? That is, how is it being received? Tocqueville's anxious query about Chevalier's ephemeral book is one that, with sympathy but with perhaps more detachment, we can direct toward his own more enduring work. For the impression an author makes in the world alters with time and circumstance—it is a dynamic historical phenomenon or series of events, each with its enveloping cloud of circumstance and judgment. And it is an especially pertinent question in American intellectual history, for to no nineteenth-century social thinker except Karl Marx have American intellectuals turned so often, and to so many different purposes, especially since World War II, than to Tocqueville.

Both the "impression" made by Chevalier's book and Tocqueville's concern about it can serve as illustrations of the opportunities and perils of undertaking a reception-history such as this. For the reverence with which Tocqueville's name is so often invoked, the canonical status of *Democracy in America*, and indeed the obscurity of Michel Chevalier, are all quite contingent facts. The game of renown might have turned out differently.

Tocqueville's unwillingness to confront Chevalier's book is emblematic of one of the fundamental problems of intellectual history, that of the relation between contingency and quality, accident and essence, or, in contemporary terms, the relation between social and political forces at work in a given historical moment and the depth of wisdom in a given author's work.

In the brief span of a single generation—the last—the field of intellectual history, which had once been the source of illumination for entire eras of American history, suddenly experienced a near total eclipse, then reemerged, somewhat abashed by its experiences in the academic wars but prepared to serve once again our understanding of cultural constructs. Early in the twentieth century, intellectual historians had succeeded in establishing the distinct viewpoint and ideology of their specialty at the center of the curricular reforms that were shaking up the American university. These reforms ushered in a fresh historical approach to the study of civilization by undergraduates. James Harvey Robinson's immensely influential course at Columbia University, "The History of the Intellectual Classes of Europe," inaugurated in 1904, became the core of the undergraduate curriculum there. By the 1940s and 1950s, two distinct approaches to the field had emerged, each identified with its own label, leading figure, paradigmatic book, and special area of inquiry. The so-called internalists took as their point of departure the inner dynamic that all ideas possess and generate. Their majestic exemplar was *The Great Chain of Being* (1936) by Arthur O. Lovejoy, the founder of the *Journal of the History of Ideas*. In this wide-ranging and deeply erudite study, Lovejoy managed, first, to capture the imagination of professional historians and students alike and, second, to propound in a programmatic first chapter an agenda for historical study itself, namely the systematic analysis "of doctrines or tendencies that are designated by familiar names ending in -*ism* or -*ity*."[5] He carefully explained the ramifications of the metaphor of the Great Chain in terms of the unfolding of its own logic. Economic and political forces and events outside the sealed-off bubble of the idea of the chain of being found no place in Lovejoy's narrative.

To the so-called externalists, by contrast, the great Merle Curti's foundational *Growth of American Thought* (1943) provided not only a method but even, in a sense, a past itself; it may be said to have fabricated, although to be sure not out of whole cloth, the very subject matter that it set out to examine. It created American intellectual history as such. In contrast to Lovejoy with his emphasis on ideas per se, Curti revealed the reciprocal interaction of ideas, events, and "outside" forces; in short, he took as his subject the effects that politics and society exercised on an evolving "growth"—American thought.[6]

Since World War II, then, scholars interested in the history of ideas have tended to favor one or the other of the above approaches. This internalist-externalist duality may appear oversimplified as it is presented here, but in the past generation (which for scholars in the humanities and social sciences in American universities might be called the Age of Binary Oppositions), the split led to bitter divisions and even opera buffa declarations of open war. The primary theater of operations in this "War between the Internalists and Externalists"—as it was actually called at the time—was the history of science. As Joyce Appleby, Lynn Hunt, and Margaret Jacob summarized it in their important history of late-twentieth-century historical controversies, for internalists the "historical development [of science] occurred as the result of empirical work and the unfolding of the rules of logic," whereas the externalists "looked for the larger interests and values at work within communities of scientists." In so doing, the latter "vastly extended the definition of the social," making it refer to "the universe beyond laboratory or university."[7]

The ascendancy of the externalists over their more hermetic rivals was in part a consequence of the growing authority of social history over intellectual history of *any* sort. Like good social historians, the externalists explained the forces and movements in the realm of ideas as a superstructural variant of more basic changes occurring in the spheres of society and politics. Indeed, the meteoric rise of social history was itself understood to be largely a product of the upheavals in society, culture, and politics that occurred in the 1960s, a time when massive social and political unrest and protests in Paris and Prague, Oakland and Detroit, Watts and Washington, Berkeley and Cornell, suddenly made the movement of ideas seem low on the priority list of historical causation. The prestige of Marxism among historians of the last third of the twentieth century was not simply the consequence of a prior political commitment; it derived also from a recognition of the fundamental Marxian insight into the primacy of social and economic deep structures and the consequent relegation of ideas, beliefs, "isms," "itys," and so on, to the category of mere reflections or echoes of deeper actualities. The dramas of swelling opposition to the war in Vietnam, of civil rights, and of decolonization seemed to empirically confirm this basic order of cause and effect. And thus it was that, as John Higham cogently summarized the situation, "the sixties did for the academic status of social history what the forties had done for intellectual history."[8]

By 1980 the ever-strengthening currents of social history had nearly cast intellectual history to the periphery of the discipline. In the mid-1970s, two leading intellectual historians, Higham and Paul K. Conkin, organized a high-powered conference on the future of intellectual history, in honor of Curti on his eightieth birthday. In the course of their planning, they were dismayed to discover how many of the most distinguished, senior people in the field saw little of value in the project, or indeed in the future of their own specialty. "I've been drifting away from intellectual history and doubt whether I personally could contribute anything of value," Higham remembered "one very distinguished scholar" responding to his invitation to participate. Others declined to respond at all.[9]

Yet younger historians, such as Dorothy Ross, Thomas Haskell, and Thomas Bender, showed enormous enthusiasm for both the conference and the field—a sure sign of its future regeneration. Bender recalled, "For many of the participants the future was bleak indeed, but several of us who were classified as younger historians were not prepared for such as pessimistic outlook on our future." He foresaw a field that would soon be rejuvenated, "perhaps chastened by its confrontation with social history but enriched as well."[10]

Conkin's own defense of intellectual history remains one of the best. Social historians, he wrote in 1977, had "pushed the issue of mass belief, or of popular mentalities, into the forefront. If intellectual historians would only explore the beliefs of the working classes, they could be on the right side politically and also make use of the newly fashionable research tools required for disciplined inferences from massive but usually thin data." Yet, the thought of scientists and philosophers exerts an immense impact on societies, albeit with a lag time sometimes spreading over generations. Therefore, "for a time it remains the property of narrow intellectual communities. . . . If specialized intellectual historians do not attend to such belief, its origin and development will remain a hidden and uncriticized aspect of our past. . . . This helps justify the exclusive focus of specialized intellectual historians."[11] The present study examines not so much Tocqueville's own thought as the reception of that thought by American intellectuals, a diverse body of "belief" that has indeed been "a hidden and uncriticized aspect of our past."

The confrontation between the history of ideas and that of changes in social structure was exemplified in the history-of-science controversy (or, as it was called by its participants, the war). What must be emphasized about the war is the fundamental and rewarding tension between these two ways of describing and explaining the origins, development, reception, and transmission of all kinds of ideas—good, bad, foolish, or clever—in American intellectual life.

We can observe precisely that tension at work in the respective fates of the books written by Chevalier and Tocqueville. Whereas Chevalier faded permanently into the background of history and remained of interest mainly to specialists in nineteenth-century travel literature, Tocqueville is widely counted among the tiny handful of the most important social thinkers of the last two hundred years. A pure internalist could ascribe the ascendancy of Tocqueville solely to the allegedly superior cogency of his ideas and exposition, while an unadulterated externalist might attribute Chevalier's eclipse to the declining relevance of his commercial and free-trade focus at a time when French national interests were defined ever more forcefully by the imperatives of industry and empire.

It is perfectly evident that neither of these explanations, or starting points for explanations, can come close to providing an adequate context for thinking about Tocqueville's reputation. Indeed, the very style of framing the problem that I have just presented, this deployment of the "Scylla-and-Charybdis" tactic, in which the writer declares his intention of steering the impartial middle course between two errors of extreme interpretation, and thereby puts himself on display as a cool-headed, lofty analyst who can navigate around the dangerous ideological shoals that ravage other interpretations—this rhetorical trick should always be read with suspicion.

And yet, in the instance of Tocqueville's reception, the dangers do lie in the clash of two extreme positions.

To begin with, there is the tendency to interpret Tocqueville's postwar fame in externalist terms as a both a manifestation and a means of advancing the interests of particular readers, especially those for whom Tocqueville was an antidote to Karl Marx during the cold war. With his thesis of liberty imperiled by advancing equality (because equality could flourish in despotic as well as in free regimes), Tocqueville seemed to have been presciently describing the post-1945 world. What is more, he cemented his reputation for prophecy by explicitly including, at the end of *Democracy in America*, his own prediction about the United States and Russia each swaying the destinies of half the globe. American commentators instantly seized upon this prediction, hardly bold in itself and already a bromide of the Paris salons when Tocqueville tacked it onto his book. It went far toward fixing one absolutely central element of Tocqueville's twentieth-century American image, that of prophet.

To be sure, Tocqueville had also enjoyed that reputation during the nineteenth century, but it had been attained chiefly as a result of his famous prediction, set forth during a speech in the Chamber of Deputies in January 1848, of impending revolution in France. When the barricades were thrown together and the monarchy came crashing down just two weeks after Tocqueville's warning, his renown as a seer was confirmed.[12] A century later, his few words on the approaching U.S.-Russia global rivalry served to secure his stature, ironically in the same prophetic role that he had enjoyed while alive but for a completely different reason—this time despotism, not revolution, was the subject of his prophecy.

In the late twentieth century, then, no single characteristic would be associated with Tocqueville more often than his prescience. And it would require little effort for the historian to mount a case for Tocqueville's stature based not on the character of his thought but rather on the supposed uncanny prescience of his predictions. One writer in the *Nation* felicitously expressed this sense of timeliness upon the 1945 publication of *Democracy in America*: "To read it in the context of these days is to feel that its republication in America . . . was a providential event devised by a higher and more witting power than Alfred A. Knopf."[13]

Yet, the "strong" version of externalism, the Scylla of the tired trope, is manifestly inadequate to explain Tocqueville's great influence and reputation in the second half of the twentieth century. After all, as we saw at the outset, Michel Chevalier was a pretty good prognosticator too, but few people remember who he was. The springs of American intellectuals' faith in Tocqueville must have a deeper source. And that source must be sought in the power of Tocqueville's thought itself. Tocqueville's canonical status derives from the fact that his life's work was a sustained meditation on the nature and direction of our modern condition, especially on the related phenomena of equality and social mobility—*démocratie*—that the violent break with Europe's feudal past had brought about. And Tocqueville's meditation produced far more than mere sociological analysis but included deep philosophic reflection, as well. Moreover, he saw—and yes, foresaw—that the greatest challenge facing a regime of equality would be the maintenance of its freedom. These are among the most urgent and intractable political issues of the past two centuries, and the warm reception Tocqueville has received from American intellectuals is owing to the generosity, subtlety, and balance of his many investigations into the still-developing modern world. As one of the profoundest of contemporary historical writers, John Lukacs, expressed it in 1997, "I have studied and read Tocqueville for nearly fifty years now, but it is only lately that I have recognized not only the essence but the meaning of the essence of his vision of history," namely the division of the past into two great "chapters," the aristocratic and the democratic.[14]

Just as one could build a case for Tocqueville's reception on the basis of external factors, then, so also could his canonization be explained by the extraordinary quality of his insights into the most basic problems of political and social institutions.

A second Scylla-and-Charybdis dichotomy which the reader should view with suspicion is this: a perpetual theoretical play, the objects of which are an indeterminate text and a kaleidoscopic reader, versus a purely descriptive presentation of undiluted data, a mere recitation of book reviews.

Little work has been done on the subject of the American reception of Tocqueville, and the few pieces that have appeared have been confined to *Democracy in America*. Almost all of this limited body of scholarship has been descriptive. But even this descriptive work can cast a useful light on Tocqueville and his many meanings. Unlike much Tocqueville scholarship in the middle of the twentieth century, the earliest account of Tocqueville's reception was, despite the impressive research that went into it, not a work of scholarly distinction. In a long appendix to the 1945 Knopf edition of *Democracy in America*, Phillips Bradley composed a "historical essay" that is the starting point for all future inquiries into the ways Tocqueville's ideas impressed his nineteenth-century contemporaries.[15] Bradley's essay will receive the separate attention it deserves later in this study; what is relevant for present purposes is its almost purely narrative character, its lack not only of theory but also almost of any thesis or argument.

The approach that will be followed in the present study is not one that can boast of steering clear of all these obstacles. Rather, it will bump off of each of them from time to time—perhaps, it might seem, somewhat like a pinball in a game machine. But honoring the profundity of Tocqueville while not only admitting but laying out for the reader the contingent elements in his changing reputation, and describing reactions to his writings while maintaining a self-conscious critical distance from the authors of those reactions, are not impossible tasks for the historian to undertake. Daunting, certainly, but not impossible.

In this study of the changing images of one crucial figure for American intellectuals, I will examine the several layers of reception from the superficial to the profound. At the end of the twentieth century, there was a sense in which Tocqueville was everywhere, part of a true "climate" of thought and opinion. Relentlessly quoted, seldom understood, he was one of the very few nineteenth-century thinkers who appeared regularly in the editorial, op-ed, and even "style" sections of not only great but also small-market newspapers.

Furthermore, since the late 1930s, Tocqueville has had the good fortune to be the subject of books and articles by some of the very best American practitioners of historical and social science scholarship, from George Wilson Pierson to Seymour Drescher and James T. Schleifer. And there are also the important American thinkers for whom Tocqueville was formative, whose own ideas reveal, if only by a kind of refraction, the light that Tocqueville shed on the questions of democracy, equality, liberty, revolution, and modernity. From Francis Lieber and Henry Adams in the nineteenth century to Hannah Arendt and John Lukacs in the twentieth, Tocqueville has operated as a leaven, imparting substance and savor to highly distinctive and often influential books, arguments, and ways of thinking.

A thinker's reputation is a cultural artifact. It is something made. As such, it is eminently suitable to analysis. That analysis is historical only insofar as one can describe a particular process, namely, the process by which that product or artifact has been fashioned. A useful term for the fashioning of a reputation is *reception*. Reception, then, is a historical *process*, reputation a *product*. But since the reception is ongoing, the product is protean. Its shape and even its seeming essence change constantly as the historical environment in which it is manufactured undergoes transformation. Thus, so important has Tocqueville become in the American imagination that writing about his reception carries with it the danger of trying to write the entire intellectual history of the United States since the age of Jackson, a task for which the present writer is unsuited, by either ability or inclination, to undertake. Instead, the attention to layers of reception, from climate of opinion to a few profound thinkers, will help to impose a modicum of structure on a potentially amorphous subject.

I begin with the situation around the turn of the twenty-first century, an ambivalent time for serious students of Tocqueville, and then try to reconstruct the process by which Tocqueville's stature reached its present paradoxical position—paradoxical because it is at once towering and very little understood. As in all good paradoxes, the two elements were intimately intertwined. By the late 1990s, it seemed no intellectual could make a reference to antebellum America without a least a mention of Tocqueville; yet at the same time concrete knowledge of Tocqueville's ideas and analyses was at a premium.

Both the sheer inescapability of Tocqueville in turn-of-the-century discussions of the antebellum United States, and the ways in which his ideas were distorted by that very inescapability, were strikingly evident in an influential 1998 study of the historiography of transcendentalism written by a leading Americanist, Charles Capper.[16] As is well known, Tocqueville never encountered, inquired about, or knew any of the central or peripheral characters in the drama of American transcendentalism, for the excellent reason that the fragile bark of transcendentalism was not launched until five years after Tocqueville's American sojourn. But this fact could not deter Capper (and countless other students of antebellum society and culture) from nudging him onto stage in his principal American role—that of prophetic sage.

Capper's study of transcendentalism is impressive from start to finish, but it contains one glaring anomaly, which becomes evident as soon as one examines the manner in which Capper employed the figure of Tocqueville. The anomaly is this: in an essay containing references to hundreds of books and articles, Capper managed on the one hand, to deploy Tocqueville as the organizing principle around which the main problems in understanding the entire recent scholarship about transcendentalism were to be arrayed and, on the other, to avoid making a single specific, paginated reference to any of Tocqueville's works or to a single work of Tocqueville scholarship.

How can such a lacuna be explained? Serious scholarly investigations like Capper's can make use of such undefined categories as Tocqueville's name summons forth only as a consequence of a protracted and nearly opaque process of substitution by which, to begin with, a thinker's specific ideas are gradually supplanted by his name's adjectival form (the actual concepts of Alexis de Tocqueville by something Tocquevillean), then, in a second, crucial stage, that adjective becomes reified in its turn; that is, it becomes transformed into a distinct entity whose properties can be assumed rather than demonstrated. In grammatical terms, a substantive morphs into a modifier, which gradually returns cloaked as a substantive. The loose term *Tocquevillean* thereby makes its appearance as a tool for historiographical analysis.

Capper's study provides a superb platform from which to observe that process, or at least its end product. For the essay, far from exhibiting shoddy research, careless composition, or slipshod conclusions, is, rather, a work of high distinction, honored in 1998 with the Binkley-Stephenson Award as the best article to appear on any subject in the leading journal in the field, the *Journal of American History*. Deeply researched and skillfully organized, Capper's study provided a new starting point for students of transcendentalism. It is not Capper's interpretations of the historiography of transcendentalism that are at issue here, however, but the way he brought Tocqueville to bear in the effort to present his findings.

To account for transcendentalism's longevity in American culture studies, Capper began by first noting its settled status in departments of both history and English; then, he ushered the indispensable Frenchman onto the stage. "Historical Transcendentalism has long been buoyed up," Capper wrote, "by that protean trio of cultural configurations that Alexis de Tocqueville, writing in the decade of the movement's rise in the 1830s (and completely ignorant of its existence), first virtually identified with 'America' itself: liberal religion, individualist democracy, and national identity" (503). Capper supported this highly debatable assertion by recourse to a scholarly appurtenance that is becoming increasingly familiar, namely the broad-gauge footnote, one that contains no specific page references but, rather, directs the reader to the entire work being cited. In this case the reference was to *Democracy in America*.

This footnote procedure can be justified, depending on the context and objectives of the work of scholarship in which it appears. Capper's article contained numerous unpaginated footnote references because it was, in large part, a guide to the literature, so that in effect the notes performed the task of a bibliographic essay. But such a method can present disadvantages for both scholarship and clear argument, as well. For example, in the case of the general reference to *Democracy in America*, if a reader were to reverse the ordinary spatial and temporal sequence of reading the sentence and the footnote—if she were first to register the footnote and then look up to the body of the text to see what is being referred to—the interpretation she would come away with would surely be misguided. She would begin by reading the footnote citing, in toto, a book entitled *Democracy in America*, by Alexis de Tocqueville, which was originally published in two volumes in 1835 and

1840. Glancing upward to the body of the text to see what the footnote validated, she would then surmise that the substance of those two large volumes is that Tocqueville identified—or at least "virtually identified"—the triad of liberal religion, individualist democracy, and national identity with the term (in inverted commas) America.

This assertion raises some difficulties, not the least of which is confusion as to its literal meaning. But more to the immediate point, the proposition that Tocqueville identified liberal religion, individualist democracy, and national identity with America is, to put it mildly, a highly questionable interpretation of *Democracy in America*. It is at once plausible, not necessarily incorrect, irrefutable, and tendentious. But it cannot reasonably be maintained that it captures the essence of Tocqueville's nearly eight-hundred-page (tendentious and plausible) tomes. Like many American commentators, Capper mistakenly identifies the *Democracy*: it is not primarily a book about America but about democracy.

Having scripted a particular version of Tocqueville as a key performer in his endeavor to interpret the historiography of transcendentalism, Capper exhibited his stage works from time to time throughout the argument. Thus, for example, Van Wyck Brooks was portrayed as having "treat[ed] the Transcendentalists' Tocquevillian individualism as nothing more than a category of moral uplift" (511); and "in the arsenal of post–World War II American historiography, Transcendentalism became, in an abrupt return to the grand theme of the grandfather of unillusioned liberalism, Tocqueville, the proof-text of consensus in America's idealist individualism" (521). Again, the literal meaning of this second sentence is not altogether clear, at least insofar as it refers to Tocqueville, although taking the two sentences together, a meaning can be constructed. It is, first, that the transcendentalists' individualism was Tocquevillean and, second, that Tocqueville's grand theme was idealist individualism. But both these assertions are simply erroneous. Indeed, in one of the most frequently quoted—yet not always best understood—passages of the second volume of *Democracy in America*, Tocqueville went to great lengths to define precisely what he meant by the term *individualism* (a brand new expression in political discourse at that time) and to differentiate it from other forms of self-regarding thought and action. The salient point about Tocqueville's discussion of individualism is that he identified it as a kind of composite or amalgam of feeling and thinking: he described it as a cold, calculating feeling of self-centeredness that was of a different order than the *égoïsme* that he associated with the French character. Egoism, he wrote, was a baser passion than individualism and, as such, much closer to the category of blind, unreflective instinct. Egoism and individualism therefore occupied opposite poles within the domain of human sentiments, with egoism being situated in proximity to instinct and individualism close to thought: "Egoism is a passionate and exaggerated love of self that impels man to relate everything solely to himself and to prefer himself to everything else. Individualism is a reflective and tranquil sentiment that disposes each citizen to cut himself off from the mass of his fellow men and withdraw into the circle of family and friends. . . . Egoism is born of blind instinct; individualism proceeds from erroneous judgment rather than depraved sentiment. Its source lies as much in defects of the mind as in vices of the heart" (DIA 585).

"Tocquevillian individualism," then, far from being "idealist" in the sense in which that term is understood in the history of Continental philosophy—which is the sense that is most relevant to the study of transcendentalism—is instead a selfish emotion that has been fused with a detached, calculated strategizing about the most efficient way to advance one's material interests. By no stretch of interpretation can it be described as idealist. I do not know precisely how to categorize the individualism of the transcendentalists, but surely theirs was not the kind Tocqueville labored so meticulously to describe. One of Ralph Waldo Emerson's biographers, Stephen E. Whicher, called it "radical egoism."[17]

But when a subject is as crucial as individualism is in Tocqueville's writings, determining the correct definition of the term is only half the task. Attending scrupulously to context is just as important. And here it must be emphasized that the rhetorical juxtaposition of Tocqueville, individualism, and America that Capper advanced (and, in doing so, followed a long tradition and legions of commentators) distorted Tocqueville's argument almost beyond recognition. Tocqueville's account of individualism occurs in a section of the *Democracy* in which the topic of America itself has almost completely vanished. In fact, Tocqueville had scarcely made any reference to the United States at all for a full fifty pages prior to his taking up the subject of individualism. That is because, at this point in his inquiry, he had all but abandoned the subject of America in favor of his passionate quest for generalizations about the effects of *démocratie* as such. Indeed, Tocqueville never mentions America until the final sentence of the two-chapter section that treats individualism, and when he does bring America back into the discussion, it is precisely in order to reveal the ways in which Americans *counteracted* individualism's baneful consequences. In short, Tocqueville forcefully detached individualism from any exclusive or necessary connection with the

United States, instead portraying it as a trait of democracy per se or of "democratic centuries" (*DIA* 585–94). He took up the subject in the section of the book that has the least to do with America and turned to the subject of the Americans only in order to illustrate the means by which individualism can be restrained.

By invoking the allegedly Tocquevillean triad of religion, democracy, and nationality, then, Capper opened up both helpful prospects and serious perils: on the one hand, the three abstractions could be brought to bear on the project of organizing the current state of scholarship about transcendentalism with great effect; on the other hand, they could be made to do so only at the expense of rendering Tocqueville himself—as opposed to a Tocquevillean mask or persona—all but invisible.

Democracy, for instance, became inexplicably transmuted into something Capper termed "the ideology of 'reform,'" again with unexplained inverted commas. Accordingly, transcendentalist socialism, abolitionism, and feminism were then squeezed into the box of a "Tocquevillian paradigm"—but only by first devising a paradigm to fit the phenomena and then affixing the Tocqueville label to it (535, 536). Admittedly, the term *démocratie*, as Tocqueville employed it, is notorious among scholars for its protean character, but general agreement does obtain that he used it to refer to a regime of broad legal and social equality and social mobility. Although Tocqueville observed that the constant agitation of democratic practices and institutions generated rhetoric and associations devoted to the promotion of social reform, it is fallacious to posit a relationship of identity between antebellum reform ideology and democracy.

Just as Tocqueville was not cognizant of a transcendentalist movement, so also only flimsy and fugitive strands of evidence reveal any awareness of Tocqueville among the transcendentalists (except in the case of Emerson, and that only late in the era of transcendentalism's ascendancy; the two men met in 1848) or indeed on the part of such nontranscendentalist figures of the American Renaissance as Nathaniel Hawthorne or Herman Melville.[18] One might concede that Capper's purpose was to show how transcendentalists can be said to have conformed to a broader American cultural paradigm that Tocqueville had presciently devised without having any awareness of transcendentalism's existence, but even allowing for the fact that the paradigm itself is lacking in empirical connection between itself and the subject under study, it does not conform to what Tocqueville himself is known to have actually thought, written, or said.

Completing the passage from the realm of grounded knowledge to that of stereotype was the task of the third, most contentious and politically sensitive facet of Capper's model, that of national identity. For at this point his text was salted with politically loaded shorthand terms that implicated Tocqueville in a conservative vision of a homogeneous and consensual United States, with phrases such as "the old Tocquevillian 'American exceptionalist' question" and "1950s Tocquevillian mythic models" (537). Capper linked this aspect of Tocqueville's reputation with the discovery, early in the essay, of a "liberal neo-consensus framework" and a "neo-liberal Tocquevillian rescue" of the transcendentalists in the work of the intellectual historian George M. Fredrickson (529).[19] Capper employed such opaque phraseology to portray Fredrickson's "rescue" as one part of an allegedly broader "Tocquevillian downplaying of contention" in scholarship about American culture in the 1950s and 1960s (528). In this manner, something "Tocquevillian" was made to signify an entire mode of approach and a generation of scholarship. This mode was portrayed as neoliberal, affiliated in an unspecified way with exceptionalism, and yet also characteristic of religiously grounded reformism in the antebellum era. These might be defensible propositions at a certain level of generalization, but their precise connection with Tocqueville was nowhere evident.

The gulf between Capper's deep research, sensitive insights, and judicious conclusions, on the one hand, and the superficiality and breadth of his deployment of Tocqueville, on the other, is so wide as to invite critical commentary in its own right. The fact that the *Journal of American History* could hold its authors to rigorous standards of evidence and argument while its most outstanding article made such cavalier use of Tocqueville's image could be taken to indicate, among other scholarly trends, a serious decline in the relevance of Tocqueville himself among American intellectuals. Capper's essay, therefore, served as a kind of milepost. It pointed to the fact that for many intellectuals, as the new century commenced, Tocqueville increasingly served a decorative rather than an analytical purpose.

The decorative was clearly in the forefront of another scholar's mind, but he hated the decoration. This was Robert Dawidoff, who does know a great deal about Tocqueville, in a puzzling study, *The Genteel Tradition and the Sacred Rage*. Reviewers of this work made note of the unfairness of Dawidoff's deployment of Tocqueville; George Cotkin called him a "straw man" for Dawidoff's tendentious argument, and Ross Posnock characterized the book as "especially interesting on James and Santayana, unoriginal on Adams, and simplistic regarding Tocqueville." Dawidoff set up a vague "Tocquevillian" feeling—completely detached from American popular culture—as a foil to a more generous "Jeffersonian" one that was inclusive, diverse, and vibrant. Dawidoff postulated a "cult of Tocqueville" and defined "Tocquevillian" as "the feeling that smart Americans have that they are better than the rest of us." So much for political philosophy.[20] Again, Dawidoff's contrast between high culture and democratic popular culture could have been drawn without reference to Tocqueville.

One additional example will underscore this crucial point. It is notable because, like the Capper essay, it used Tocqueville in a manner that was manifestly outside Tocqueville's own expressed area of interest. Also like Capper, the author-editors of the work in question are distinguished scholars, Christopher Waldrep and Donald G. Nieman. In *Local Matters: Race Crime, and Justice in the Nineteenth-Century South* (2001),[21] a collection of essays on Southern legal history, these two respected historians opened their introduction by adverting to the observations of "de Tocqueville" that the law in America stood as a bulwark against the unrestrained force of public opinion and majoritarian tyranny. "But was de Tocqueville correct?" they inquired (ix). Their "book examines crime, justice, and community in the nineteenth-century American south, a region better known for honor and vigilantism than the rule of law" (ix). This was precisely why Tocqueville had excluded the South from his conclusions about both democracy and America. Not surprisingly, as the editors explain, the essays in their book demonstrate that "de Tocqueville overstated his case" (x). That is, the law only marginally, if at all, protected African Americans from the majoritarian tyranny of white supremacy in the postbellum South. "De Tocqueville's faith in the law ultimately proved elusive in a society more devoted to protecting white privilege than to the rule of law" (xvii).

The Tocqueville theme was picked up in the reviews of this book. Dickson D. Bruce Jr. followed the lead of Waldrep and Nieman by opening his review in the *Journal of American History* with Tocqueville's observations; the book's contributors, Bruce wrote, present "important discussions of that devotion to law Tocqueville observed among Americans." Certainly after reading this review, a reader could reasonably expect to encounter important discussions of Tocqueville's observations about Americans' devotion to law, and those expectations would be reinforced by reading the editors' introduction. Such a reader would be sorely disappointed, however, to discover that not one of the book's nine essays contained a single reference to Tocqueville.[22]

Tocqueville had been pushed on stage to serve as reinforcement for a banal point about the institution of the law, as if his authority were necessary to endorse the point that Waldrep and Nieman, who, it bears emphasizing, were extremely respected in their field and hardly needed the literary crutch of a venerated and ill-understood name, desired to make. The idea that law functions to dam the stream of popular prejudice is in any case common-place, if not tautological.

When Tocqueville is not incorporated into a writer's analysis, in other words, but is instead mined for observations that that writer wishes to make—or in this case, refute—we have an example of a decorative marker. The litmus test, therefore, of Tocquevillean ornamental status is whether using him helps the reader to understand the point because his ideas are incorporated into the analysis—whether he is part of the theory that helps us understand the phenomenon under observation—or whether he illustrates, through quotation or paraphrase, a point an author wishes to underscore. In other words, if the arguments of an author would be unchanged if Tocque-ville were absent from them, his status is ornamental. That was the case with Waldrep and Nieman's treatment of Tocqueville.

But this ornamental function proves to be an illusion at a deeper level, as well. For authors like Waldrep and Nieman, and so many others, gave the impression that Tocqueville's thought was being confronted at a serious level and woven into the analysis. It did not appear as if he was just being mined for epigrams, as, for example it would be easy to accumulate from the works of Shakespeare or Voltaire. While the argument on the page gave the appear-ance of Tocquevillean analysis, the reality was that Tocqueville's observa-tions were utterly dispensable for the authors' purposes—and absent from the essays in the book.

In fact, Tocqueville excluded the South from his generalizations about American culture and took pains to explain why. Simply put, his book was about democracy in America, and the South was undemocratic, so he would just leave the discussion of the South to others, and especially to Beaumont, whose romantic novel, *Marie,* Tocqueville wholeheartedly recommended to readers as illustrative of both his and Beaumont's observations and conclu-sions about the American South (*DIA* 365, 392n30). And those observa-tions, far from showing that "de Tocqueville overstated his case," *coincide* almost exactly with those of the essayists in Waldrep and Nieman's collec-tion—for "faith in the law ultimately prov[ing] elusive in a society more devoted to protecting white privilege than to the rule of law" is the theme, and the moral, of Beaumont's *Marie,* as well. The editors, then, applied Tocqueville's generalizations to a region of the United States that Tocque-ville pointedly excluded them from, then challenged those generalizations as not being applicable to that region, and finally concluded that it was Tocqueville who had been in error.

Yet how misleading would the image of turn-of-the-century scholarship on Tocqueville be if the account were abruptly to halt here. For the late twentieth century could also be seen as a true golden age of Tocqueville scholarship, with breakthrough studies in several important and relatively neglected areas of Tocqueville studies, excellent new editions of a kind that had never been successfully attempted before, attention to Tocqueville's more overlooked or marginal works by major historians and political theorists, and greater stress than ever before on the comparative dimension in Tocqueville rather than a dogged continuation of the tradition of treating his *Democracy* as the epitome of his life and a work of more pressing importance to his American than his European readers. There was a Tocqueville Society and a bilingual *Tocqueville Review/Revue Tocqueville*.[23] Some of the new work included an intelligently abridged new translation of *Democracy in America* and even, *mirabile dictu*, a comprehensive anthology with a brilliantly informative introduction. The anthology by two leading Tocquevilleans, Olivier Zunz and Alan Kahan, both students of the great *Tocquevillien* François Furet, not only surmounted the traditional dangers that afflict efforts to present a comprehensive picture of Tocqueville's thought, but also gave students and scholars alike a biographical overview, through the anthologized selections, of that body of work.[24]

Studies of Tocqueville's relation to French imperialism illustrated the vigor of turn-of-the-century scholarship. Anyone contemplating the role that imperial conquest played in French history during the years of Tocqueville's active involvement in politics can see immediately that France's leaders had undertaken a foreign policy that, however vigorously it might have supported national interests, cannot be said to have advanced those causes of liberalism and human freedom with which Tocqueville is so often and so closely associated. Universally recognized as one of the pillars of liberal thought in the nineteenth century, Tocqueville was also a firm and at times violent supporter of French colonial conquest in Algeria. In other words, Tocqueville's stance in relation to the crucial question of colonialism seems to present a paradox: how can the liberal be at the same time an imperialist? And how can Tocqueville's support of imperial expansion square with his expressed belief in fundamental racial equality and his active support of slave emancipation?

Tocqueville's writings on these questions (including some that Tocqueville did not intend for publication) first appeared in Volume III of the Gallimard edition of the *Oeuvres complètes* in 1962. In their introduction to that volume, André Jardin and J.-J. Chevallier contended that Tocqueville's texts were consistent with his political and moral values: the Algerian reports, they wrote, were "treated by the same expert and lucid pen" that composed *Democracy in America*. "But this pen serves as well France's major interests, in addition to those values—truth, justice, and liberty so dear to its author."[25]

This interpretation provoked a whirlwind of research by Melvin Richter culminating in one of the most important of all Tocqueville articles, published in the following year. Far from harmonizing with the Tocqueville of the *Democracy*, Richter argued, the Algeria reports show him to have abandoned his political principles: "When this issue forced him to choose, he placed nationalism above liberalism." Tocqueville seems indeed to have actively repressed his feelings about the violence that accompanied France's actions in North Africa; and fearing lethargy in France itself, he also approved of war as a means of rousing the French citizenry to great thoughts and stirring actions. As the German political scientist Michael Hereth put it in a discussion much indebted to Richter, "any admirer of Tocqueville is baffled" by the Algerian texts.[26] Richter's essay was for a long time the last word on the Algerian question in Tocqueville's career.

Then, in 1990, the historian and critic Tzvetan Todorov launched a pitiless attack on Tocqueville's colonialist writings and took issue with Richter's position that they constituted a simple contradiction with the liberalism of the *Democracy* and *The Old Regime and the Revolution*. To Todorov, Tocqueville's devotion to the principles of human rights vanished under the pressure of international relations. Human rights inhere in individuals, but, Tocqueville believed (according to Todorov), nations are in a state of nature vis-à-vis one another (as Locke had pointed out). But states, as such, are also analogous to individuals. Todorov's claim was straightforward: "Liberalism seeks to guarantee to each the right to exercise his abilities freely; thus colonizers have the right to colonise. Tocqueville's colonialism is no more than the international extension of his liberalism."[27]

How to reconcile these two views? Perhaps they cannot, or should not, be reconciled. But such is the healthy state of the field that even after such excellent scholarship, a new perspective was still possible. It was provided by Jennifer Pitts in 2001. Her study was especially welcome—and emblematic of the state of the field at the time—because it combined new translations of the key texts with clear analysis. Contra Richter, Pitts perceived more similarities than differences between the Algeria writings and the *Democracy*, especially because the *Democracy* itself is a far more indeterminate text than many commentators have been willing to concede. "Tocqueville's writings on European expansion in North America are tinged with the same ambivalence that would permeate his writings on Algeria. His protests at the cruelty of the American settlers and his laments over the extermination of noble cultures were heartfelt. Still, he could not help admiring the energy and perseverance of the English settlers in North America." But, as against Todorov's tone of fury at liberalism itself, Pitts emphasized a transformation in Tocqueville's attitudes during the 1830s and 1840s. "Tocqueville had been chastened by the wanton violence of the French army. . . . [He] came to see that the very means he had countenanced five years before had sown disaster among the native population and produced a society of settlers more violent and oppressive than the army itself."[28]

Thus, Jardin and Chevallier interpreted the Algerian writings benignly, seamlessly connecting French national interests with the values of liberty and justice. Richter argued that Tocqueville's embrace of colonial domination in Algeria stood in sharp, deplorable, and puzzling contrast to both the liberal values and the sociological method of *Democracy in America*. Todorov maintained that the *Democracy* did not particularly conflict with the Algerian writings but neither did it matter because liberalism was implicated in imperialism. And Pitts showed that the *Democracy* and the Algerian writings did not conflict as much as Richter thought, but that was because of the *Democracy*'s ambivalences and the evolution of Tocqueville's ideas. Here indeed were the elements of a serious argument on an important question bolstered by excellent scholarship and clear argument. Cheryl Welch then stepped in with a magisterial overview of the literature combined with a profound investigation of the moral psychology leading to Tocqueville's inconsistencies, evasions, and dishonesty in an article that reached Richter's standard, forty years later.[29]

As a third aspect of Tocqueville's turn-of-the-century standing, I would point to the seemingly endless controversy over the question of what constitutes the proper relationship between civil society and government and the degree to which broad-based participation in associations is a measure of the health of a democratic culture. In 1999, the *Chronicle of Higher Education* published a review of the major book-length literature on the question until that time, entitled "Perhaps We Bowl Alone, but Does It Really Matter?" Within a few years, many of the participants in the controversy were asking, "Here Is Another Bowling Alone Article, but Does Anyone Really Care?" The research of Harvard sociologist Robert Putnam had shown that

Americans were devoting less and less time and attention to voluntary associations and voluntary and quasi-voluntary civic responsibilities, and he used the decline in bowling-league membership as a marker for civic disengagement. Conservatives and left-leaning scholars viewed the whole controversy differently. Francis Fukuyama, with characteristic fluency, put it this way: "the left-wing vision of civil society is you have a community-action group mobilizing to stop Wal-Mart. . . . The right-wing vision is that these groups are an antidote to government." The merits of the many sides of the debate are not of concern here. The key point about the arguments over civil society is that the concept itself is derived from the observations of Tocqueville in the *Democracy* about the importance of associations and Americans' using them to counteract the evils of individualism and democratic excess. Of sixteen books listed in the *Chronicle*'s review, thirteen paid extended tribute or attention to Tocqueville and his chapters on associations. For the most part, however, the debate over civil society, considered strictly as an issue in recent American politics and society, could have occurred without Tocqueville's help. For example, one of the soundest and most empirically and methodologically sophisticated contributions to the discussion was an article about the effect of the GI Bill on civic participation; Tocqueville was absent from the analysis and the literature search.[30]

Yet, Tocqueville's role in this controversy is not, as in the cases of Capper and Waldrep and Nieman discussed earlier, that of decorative embellishment *tout court*. For the genesis of the notion of civic associations' playing a distinctive part in the day-to-day agitation of democratic culture is to be sought in Tocqueville, and not only in the *Democracy* but, as is almost always overlooked in the debate, in *The Old Regime* as well. Therefore, it is necessary and right for the civic-participation writers to cite and explicate Tocqueville, even though his particular conclusions or methodology are not woven into the accounts such writers present.

So flowed the currents of Tocqueville's reception at the turn of the twenty-first century. The scholarly trends were as follows: Greater attention to Tocqueville's works besides *Democracy in America*. Complementing this turn, more work with a comparative dimension, picking up on studies by comparativists of an earlier generation like Drescher. New editions and translations of works from all sides of Tocqueville's oeuvre, including the *Democracy*. Less attention to Tocqueville as a commentator on American life and institutions. Tocqueville's non-American works being examined using the insights and methods of poststructuralist reading strategies.

Side by side with the scholarship specifically devoted to Tocqueville was the ornamental use of the French seer with his prescience who could always be used as a prop or straw man. Finally, Tocqueville was also brought into discussions in which he did not contribute to the analysis but was important because key concepts in political thought derived from his work.

In 1962, the historian Richard Herr wrote a discerning study of Tocqueville's *The Old Regime and the Revolution*. He approached *The Old Regime* in Dantesque fashion as a text that could be interpreted at varying depths. Tocqueville's description of the faltering society and government of the Old Regime, presented to the reader by means of the themes of centralization and an increasingly decorative aristocracy, are like waves on the surface of the sea, Herr wrote. Beneath the waves on the surface, however, are the ocean tides, the forces delivering those institutions to the point of revolution's inception. But still deeper, running below even the tides, are the mighty ocean currents of the beliefs, mores, and habits of heart and mind of the people.[31] Some metaphors are meant to induce visual correlatives; some conceptual parallels; a few are aids to philosophical insight. In my judgment, Herr's metaphor of the waves, tides, and current is a hermeneutical tool and not merely a visual aid. I would borrow the trope, and venture the proposition that the decorative use of Tocqueville, while a surface wave, is yet significant as a marker of Tocqueville's indispensability; running deeper, however, than such references or than injections of Tocquevillean concepts into social and political analysis runs a current of scholarship that is flowing away from the older concerns with America and democratic mores.

Notes

1. Michel Chevalier, *Society, Manners, and Politics in the United States: Letters on North America*, ed. John William Ward, trans. T. G. Bradford (New York: Doubleday Anchor, 1961), 95, 367; *TBA*, 175. On the Russia–United States prophecy, see Theodore Draper, "The Idea of the 'Cold War' and Its Prophets," *Encounter* 52, no. 2 (1979): 34–45.

2. Arthur Louis Dunham, *The Anglo-French Treaty of Commerce of 1860 and the Progress of the Industrial Revolution in France*, University of Michigan Publications in History and Political Science, vol. 9 (Ann Arbor: University of Michigan Press, 1930), 28–34.

3. Alexis de Tocqueville to the editor of the *London Times* [published December 11, 1851], *Letters*, 266–78.

4. Alexis de Tocqueville to Gustave de Beaumont, November 4 [December 3], 1836, *OC*, VIII, pt. 1, 176. (The letter is dated November 4 and postmarked December 3.)

5. Arthur O. Lovejoy, *The Great Chain of Being: A Study of the History of an Idea* (Cambridge, Mass.: Harvard University Press, 1936), 5.

6. Merle Curti, *The Growth of American Thought* (New York: Harper and Brothers, 1943); on the contrast with Lovejoy see Thomas Bender, "Intellectual and Cultural His-

tory" in *The New American History*, ed. Eric Foner, revised and expanded ed. (Philadelphia: Temple University Press, 1997), 3–4.

7. Joyce Appleby, Lynn Hunt, and Margaret Jacob, *Telling the Truth about History* (New York: Norton, 1994), 172.

8. John Higham, introduction to *New Directions in American Intellectual History*, ed. John Higham and Paul K. Conkin (Baltimore, Md.: John Hopkins University Press, 1979), xiii. For specific application of this theme to Tocqueville's work, see Delba Winthrop, "Tocqueville's *Old Regime*: Political History," *Review of Politics* 43, no. 1 (January 1981): 88–111; and Olivier Zunz, "Tocqueville and the Writing of American History in the Twentieth Century: A Comment," *Tocqueville Review* 7 (1985–1986): 131–35.

9. Higham, "Introduction," xiv.

10. Thomas Bender, *Intellect and Public Life: Essays on the Social History of Academic Intellectuals in the United States* (Baltimore, Md.: John Hopkins University Press, 1993), 3.

11. Paul K. Conkin, "Intellectual History: Past, Present, and Future," in *The Future of History*, ed. Charles F. Delzell (Nashville, Tenn.: Vanderbilt University Press, 1977), 126.

12. "Your conversations have so much prepared me for the events which have passed since May, that I seem to be looking at a play which I have read in manuscript." Nassau William Senior to Tocqueville, November 30, 1851, in *Correspondence and Conversations of Alexis de Tocqueville with W. Nassau Senior*, ed. Mrs. M. C. M. Simpson, 2nd ed., 2 vols. (London: Henry S. King, 1872), I:271.

13. Margaret Marshall, "Notes by the Way: Alexis de Tocqueville's Discussion of Cultural Matters," *Nation* 162, no. 5 (February 2, 1946): 130.

14. John Lukacs, "Fear and Hatred," *The American Scholar* 66, no. 3 (Summer 1997): 441.

15. Phillips Bradley, "A Historical Essay," appendix II in Alexis de Tocqueville, *Democracy in America*, trans. Henry Reeve, 2 vols. (New York: Vintage, 1945), II:389–487.

16. Charles Capper, "'A Little Beyond': The Problem of the Transcendentalist Movement in American History," *Journal of American History* 85, no. 2 (September 1998): 502–39; subsequent references appear parenthetically in the text.

17. Stephen E. Whicher, *Freedom and Fate: An Inner Life of Ralph Waldo Emerson* (Philadelphia: University of Pennsylvania Press, 1953), 51–57.

18. Robert D. Richardson, *Emerson: The Mind on Fire: A Biography* (Berkeley: University of California Press, 1995), 453; the exhaustive research conducted by Merton M. Sealts Jr., *Melville's Reading*, rev. and enl. ed. (Columbia: University of South Carolina Press, 1988), reveals no reference to Tocqueville; no record of either Tocqueville or Beaumont, including the *Penitentiary System*, appears in Marion L. Kesselring, *Hawthorne's Reading 1828–1850: A Transcription and Identification of Titles Recorded in the Charge-books of the Salem Athenaeum* (New York: New York Public Library, 1949).

19. George M. Fredrickson, *The Inner Civil War: Northern Intellectuals and the Crisis of the Union* (New York: Harper and Row, 1965).

20. George Cotkin, review of *The Genteel Tradition and the Sacred Rage*, by Robert Dawidoff, *American Historical Review* 98, no. 1 (February 1993): 250; Ross Posnock, review of *The Genteel Tradition and the Sacred Rage*, by Robert Dawidoff, *Journal of American History*

80, no. 1 (June 1993): 293; Robert Dawidoff, *The Genteel Tradition and the Sacred Rage: High Culture vs. Democracy in Adams, James, and Santayana* (Chapel Hill: University of North Carolina Press, 1992), xvii.

21. Christopher Waldrep and Donald G. Nieman, eds., *Local Matters: Race Crime, and Justice in the Nineteenth-Century South* (Athens: University of Georgia Press, 2001). References appear parenthetically in the text.

22. Dickson D. Bruce Jr., review of *Local Matters: Race Crime, and Justice in the Nineteenth-Century South*, edited by Christopher Waldrep and Donald G. Nieman, *Journal of American History* 89, no. 1 (June 2002): 227–28.

23. Theodore Caplow, "The Early Days of the Tocqueville Society," *La Revue Tocqueville/The Tocqueville Review* 21, no. 1 (2000): 5–9; Olivier Zunz, "Twenty Years with *The Tocqueville Review*," *La Revue Tocqueville/The Tocqueville Review* 21, no. 1 (2000): 13–15. As these articles imply, the society was very much a closed affair, with membership by invitation only in a classic old-boys and -girls network.

24. Alexis de Tocqueville, *Democracy in America*, abridged by Sanford Kessler, trans. Stephen D. Grant (Indianapolis, Ind.: Hackett, 2000); Olivier Zunz and Alan S. Kahan, eds., *The Tocqueville Reader: A Life in Letters and Politics* (Malden, Mass.: Blackwell, 2002).

25. OC, III, Pt. 1, 9.

26. Melvin Richter, "Tocqueville on Algeria," *Review of Politics* 25, no. 3 (July 1963): 362–98 quote, 364; Michael Hereth, *Alexis de Tocqueville: Threats to Freedom in Democracy*, trans. George Bogardus (Durham, N.C.: Duke University Press, 1986), 158.

27. Tzvetan Todorov, "Tocqueville's Nationalism," *History and Anthropology* 4 (1990): 357–71 quote, 366; reprinted in Todorov, *On Human Diversity: Nationalism, Racism, and Exoticism in French Thought*, trans. Catherine Porter (Cambridge, Mass.: Harvard University Press, 1993), 191–207.

28. Jennifer Pitts, introduction to *Writings on Empire and Slavery*, by Alexis de Tocqueville, ed. and trans. Jennifer Pitts (Baltimore, Md.: Johns Hopkins University Press, 2001), xv, xxvi. Hereth had also noted a change over time, without developing the theme; Hereth, *Tocqueville*, 145–65.

29. Cheryl Welch, "Colonial Violence and the Rhetoric of Evasion: Tocqueville on Algeria," *Political Theory* 31, no. 2 (April 2003): 234–64.

30. D. W. Miller, "Perhaps We Bowl Alone, but Does It Really Matter?" *Chronicle of Higher Education* 45, no. 45 (July 16, 1999): A16–A18; Fukuyama quote, A16; Robert Putnam, *Bowling Alone: The Collapse and Revival of American Community* (New York: Simon & Schuster, 2000); a comprehensive study focused on Tocqueville's role is Chad Alan Goldberg, "Social Citizenship and a Reconstructed Tocqueville," *American Sociological Review* 66, no. 2 (April 2001): 289–315; Suzanne Mettler, "Bringing the State Back into Civic Engagement: Policy Feedback Effects of the G.I. Bill for World War II Veterans," *American Political Science Review* 96, no. 2 (June 2002): 351–65; Theda Skocpol, "The Tocqueville Problem: Civic Engagement in American Democracy," *Social Science History* 21, no. 4 (Winter 1997): 455–79, is the best critique of Putnam.

31. Richard Herr, *Tocqueville and The Old Regime* (Princeton, N.J.: Princeton University Press, 1962), 35–36.

✳

CHAPTER TWO

At Old Mrs. Otis's

If there is a tendency to trot out Tocqueville as spokesman for conclusions that a writer has formulated beforehand, such a tendency has deep roots in the earliest encounters between this French aristocrat who was both wise and shrewd, even in his twenties, and the nation he studied with such intense curiosity from 1831 until his death in 1859. From the moment Tocqueville and Beaumont disembarked in New York, on May 11, 1831, American citizens both prominent and obscure not only sought their company but also cultivated public awareness of having been in it. To have made the acquaintance of Tocqueville and Beaumont, it seems, was not enough; one had to be known to have made it.

Even before their arrival, the two handsome young commissioners created a stir among the Americans on board the Le Havre, the American ship on which they sailed from Le Havre to New York City. The idea that the brand-new government of Louis Philippe would turn to these United States for help and advice on the difficult question of how a free society should deal with crime and punishment was a deeply flattering signal to Americans of all classes. It betokened at last a recognition on the part of the Old World of the potential usefulness of the New. It was not so much a sense of superiority that Tocqueville and Beaumont encountered on their travels, but rather a generous if occasionally condescending eagerness by Americans to impart their appraisals of American social institutions to these European emissaries. And for their part, the young Frenchmen knew how to magnify the always-pleasant sensation that their informants' knowledge and opinions were highly valued. They were not only assiduous in their inquiries but also transparent in their openness to having Americans instruct them about their land, society, and politics.

One of their first requirements was to attain fluency in English. On board the *Le Havre*, they experienced an extremely pleasant immersion course, assisted mightily by "a most agreeable and gracious American girl, Miss Edwards," with whom Beaumont took great pains to assure his family (and no doubt himself) he was not in love, "in spite of her 18 years, her fresh complexion, her kindness, and all the charms of her person."[1]

It was also aboard the *Le Havre* that Tocqueville and Beaumont met their first important informant about politics. He was a New York merchant of considerable distinction named Peter Schermerhorn, and he managed to start off their investigations by providing them with misleading information on several different subjects. But conversations with Schermerhorn also furnished Tocqueville with an idea that would eventually become central, if not to Tocqueville's work itself, then to subsequent Americans' reception of it— the idea of national character. This crucial phrase makes its first appearance in Tocqueville's notebook on April 24. Under the heading "NATIONAL CHARACTER OF THE AMERICANS," Tocqueville noted: "Mr. Schermerhorn . . . told me that the greatest blot on the national character was the avidity to get rich and to do it by any means whatever."[2] Such an observation—that the drive for wealth is the greatest blot on America's character— seems oddly complacent in the era of Indian removal and of a burgeoning movement for the abolition of slavery. Just eleven months earlier, on May 28, 1830, Congress had passed the Indian Removal Act, the crowning achievement of Andrew Jackson's domestic program, while during Tocqueville and Beaumont's travels, on August 29, 1831, Nat Turner would ravage the Virginia countryside in the bloodiest slave revolt in American annals, murdering fifty-five whites, over half of them children. While Schermerhorn obviously cannot be faulted for not having foreseen the Turner revolt, what is striking about his insipid assertion is not its specific application to the American people but rather its bland universality; it may be applied to any people, to all people, to the human race. By singling out cupidity as a character trait, rather than a conditioned response to culture and institutions, Schermerhorn managed at once to utter a platitude and to disguise the source of any insight the platitude might have potentially contained.

But what affected Tocqueville the most was the notion of a nation's possessing a character rather than any purported specific components of it. And although Tocqueville would pursue the theme of riches with a passion comparable to that of the Americans' pursuit of the real thing, he would also perceive very early in the journey the centrality of race in forging and maintaining the nation's character and institutions. At the end of Volume I of

Democracy in America, he would compose a great essay on the triangular relations of the three American races—red, black, and white—that remains one
of the classic documents of the history of American race relations.

On the day after their arrival, the New York *Mercantile Advertiser* printed
a notice that conferred an immediate and highly useful notoriety on the two
Frenchmen: "We understand that two magistrates, Messrs. de Beaumont and
de Toqueville [*sic*] have arrived in the ship *Havre*, sent here by order of the
Ministry of the Interior, to examine the various prisons in our country, and
make a report on their return to France. . . . We have no doubt that every
facility will be extended the gentlemen who have arrived."[3]

Although Tocqueville and Beaumont arrived in America armed with seventy letters of introduction to leading intellectual and political figures, they
"found it so easy to enter New York social circles that the letters were almost
unnecessary."[4] Indeed, they were so heavily showered with invitations and
offers of help that Tocqueville could not forbear, as he confessed to his
beloved tutor, Abbé Lesueur, "laughing up my sleeve when I thought of the
difference that fifteen hundred leagues of sea makes in men's situations. . . .
I pictured to myself the extremely minor role that I played in France two
months ago and the comparatively elevated situation in which we found ourselves here."[5]

Tocqueville and Beaumont's first "reception" in America, then, was warm,
energetic, flattering, and exhausting. The list of their hosts in George Wilson
Pierson's exhaustive chronicle of their sojourn runs to upwards of two hundred names. These friends and informants—politicians, lawyers, educators,
merchants, businessmen, their wives, and sometimes their children—have
struck some commentators as being too heavily tilted toward the elite of
American society.

Using the growth and expansion of Tocqueville's own influence as a measure of importance, however—an influence that the duo can hardly have
anticipated in those early days in the spring of 1831—their most important
American acquaintance was young Dr. Franz Lieber of Berlin and Boston.

This Dr. Lieber never lacked for admirers, and eventually he reached the
pinnacle of American intellectual culture. By the time of the Civil War, he
was one of the most respected professors in the United States and an
acknowledged founder of an academic discipline.

"Your publications . . . furnish us with a proof of how it is possible with a
profound scientific culture to introduce ideas from the old European world
into a virgin state such as the Union is and there to make them practical—
ideas which return to the old world fettered by political and military *routine*,

and then there become instructive and enlightening in turn."⁶ This ponder-
ous encomium, which seems fitting as a judgment on Tocqueville's writings,
was instead directed by an eminent European academic toward this now
nearly forgotten political theorist, expert on international law, and exiled
immigrant intellectual. At once a transmitter, interpreter, and appropriator
of the thought of Tocqueville, as well as the Frenchman's close friend, tireless
correspondent, occasional petitioner, and—in his own mind at least—
intellectual rival, Lieber is one of the most interesting figures in mid-nine-
teenth-century American intellectual history. He is one of those authors
whose career had both an intrinsic interest and an influence that is dispro-
portionate to the quality of his thought. A citizen of that crowded domain
inhabited by people of talent but well short of genius, possessing great ambition and a tremendous capacity for work, Lieber made a notable imprint on
nineteenth-century American intellectual culture. *Century Magazine* perceptively said of him in 1883: "As a writer, he was too profound for the general
reader; as a teacher and lecturer, he was adapted to superior and not to inferior intellects; and so he seemed to have less influence than he really possessed. But he had the power of attracting, informing, and inspiring strong
minds."⁷

Lieber was born in Prussia precisely at the dawn of the Romantic era, in
1798. During his eventful youth he was struck full force by the *Sturm* of the
Napoleonic onslaught and the *Drang* of suspicion, arrest, and jail at the
hands of the assiduous Prussian police for his liberal convictions. As a lad of
only sixteen, Lieber sustained serious wounds at the battle of Namur, during
the Waterloo campaign. Lying on the field, in profound agony and nearly
unconscious, he was stripped of his valuables by scavenging peasants. Seeing
his eyelids quiver, one peasant exclaimed, "Ah, mon camarade, tu est dans
un état qu'il faut que tu crèves!"—You are surely about to die.⁸

Like some of his British and American contemporaries, Lieber gradually
developed a conception of French culture, and especially French government
and administration, as a kind of negative ideal—a type or exemplar of what
should be avoided in the science of effective government. In effect, his prejudices would serve to organize nearly all his thinking in the realm of political
science, a field he did more than anyone in the United States to establish as
an academic discipline.

Lieber possessed one quality in particular that is somewhat difficult for
later generations to apprehend, but that is best conveyed by the nearly obso-
lete word "complaisance." That is, he had the ability or characteristic of
making it seem to others that he was of one spirit with them. Signifying
something more subtle and sincere than simply being ingratiating (a term

that hints at a Uriah Heep–like affectation or phoniness), complaisance con-notes a cheerful willingness to oblige, an ability to please others without endangering one's own separate selfhood or authenticity. Taking his lead from James Boswell, Walter Jackson Bate sensitively elaborated on this trait in the psychology of the young Samuel Johnson. Bate pointed out that com-plaisance was "a stronger word at the time than it is now in suggesting cour-tesy and 'eagerness to please or oblige.'"[9] Many acquaintances, and especially women, recalled this obliging, socially fluent aspect of Johnson's youthful character. In fact, they depict an adolescent who is almost completely at odds with the more familiar figure of the mature Johnson, with the magnifi-cent force of his character emerging despite his violent tics and convulsions, bad hearing, and apparent social ineptitude.

Like young Sam Johnson, young Francis Lieber, too, displayed a remark-able natural gift for eliciting sympathy and support from others, in his case particularly from older or more powerful men. He did so partly because of his unaffected, obliging nature and partly because of the historic conjuncture that seemed to make the major events in his own life story—his suffering wounds in the final campaign against Napoleon, dashing off to aid the Greek struggle for independence, imprisonment by the Prussian police for his lib-eral political views, and emigration to America—virtually identical with the great political and social upheavals of his day.

Writing in the *Southern Literary Messenger* for January 1836, Edgar Allan Poe reviewed Lieber's first major book, the *Reminiscences of an Intercourse with Mr. Niebuhr, the Historian*. In the review, he drew particular attention to Lieber's "style of irresistibly captivating *bonhomie* and *naiveté*" and concluded that the reminiscences evinced "an interest altogether their own" as well as that conferred on them by their august subject, the great historian Barthold George Niebuhr.[10] At about the same time that Poe observed the complai-sant qualities in Lieber's prose, Chancellor James Kent of New York, the Jack-sonian era's greatest conservative and jurist, told Lieber, "You are such a temperate and reasonable reformer."[11] No stronger tribute could come from the redoubtable pen of Chancellor Kent, who was clearly aware of the ambig-uous—not to say oxymoronic—nature of the compliment.

But with only a slight change of perspective—just a small shift to a harsher and less generous angle—Lieber's complaisance and bonhomie appear in a less endearing light. Indeed, he can be made out to have been an ambitious toady whose assiduous cultivation of the powerful and the influ-ential—of the Niebuhrs and the Kents—seems the crassest sort of careerism. Such was the portrait of the immigrant intellectual drawn by two militant New Dealers, Joseph Dorfman and Rexford Guy Tugwell, in two jointly written articles that appeared in 1938. Scintillating in their wit and sneering in their condescension, these essays are important as the first sustained study of Lieber that had appeared in more than half a century. In the unsympathetic hands of Dorfman and Tugwell, Lieber, with his "mentality so typically Prussian," was mainly of interest as "a pre-Bismarckian supernationalist" whose ungainly efforts at cultural assimilation only served to "illustrate . . . the unsuccessful grafting of one civilization on another."[12] His distinguishing characteristic as an intellectual was his unrelenting restatement of the safest opinions held by the best men. "Lieber merely stated what all the best people would have agreed to" in his *Manual of Political Ethics*, Dorfman and Tugwell contended. "Thus after a long excursion through the far country of first principles Lieber came home again laden with propitiatory gifts for the mighty."[13]

There is much value, much truth, and certainly much wit in Dorfman and Tugwell's portrait, but its features are distorted by their lack of sympathetic engagement with their easily lampooned subject. Lieber was more than a maniacally ambitious striver with a superhuman work ethic. He was also one of the first political thinkers to apply the insights of Tocqueville to the study of American political institutions, a systematic thinker and planner in the field of international law, and an academic who lobbied with administrators and trustees to see his educational ideas become part of the standard college curriculum. His ceaseless self-promotion and self-dramatizing must have been tiresome to his American and European friends, yet so many of them were nevertheless able, and apparently happy, to provide support for his projects and ambitions.

Two of Lieber's most consistent supporters and friends were Tocqueville and Beaumont. At first, this seems an unlikely connection. To begin with, Lieber was bitterly anti-Catholic as well as a Francophobe who articulated his political philosophy by employing a facile metaphorical contrast between "Anglican" and "Gallican" notions of liberty. According to his theory, English political institutions had developed in a manner that fostered "individual independence, and . . . a feeling of self-reliance," whereas "In France, liberty is expected to begin practically with government organization, and to descend to the people."[14] Such observations were hardly innovative, and in fact constitute a severe dumbing-down of conclusions that Tocqueville had reached many years before Lieber published the 1848 essay in which these ideas appeared. Moreover, Lieber was a slaveholder during most of the time the strongly antislavery Tocqueville knew him (Lieber moved from South Carolina to New York and Columbia University in 1857; Tocqueville died in 1859).

Yet, in spite of these differences, the bonds that bound Lieber to his two French friends were close and permanent. They were forged during Tocqueville and Beaumont's 1831 journey, strengthened by continual correspondence, and further solidified in 1844, when Tocqueville recruited Lieber to write about American affairs for the newspaper Tocqueville had just purchased, *Le Commerce*.

The thirty-two-year-old Lieber laconically recorded the following entry into his diary, in Boston, on Sunday, September 18, 1831: "Meet De Beaumont and De Tocqueville at old Mrs. Otis's. They are here to study the prisons."[15] "Old Mrs. Otis" was the wife of the last great Federalist politician, and the retiring mayor of the city, Harrison Gray Otis. At her home that afternoon, Beaumont, Tocqueville, and Lieber struck up an immediate spark of comradeship and mutual interest. "The three young men were delighted with each other," Pierson noted, adding that Lieber was attracted to Beaumont in particular.[16] This special affinity between Beaumont and Lieber would endure for four decades. Later that very day, the Frenchmen visited Lieber at the latter's modest home. The three were frequent companions during Beaumont and Tocqueville's visit to Boston and were never thereafter out of contact by correspondence for the remainder of Tocqueville's life.

At the time of Tocqueville and Beaumont's visit, Lieber was enjoying the first blush of fame and reputation, for his audacious project to publish an *Encyclopedia Americana* had proven a success. Its thirteen volumes constitute an appropriate monument to Lieber's doggedness, tact, and great capacity for labor. He translated hundreds of articles from a German encyclopedia and contributed dozens of articles himself, as well as coaxing scores more from American collaborators. When Tocqueville returned to France, he lugged a copy of the *Encyclopedia Americana* back with him. Lieber had made a close study of the famous legal *Commentaries* of Joseph Story, and Story's ideas can be detected throughout the articles Lieber contributed. As Frank Freidel shrewdly conjectured, "Perhaps from [the *Encyclopedia*] rather than from the *Commentaries* came the many ideas of Joseph Story," ideas that, Story complained, Tocqueville had relied on excessively in writing *Democracy in America*.[17]

The greatest immediate benefit to Lieber from his relationship with Beaumont and Tocqueville was his receiving the commission to translate *Du Système pénitentiare*, their outstanding study of the American prison system. It was, of course, the research for this pioneering work that had furnished the occasion for their visiting the United States in the first place.

"MM. De Beaumont and De Tocqueville had the kindness to send me, a few months ago, their work on the *Penitentiary System in the United States*, before it had issued from the press in Paris," Lieber wrote in a lengthy translator's preface that contained a massive dose of self-promotion. According to Lieber's account, he had been quite reluctant to undertake the task of translation. "My time was, at that period, and is still so much occupied by previous engagements" that he was inclined to turn down the request, he wrote, despite the high level of "my personal regard" for "my friends." But, in the end, "the great importance of the subject . . . induced me to undertake the task."[18]

This version of events is unusually misleading, even for Lieber, as convincing evidence shows that it was the ambitious Lieber, not the French authors, who had first proposed the idea of providing an English edition of the penitentiary volume. Beaumont wrote to Lieber on November 16, 1832, "Our report on the penitentiary system of America is finally finished. We want very much for you to carry out the project *that you have devised* of publishing the translation before it is completed, as being based on the *manuscript of the authors.*"[19] Beaumont's letter clearly shows that the impetus for the project came from the translator, not the other way round.

But this letter of Beaumont's also reveals a note of easy warmth that would suffuse the correspondence of the two friends for years to come. In it, he recollected with fondness "our conversations and our excursions around Boston" and reminisced gallantly about "Mme. Lieber . . . mille fois plus aimable que toutes les américaines de Boston." He also he touched on a motif that Marie de Tocqueville echoed years later and that may help to account for the depth and duration of the friendship between Lieber and the Tocquevilles. It is the idea that Lieber, the exiled immigrant intellectual who was formed by his European origins in every way, belonged finally in Europe rather than the United States. Somehow, Beaumont wrote, "I just cannot persuade myself that you live *in America*. It is Europe that suits you, and by which you have been *made into a friend to the world.*"[20] And yet Lieber himself said, at about the time of Tocqueville and Beaumont's visit, "Only here in America have I learned the true value of liberty; and here is the turning point of my life."[21] Lieber was a genuinely cosmopolitan character, bestriding European and American mores, and Beaumont's expression of feigned incredulity at Lieber's residence in America was somewhat forced. But it was Lieber's very Europeanness that continued to endear him to his old acquaintances from Boston.

Fifteen years later, Mme. Tocqueville, in a charming burst of sentiment, inquired, "Why are you so far away across the Ocean? When I think that perhaps we shall never meet again it quite damps my courage. Are you really fixed in America forever? Pray tell me when you next write your plans for the future, for I should be too sad if I thought you would never take up your permanent abode in Europe. It would give me so much pleasure to make Mrs. Lieber's acquaintance."[22]

As to the *Système pénitentiare*, Lieber's pursuit of this high-profile contract was an astute tactic that not only cemented his friendships with Beaumont and Tocqueville but also created his own reputation as an expert in the field of criminal punishments. In fact, however, the English-language edition of *The Penitentiary System in the United States* is a very different volume from its French original. For not only did Lieber supply his long-winded preface to it, but he also affixed no fewer than seventy-one often rambling, discursive footnotes to the Frenchmen's text, thereby ostentatiously intruding himself onto the pages of the original study.

Lieber's manic energy, huge capacity for work, and verbal hyperactivity, combined with the scarcity of real depth in most of his output, make him an exhausting subject to study. He is so hard to keep up with, and at the end of the day one wonders if the chase has been worth it. Indeed, Lieber seems to have been something of a graphomaniac. One example of his overflowing verbal industry can be examined in the special collections department of the Milton S. Eisenhower Library at Johns Hopkins University. It is described in the library's catalog as Lieber's interleaved copy of the first edition of his translation of the *Système pénitentiare*. It is a massive tome that might surprise anyone with a conventional understanding of the word "interleave"—that is, to insert a blank sheet between two leaves of a book. An interleaved volume is one with sheets of writing paper slipped between some of the pages, on which a reader has jotted or intends to jot notes or queries about the subjects treated in that portion of the volume. But such is not the appearance of Lieber's copy of the *Penitentiary System*, for what Lieber did was to remove the book's original binding and stitching, cut the fascicles, place a large sheet of paper between every single page in the book, restitch and rebind the volume, and cram the sheets with all sorts of notes, editorial changes, typographical corrections, further remarks on his own footnotes, pasted newspaper clippings, notes on the clippings, and even correspondence. It is a remarkable, bulging, ongoing, palimpsestical conversation with himself (and only secondarily with Beaumont and Tocqueville) about every aspect of the great social question of prison discipline.

It is startling to compare Lieber's version of the *Penitentiary System* with the French original. For every two pages of large-type text (on average), Lieber inserted one small-type narrative footnote. Indeed, one cannot escape the conclusion that the distorted Lieber edition, taken as a whole, represents more of an effort to grab attention for Francis Lieber than a means of introducing Americans to the ideas of Beaumont and Tocqueville.

Worse, Lieber very nearly succeeded in changing the very focus of the study in his edition, even though ostensibly it was only a translation. Beaumont and Tocqueville's objective had been to investigate America's system of criminal punishments as dispassionately as they could and to assess the degree to which that system, or elements of it, might be "applied" in France. Lieber's purpose, however, was totally different—for in the course of pursuing his own investigations, he had become a passionate, loud, and inflexible supporter of one side of a strange and now-forgotten controversy.

The issue in this battle was whether prisoners in the new penitentiaries should be kept strictly separated at all times of the day and night, or whether they ought to be allowed to labor in the company of their fellow prisoners during a portion of each day. When penitentiaries first began to be erected (thanks to the humane vision of the Quakers, "who abhor all shedding of blood"[23]), total isolation, utter silence, and complete idleness were considered the three indispensable, mutually reinforcing components of convict reformation, and rules enforcing the regime were put in place in the new reformatory institutions. The outcome was tragic. "This absolute solitude, if nothing interrupts it, is beyond the strength of man," Beaumont and Tocqueville wrote. "It destroys the criminal without intermission and without pity; it does not reform, it kills."[24] Reformers thought they could overcome the problem by eliminating not the solitude but the idleness. So all agreed that the prisoners would be put to work. As to the other two building blocks of reformation, silence and solitude, the first was everywhere retained, but the second was modified at the prison located in Auburn, New York. There the prisoners worked according to a congregate system during the day and retired to their single cells at night. In Pennsylvania's two prisons, in Pittsburgh and Philadelphia, however, more of the old-time faith was retained; there prisoners labored in isolation in specially designed cells, working to produce items that could be fabricated individually, such as shoes and harnesses.

The great battle of the systems, Auburn and Pennsylvania, was waged over the course of an entire generation. "The debate raged with an incredible rancor," wrote the pioneer historian of the penitentiary, David J. Rothman. "In retrospect [the two programs] seem very much alike, but nevertheless an extraordinary amount of intellectual and emotional energy entered the argument. The fervor brought many of the leading reformers of the period to frequently bitter recriminations, and often set one benevolent society against another. . . . Every report from the New York and Pennsylvania penitentiaries was an explicit apology for its procedures and an implicit attack on its opponents."[25]

In the *Système pénitentiare*, Beaumont and Tocqueville described the two systems and the dispute over their respective morality and efficacy with an admirable impartiality and restraint. Indeed, it is difficult to determine which side they favored simply by reading the book. Years afterward, in fact, Beaumont was admonished in the Chamber of Deputies for having side-stepped the issue. The occasion was a seventeen-day debate over the report of a committee of which Tocqueville was *rapporteur*. (Beaumont then admitted their preference for the Pennsylvania scheme.)[26] In their book, the controversy is really a side issue, occupying only a short portion of an extensive chapter on the purpose of penitentiaries.[27] But for Lieber, the translation provided an opportunity to proselytize vigorously on behalf of the Pennsylvania plan, to which, in characteristic fashion, he had become ardently attached during his research. Thus it transpired that a book notable in its original form for scrupulous detachment was presented to the American public as a stridently partisan argument in favor of one side.

Lieber's intrusions in the *Penitentiary System* were ubiquitous. For example, he attached his own separate dedication to the volume, and that dedication was to three men. Then again, on the title page, a pair of horizontal lines set off Lieber's name, written in a typeface the same size as that used to identify the authors. In the abundant footnotes, he frequently made reference to his *Encyclopedia Americana*. He even appended his encyclopedia article, "Penitentiary System of Pennsylvania," a polemic in the guise of a report, to the volume. "The system of solitary confinement, as now practiced in the Eastern Penitentiary in Philadelphia, is the only effectual mode of making prisons schools of reformation, instead of schools of corruption," he gruffly argued. "The more light there is thrown upon this subject, the better for the cause."[28]

Indeed, the very opening sentence of Beaumont and Tocqueville's text is defaced by a brusque and tasteless Lieber intervention. It distorts the all-important beginning of their book while it mars the appearance of the printed page with its sleeve-tugging bid for attention. "Society, in our days, is in a state of disquiet, owing, in our opinion, to two causes," began Beaumont and Tocqueville in their preface. But before they could even identify what those causes of social disquiet might be, Lieber intruded with an asterisk. The footnote to which the asterisk draws attention occupies two-thirds of the printed page, in small type. In both manner and meaning it clashes with Beaumont and Tocqueville's argument:

> We live, every one will admit, in an agitated period—one of those epochs (in the opinion of the translator) which are characterized in history by the conflict of new principles with old, and whose agitation can cease only when the former acquire a decided ascendancy over the latter. We must be careful, however, that the Present does not appear to us in those magnified dimensions, with which it never fails to impress itself on our minds, if we do not view the Past and the Present with conscientious impartiality, and examine both with unprejudiced scrutiny.[29]

And so on, and on, and on—for four hundred words. To examine with scrutiny . . . the new conflicts with the old . . . the times are agitated . . . the present looms too large: such were the convictions that gripped Lieber with a force so violent that he felt compelled to interrupt the authors he was translating before they could even draw their first breath.

Perhaps it is not surprising, then, to find Tocqueville expressing considerable irritation with his old friend from Boston. Privately, he complained to Beaumont about the appearance of the volume and Lieber's interpolations. "I have just received Lieber's English translation. . . . Lieber has not written [to me], perhaps his letter was addressed to you. Moreover, I have not been completely satisfied with his translation. It is laden down with notes in which in his capacity as a *foreigner*, he believes himself obliged to contradict the tiniest truths that we have said about America. One sees that he is singularly afraid of centralization (*solidarité*). The whole of his work has made me believe that the Americans have not found themselves well enough treated by us."[30]

Yet, in spite of his exuberant liberties, relations between Lieber and his friends from "old Mrs. Otis's" seem not to have been permanently damaged. Evidently, Lieber's complaisance was still a powerful force. Throughout the 1830s and 1840s, the three comrades maintained their warm correspondence. Lieber had entered his sad "exile" at rough-edged South Carolina College in 1834, the year after the *Penitentiary System* appeared, while Tocqueville published the first volume of his immediately and immensely successful *Democracy* the following year.

In July of 1836, in an act with marvelous symbolic overtones for all students of American history and culture, Beaumont married Clémentine de Lafayette, the granddaughter of that great marquis who was the most revered

PREFACE.

Society, in our days, is in a state of disquiet, owing, in our opinion, to two causes:*
The first is of an entirely moral character; there is in the minds of men an activity which knows not where to find an object; an energy deprived of its proper element; and which consumes society for want of other prey.
The other is of an entirely material character; it is the unhappy condition of the working classes who are in want of labour and bread; and whose corruption, beginning in misery, is completed in the prison.
The first evil is owing to the progress of intellectual improvement; the second, to the misery of the poor.
How is the first of these evils to be obviated? Its remedy

* We live, every one will admit, in an agitated period—one of those epochs (in the opinion of the translator) which are characterized in history by the conflict of new principles with old, and whose agitation can cease only when the former acquire a decided ascendency over the latter. We must be careful, however, that the Present does not appear to us in those magnified dimensions, with which it never fails to impress itself on our minds, if we do not view the Past and the Present with conscientious impartiality, and examine both with unprejudiced scrutiny—in many cases the most difficult task of the historian. The present evil always appears the greatest; but if we allow ourselves to be thus biassed, we shall be liable to mistake the real aim after which we ought to strive, and the means by which we endeavour to arrive at it, and unconsciously will lend assistance to those who, more than any others, raise in our age the cry at our disturbed times—the advocates of crumbling institutions. They ought to be aware, that few times were more peacefully disposed than that in which we live, and which they are so anxious to represent as deprived of all solid foundation. If we examine century by century, from the seventeenth up to the beginning of the common era, where and when do we find peace? We meet every where with war, turmoil and party strife, contests often originating in frivolous cabinet intrigues, or kindled by religious fanaticism, or by interest and ambition hiding themselves under the pretence of defending sacred rights, inherent in individuals, for the purpose of obtaining sway over nations. The sober student of history must admit, that there never was a period possessing more powerful elements of peace, than our own; since the interests which determine the condition of society have become more and more expanded; are of a general and national, not of a limited, individual, and therefore, arbitrary character. These observations are by no means directed against the writers of the present work, but merely intended as a general remark on what we conceive to be a misconception very common in our time; and particularly against those who, taking for granted that the time we live in is more unsettled and disturbed, and that society is in a more feverish state than heretofore, are opposed to salutary and necessary reforms, extolling former times as those of happy ease.—Trans.

Lieber's Intrusion. Gustave de Beaumont and Alexis de Tocqueville, On the Penitentiary System in the United States and Its Application in France, trans. Francis Lieber (Philadelphia: Carey, Lea, and Blanshard, 1833). Nineteenth-Century Collection, Saint Louis University Law Library.

of all foreign friends of the United States. It was not a match calculated to please Beaumont's legitimist family, who predictably opposed it. But Beaumont was too independent, and perhaps too much of a friend of America, to be swayed by their objections. Indeed, the young lovers made a splendid couple. Five years later, Beaumont, healthy and happy, wrote to his old friend in South Carolina that he had such "fond memories [of America] . . . all the more dear since, due to my marriage with the granddaughter of General La Fayette, I am half American."[31]

However, it is clear that Lieber's relations with Tocqueville himself were somewhat cooler than those with Beaumont. Tocqueville's temperament was always of a reserved and emotionally cautious nature, and this reserve certainly stands out in comparison with the more effervescent Beaumont. Beaumont, an accomplished draughtsman who produced marvelous sketches and watercolors from the American journey, also shared Lieber's affinity and enthusiasm for the visual arts. Yet, the chief explanation for the disparity in Tocqueville's and Beaumont's responses to Lieber must lie in the South Carolinian's exaggerated notion of his own importance as an American intellectual, which was admittedly considerable. But considerable or not, Lieber came to see himself as a sort of American Tocqueville and was, at times, not shy about drawing the comparison for the benefit of others.

But Tocqueville's was a relative coolness only, a kind of friendliness held in reserve, and the general tone of Tocqueville and Lieber's correspondence is businesslike, but warm. One specific piece of business came to the fore during the mid-1840s, when Tocqueville made a full-blown foray into political journalism. He purchased and ran a "faltering and somewhat leftist newspaper," changed its name to Le Commerce: journal politique et littéraire, and exercised the controlling voice over its editorial position (Le Commerce "represented only me," he wrote to Beaumont). Roger Boesche has explored fully the significance of this rather neglected episode and concluded that "except for his 1831–1832 sojourn in the United States that produced De la démocratie en Amérique and for the tumultuous year of 1848, Tocqueville's year of control over Le Commerce may well have been the most courageous, the most distressing and the most revealing of his personal life."[32] And for such success as Le Commerce could attain, he had to rely to a considerable extent on the contacts, talents, and insights of Francis Lieber.

In fact, Lieber owed Tocqueville a big favor, because he had been pestering Tocqueville for years about being made a corresponding member of France's prestigious Academy of Moral and Political Sciences. It was a high honor and one Lieber sorely longed for. He began lobbying for the appointment in 1839, as soon as Tocqueville was elected to the Chamber of Deputies.[33] Tocqueville had many other things on his mind at that time—notably a ground-breaking report to the Chamber on the abolition of slavery in the French colonies, a neglected classic of the abolitionist literature, not to mention the still-unfinished second volume of *De la démocratie en Amérique*—and probably also thought Lieber's election would be a pretty sure thing. But it was not to be accomplished for several more years. "I consider [my election] the highest honor of the kind which can reward the labors of the scholar," Lieber wrote on November 24, 1839, "and, my friend, let me ask you in confidence, do we in America not require to be cheered on from Europe?"[34]

In 1844, Lieber received a pardon for his past political sins from the king of Prussia and decided to tour Europe with his wife, Matilda. The couple visited the Tocquevilles in Paris in May, when they undoubtedly discussed the impending elections to the Academy. After a trip to London, they returned in late summer, where Lieber spent ten days in the Louvre, feeling, as he wrote to Charles Sumner, like "a long dried sponge thrown into the water."[35]

As the Liebers were about to depart for home, Marie de Tocqueville wrote a letter to Francis that revealed the considerable services she performed for her husband while he was engaged with *Le Commerce*. The letter is most persuasive and friendly. "Mr. de Tocqueville is more than ever occupied," she explained, before describing exactly what Tocqueville wanted Lieber to do in his new capacity as a contributor to the paper: "Perhaps you will be able to get some subscribers to the *Commerce* in America, in New York it might be possible to place a few or in any part of the Union it would be very desirable to introduce that Newspaper; if the American Newspapers could give extracts from it, I think it would produce an excellent effect. What M. de Tocqueville desires is that the *Commerce* should obtain as much publicity as possible out of France as well as within."[36]

Marie de Tocqueville's letter revealed how staunchly she acted as a refuge for her overburdened husband. As André Jardin wrote of her, "More than anything else, she was and remained for him a calm, soothing refuge. 'You reconcile me with the world and with myself,' he wrote to her. He felt that this calm, and the confidence he had in her provided support that was essential to his very life."[37]

Lieber sent but four letters to *Le Commerce* from America. It did not greatly matter; little was to come of Tocqueville's enterprise. He ceased his connection with the paper on June 30.[38] But Lieber did finally succeed—he was made a corresponding member of the Academy in 1851.

One can detect indications of less than fulsome feeling toward Lieber in Tocqueville's silences, in his failures to respond to the Prussian's overtures, and in his turning over to Mme. Tocqueville some portions of their correspondence. And one additional source of Tocqueville's irritation is also evident in Lieber's correspondence—his overflowing self-esteem. As he attained middle age, Lieber's outsized ego combined with his lack of circumspection to overbalance the effects of his charming youthful complaisance.

Like many considerably talented, intensely ambitious people with a focused, highly developed work ethic, Lieber lacked a sense of proportion about his own superiority. Although he was a significant figure in the development of American political thought and possessed a fine critical intelligence, he could not find the right standard by which to measure his own accomplishments. When Tocqueville's great *L'Ancien Régime et la Révolution* appeared in 1856, Lieber issued to Samuel Ruggles, a trustee of Columbia University—the institution, which had, to his infinite gratitude, delivered him from his long Southern exile—the following remarkable judgment: "Are you reading De Tocqueville's *The Old Regime* [which had not yet been translated]? In spite of a few apparent contradictions, it is an excellent book and a very Commentary upon 2 or 3 chapters of my Civil Liberty." And he proceeded generously to rank Tocqueville as one of the three most prominent "historico-philosophical publicists" of the modern world—along with the Baron de Montesquieu and . . . Francis Lieber. "I really write this with perfect calmness."[39]

It was just as well for Lieber that he interpreted the *Ancien Régime* as a commentary by Tocqueville on his own important book, *Civil Liberty and Self-Government* (1853), for receiving such a commentary in a direct way was precisely what Lieber had been unable to obtain, despite repeated direct requests. In 1853, Lieber had sent copies of his book to Beaumont and Tocqueville. "I do not know that there is a man living, whose opinion that there is some substance in the work, I should value more than yours," he wrote to the latter on September 29, 1853. "You will see that I have several times quoted you in that esteem which I sincerely feel for you." But a year later, he had still not received a reply and felt constrained to ask for it again "before I return to my everlasting South [for the school term]."[40] But he never received that response.

It is likely, as I have suggested, that Tocqueville's unwillingness to provide an appraisal arose in part out of pique at Lieber's elevated opinion of his own work. Lieber's lack of proportion about his achievements—his conviction that he was in fact a second Tocqueville—appeared as early as the 1830s. "It is possible that I shall soon write a book on Politics, in which, as a matter of course, I should make use of your 'Democracy'," Lieber condescendingly wrote in 1839. The book in question turned out to be the turgid *Political Hermeneutics*, a suitable example of Lieber's research technique, which, as Charles Robson put it, consisted of "collect[ing] data . . . by prodigious exertion rather than any precise and efficient system."[41]

In the *Political Ethics*, which was also published that year (the heart of the *Political Hermeneutics* had appeared as a chapter in the *Ethics*, which Lieber subsequently expanded), Lieber included a lengthy chapter on the concept of *instruction*, his term for the supposed responsibility of senators to follow in detail the explicit wishes, or instructions, of the state legislatures that elected them. In the manner of Edmund Burke, whom he did not credit, Lieber classified the principle of responsibility to constituents into two categories, which he labeled the representative and the deputative. Representatives are the true glory of the emerging systems of republican government, while deputies are outgrowths of the feudal era. "It was the common principle in the feudal estates, respecting communities, professions, provinces, classes, and estates, because their deputies represented their respective bodies as a whole, and only them." Upon this distinction Lieber constructed an elaborate argument for the freedom of senators to vote as representatives with free consciences, not mere deputies recording the interests of the legislatures that had appointed them for that duty. In short, Lieber considered the deputative principle a feudal relic and the doctrine of representation a great advance in the art and science of government. With perhaps less than perfect tact in addressing a man who had just been elected to his nation's Chamber of Deputies, Lieber drew particular attention to this chapter in his *Political Ethics*. "If there is anything worth reading in the book, it must be there," he wrote to Tocqueville. "I beg you . . . to look at it. [It] includes some of the most essential points of the representative principle, and in what it is contradistinguished from the deputative principle in the Middle Ages."[42] But Tocqueville still demurred. There is no record of a response to Lieber's request.

Within weeks of his appeal to Tocqueville, he told his friend Samuel Hilliard, "I know that my work belongs to the list which begins with Aristotle, and in which we find the names Thomas More, Hobbes, Hugo Grotius, Puffendorf."[43] This hyperbolic reflex extended to specific components of the vast body of his work. Examples of Lieber granting the highest importance to diverse and hardly related aspects of his writings abound. Some of his references to particular short sections, chapters, and pamphlets may have misled certain scholars, such as Merle Curti, into accepting Lieber at his word.

For example, in a manuscript at the Huntington Library entitled "What I Have Done," which was probably written for his son Norman in about 1854, the first item on the list reads, "First established the idea of *institutional* liberty." And yet he had written to Tocqueville, concerning the second volume of the *Political Ethics*, "I consider this second part the chief one of this work, and the whole work that of my labors to which I am willing to stake my name and reputation." Many years later, it was about a paper on land reforms in Russia that he wrote to Daniel Coit Gilman:

> When Haydn 72 years old heard his own "Creation", and that sublimest of musical passages came: *Let there be light*, he rose, stretched forth his hand, and cried: 'Not from me, not from me; from Thee oh God", and was carried home. Small things—very small things may remind us of great things—very great things. Perhaps I would be as willing to stake my name as a lover of freedom and as a statesman upon these 7 pages, as upon anything else I may have published.

But a year later he told Charles Sumner it was his work on nationalism that was absolutely central to understanding his thought: "My pamphlet *Nationalism* will be found sticking in my bones, instead of my marrow, when I am dead and people should take the trouble of applying the cleaver to my shins."[44]

Nationalism, institutional liberty, land reform, representative versus deputative principle: where was the real core of Lieber? Was there such a core? Or was the net he cast over the turbulent sea of politics and history simply too vast to manage? I believe, with Curti, that one theme in Lieber constitutes his most important legacy. And because of his enormous influence on the development of political science, his contacts with virtually every important educator in the mid- to late-nineteenth century, and his specific impact on key thinkers who came after him—such as William Graham Sumner, Thorstein Veblen, Daniel Coit Gilman, and John W. Burgess—this was also one means by which Tocqueville's legacy was kept alive when direct scholarly attention to his life and thought had not yet been developed. This was the theme of nationalism.

Lieber's American nationalism was passionate as it was sincere, but there is a sense in which it was a derivative nationalism, an outgrowth of the ideology of his youth. The German yearning for national unification and self-assertion, which was of the same age as Lieber, was in important respects echoed in the American nationalism of the Civil War period, and it exerted an emotional pull on Lieber that never relinquished its hold. In the last year of his life, as the tensions between Prussia and France intensified to a fever pitch, Lieber's anti-French, anti-Catholic, Prussian nationalism spilled over in a letter to Yale's Theodore Dwight Woolsey. "This day—perhaps this very hour," he dramatically proclaimed, "the Protestants meet near the Luther Monument in Worms, 'to say an open word to Rome,' on the impending [Vatican] Council, the reigning Jesuitism and the apprehended War between the Latin, Catholic, and [illeg.] race on the one hand, and the Germanic, Protestant and Liberty race on the other hand."[45] When the Franco-Prussian War did come in 1870, it wiped out one of the oldest and closest friendships of Lieber's life, that with pro-American French publicist Édouard Laboulaye.[46]

Tocqueville's works were transmitted and interpreted for American readers not solely through the work of academic intellectuals like Lieber but also through journalists and publicists (a word invented by Lieber) on a variety of subjects unrelated to politics. Completely overlooked in accounts of Tocqueville's growing prestige in antebellum America has been the part played by women in elevating it. At the time of Tocqueville and Beaumont's American journey, a new genre of nonfiction was making its appearance before an immense readership: the manual of domestic advice. Its originator, Boston's Lydia Maria Child, was one of the most popular American writers of the nineteenth century. A poet, short story writer, and novelist, as well as a skilled magazine editor, Child was also noted as a devoted soldier in the cause of abolitionism. She edited the *National Anti-Slavery Standard* along with her husband, Rev. David Lee Child, as well as the first American magazine for children, the *Juvenile Miscellany*. In 1828 she published the first book on the subject of the organization and disposition of resources for the American home. It was called *The American Frugal Housewife: Dedicated to Those Who Are Not Afraid of Economy*, and it went through twelve editions in just four years. It was one of the most popular books in America at the time of Tocqueville and Beaumont's sojourn.[47]

Mrs. Child, however, was destined to be overshadowed by an author even more successful, more widely known, and more conservative in both gender and national politics: Catharine Beecher, whose sister Harriet was an acquaintance of Tocqueville's. Beecher's *Treatise on Domestic Economy for the Use of Young Ladies at Home and at School* (1841) introduced Tocqueville's second volume to probably more readers than any other single source. It presented the Frenchman as a perspicacious observer of American domestic manners. In her opening chapter, Beecher quoted Tocqueville's chapters on American women and girls at great length and with copious indications of approbation. It was not only those chapters' accuracy as descriptions of the roles performed by wives and daughters in shaping American democratic mores that Beecher commended but also the moral superiority of such roles to those played by the Americans' European sisters. It is an impossible argument, and however fervently one wishes to evade the snares of presentism, it is difficult not to wonder how far it was really accepted even in the 1840s—as opposed to being ignored *as* argument and understood simply as a description of mores. "It is in America, alone, that women are raised to an equality with the other sex," was Beecher's Tocquevillean claim. "[Here] women have an equal interest in all social and civil concerns. . . . But in order to secure her the more firmly in all these privileges, it is decided that, in the domestic relation, she take a subordinate station, and that, in civil and political concerns, her interests be entrusted to the other sex, without her taking any part in voting, or in making and administering laws." The *Treatise* was a huge commercial success, reprinted every year between 1842 and 1857; like the *Democracy* itself, it was adopted by the Commonwealth of Massachusetts for use in the schools. It was Beecher—borrowing directly from Tocqueville—who gave the nation the metaphor that would shape the discourse about America's white female population for more than a century: that of the "sphere," or enclosed circle of domesticity within which they were to perform their sacred duties to family and republic.[48]

Beecher's laudatory insertion of Tocqueville into the discussion on domestic economy furnished more American readers with their introduction to the *Democracy*'s second volume than did the reviews in the magazines. That volume appeared in the Reeve translation on April 20, 1840, the same day that it was published by Gosselin in Paris. John Stuart Mill devoted a long article to both volumes of the *Democracy* in the *London and Westminster Review* for October 1840. The first comment on the second *Democracy* in the American periodicals came in July 1841. Thus, the *Treatise on Domestic Economy* coincided with the earliest notice of that second volume.[49]

As Kathryn Kish Sklar showed in a masterful essay on Beecher's *Treatise*, the work was something new in American letters. It contained the first and most comprehensive argument for the idea of the separate sphere, as well as for "the spiritualized, specialized, and politicized view of motherhood." It was a novel kind of work because of the comparatively narrow scope of its intended audience. According to Sklar, earlier manuals on household management—including, despite its title, even Child's *American Frugal Housewife*—had been directed to an audience of both women and men. Beecher's, by contrast, was just for women and girls. Appearing at the historic conjuncture of the "demographic transition" of declining birth rates and improved rates of infant mortality, the *Treatise* was in a sense the complement in the realm of gender politics and ideology to these changes in family structure and future expectations.[50]

Three years before Beecher composed her hymn to the virtues of the domestic sphere, John C. Spencer had published the first American edition of the *Democracy*. That volume comprised only what we know as Volume I, of course, because Volume II was not completed until 1840. As a consequence of the slightly belated appearance of Volume I in a widely available edition and Volume II coming out just a couple of years afterwards, Tocqueville enjoyed a sustained period in the public consciousness.

Spencer had been one of Tocqueville's most trusted and influential sources of information. Yet the Canandaigua lawyer maintained a curious silence during the time surrounding Tocqueville and Beaumont's visit, while for his part Tocqueville himself never seems to have grasped the significance, either to American political history or to the personal career of his best-informed host, of the popular movement that swept upstate New York shortly before their visit: Antimasonry.

Spencer had first met Tocqueville and Beaumont in Utica on July 5. Beaumont wrote to his family that Spencer was "the most distinguished man whom I have yet met in America." This was an accurate description. In 1830, Spencer had completed the Revised Statutes of New York and, more importantly, had served as the special counsel appointed by President Martin Van Buren in the matter of the disappearance and almost certain murder of William Morgan in 1826—the episode that spontaneously generated the popular movement of political Antimasonry. The tragic Morgan affair sparked a passionate defense of law, constitutional government, and popular democracy against what was perceived, correctly in the event, as the forces of privilege and arrogant secrecy. Spencer was squarely in front of the Antimasonic movement as one of its most respected early leaders. By the year of Tocqueville and Beaumont's stay at Spencer's stately Canandaigua home (now the Elm Manor Nursing Home on Canandaigua's Main Street), Antimasonry had evolved into a political party, albeit without the active involvement of Spencer himself. "Antimasonry's impressive but brief showing in politics actually understated its achievement," the historian Daniel Feller concluded. "Thriving on the new democratic ethos," the Antimasonic Party held the first presidential nominating convention and issued the first written party platform on September 26, 1831, while Tocqueville and Beaumont were busy visiting prisons and workhouses in the vicinity of Boston.[51]

In spite of the fact that Spencer was one of their most important informants, however, and notwithstanding the remarkable coincidence that Tocqueville and Beaumont were in Baltimore, the city that hosted the Antimasonic Party convention, just one month after the party nominated William Wirt for president, the whole Antimasonic movement—an epitome of the democratic political mores that Tocqueville would soon analyze—eluded their notice. In notes about his Spencer interview, Tocqueville recorded the sole reference to Antimasonry in all his writings. Tocqueville had inquired about limits on press freedom. "When a paper publishes libelous facts . . . then it is prosecuted and generally punished with a heavy fine," Spencer responded. "I recently had an experience of an example. At the time of the case in connection with the disappearance of Morgan (a Masonic affair) a newspaper printed that the jurors had pronounced their verdict of guilty from motives of 'party spirit.' I prosecuted the writer of the article and had him punished."[52] Tocqueville, subsequently renowned for his powers of observation, did not notice one of the clearest empirical examples of his theoretical position when it was set before his eyes. And, with a sort of symmetrical cluelessness, Spencer himself failed to make any mention of Tocqueville's visit in his correspondence of that summer. It was as though the Frenchmen's stay, however celebrated afterward, had made little impression on Spencer at the time.[53]

Seven years later, Spencer arranged for an American publication of the first *Democracy*. For this historic volume he provided a preface and some notes that in their very brevity led to an augmentation of Tocqueville's reputation. "We repose on the authority of the work with more confidence than ever, when we see how little it contains, which so acute and well-informed an annotator as Mr. Spencer found to require correction or explanation," the *North American Review* pronounced in October 1838. One careful historian of Antimasonry heard echoes of Spencer's Antimasonic convictions in Spencer's preface, especially in his affirmation that "all republics depend on the willingness of the people to execute the laws," words that "could have been written by the citizens of Genesee County in 1826." Perhaps so, but to a reader unfamiliar with the details of the controversies in Genesee County even in 1838, such a remark must have seemed more of a bromide than a unique or bold political observation. Spencer later became so closely identified with the *Democracy* that one wag in 1864 facetiously proposed, in Baconian-Shakespeare fashion, that he had been its secret author.[54]

But Tocqueville's book was by no means greeted with unrestrained approbation.

"Monsieur de Tocqueville/may pass *in Europe* for American history/ . . . And New Orleans occurred in 1815, Monsieur de Tocqueville/may pass in Europe for American history/in a foreign tongue," wrote Ezra Pound contemptuously in the *Cantos*. Pound's verses were derived directly from and echoed almost verbatim the hard and unforgiving voice of the great frontier senator Thomas Hart Benton of Missouri, a man who, like Pound, never forgave a slight, real or imagined. Benton once merely wounded an adversary in a duel, so he called him out again for a second in which he shot him dead. Pound referred to Tocqueville four times in the *Cantos,* each reference more disparaging than the last and all based on the animus of Benton.[55]

In his massive autobiography, *Thirty Years' View*, Benton attacked Tocqueville in two extended and one brief passage because Tocqueville had shown a disregard bordering on contempt for Benton's hero, Andrew Jackson. In January 1832, at the very moment when the Congress and president were wholly engrossed in the struggles over the bank, the tariff, and nullification, Tocqueville and Beaumont were presented to Jackson at the White House. None of the three was impressed with his new acquaintance. In the *Democracy* Tocqueville wrote:

> General Jackson, whom the Americans have twice elected to be the head of their government, is a man of violent temper and very moderate talents; nothing in his whole career ever proved him qualified to govern a free people; and indeed, the majority of the enlightened classes of the Union has always opposed him. But he was raised to the Presidency, and has been maintained there, solely by the recollection of a victory which he gained, twenty years ago, under the walls of New Orleans; a victory which was, however, a very ordinary achievement and could only be remembered in a country where battles are rare.

Beaumont was in full accord; as he wrote on the following day to his mother, "He is not a man of genius. Formerly he was celebrated as a duelist and hothead; his great merit is to have won in 1814 the battle of New Orleans against the English . . . so true is it that in every country military glory has a prestige that the masses can't resist."[56]

During those tumultuous January days, Benton strove to marshal every scrap of support he could find as Jackson's floor leader in the Senate on the bank issue. To Benton—"Old Bullion" as he became known for his obdurate hard-money views—Jackson's war on the bank and support of a tariff constituted a life-or-death struggle for civilization and republican government. If Tocqueville tended to view and portray Jackson through the gauzy filter of his preestablished ideas about centralization and local powers—as in his words "a Federalist by taste and a Republican by calculation"—Benton understood Tocqueville in terms of the emerging Whig-Democratic party division. Because Tocqueville had warned readers of a tyrannical inclination in President Jackson, he sounded to Benton like Henry Clay and the Whigs of 1834, who actually managed to pass a resolution of censure against Old Hickory for having removed the government's deposits from the bank. Three years later, the Senate, led by the relentless Missourian, ordered that thick black lines be drawn around the words of the censure in the official record and the following words be written across it: "Expunged by order of the Senate, this 16th day of January, 1837." Benton, in short, could not abide Tocqueville's portrayal and took his revenge in the *Thirty Years' View*.[57]

Yet it is one measure of the deference that Tocqueville was able to command in the 1850s that, at the conclusion of a chapter enumerating the "errors of Mons. de Tocqueville" with regard to Jackson, Benton proffered a conciliatory bouquet: "Regard for Mons. de Tocqueville is the cause of this correction of his errors: it is a piece of respect which I do not extend to the riffraff of European writers who came here to pick up the gossip of the highways, to sell it in Europe for American history, and to requite with defamation the hospitalities of our houses."[58]

No such regard can be detected in Pound's *Cantos*, where Tocqueville operates as a foil to Jackson, Benton, and other upholders of a metallic currency. Benton's championing of Jackson stood for Pound as a crucial event in American banking and financial history. Pound's contempt for Tocqueville was in part a means for him to express his crank economic theories. Central to this portion of the *Cantos* is Pound's quotation from Benton's Senate speech defending Jackson's bank and hard-money policies in Canto LXXXVIII, where Tocqueville is disparaged and hard currency extolled in nearly the same poetic breath: "a currency of intrinsic value FOR WHICH/ They paid interest to NOBODY/page 446/column two/("Thirty Years," Benton) . . . Tariff/Monsieur de Tocqueville may pass *in Europe* for American history."[59]

Notes

1. Gustave de Beaumont to his father, April 25, 1831, quoted in *TBA*, 45.
2. Quoted in *TBA*, 49.
3. Quoted in *TBA*, 58.
4. André Jardin, *Tocqueville: A Biography*, trans. Lydia Davis with Robert Hemenway (New York: Farrar, Straus & Giroux, 1988), 107.

5. Quoted in Jardin, *Tocqueville*, 109.

6. Dr. [August] Heffter to Francis Lieber (translation), August 26, 1863, Lieber Papers (JHU).

7. Daniel Coit Gilman, "A Romantic Career," *Century* 26, no. 5 (September 1883): 792.

8. Francis Lieber, *The Miscellaneous Writings of Francis Lieber*, ed. Daniel C. Gilman, 2 vols. (Philadelphia: J. B. Lippincott, 1881), I:162–64.

9. Walter Jackson Bate, *Samuel Johnson* (New York: Harcourt Brace Jovanovich, 1977), 84.

10. Edgar Allan Poe, *Essays and Reviews*, ed. G. R. Thompson (New York: Library of America, 1984), 665, 669.

11. Quoted in Frank Freidel, *Francis Lieber, Nineteenth-Century Liberal* (Baton Rouge: Louisiana State University Press, 1948), 96.

12. Joseph Dorfman and Rexford Guy Tugwell, "Francis Lieber: German Scholar in America," *Columbia University Quarterly* 30, no. 3 (September 1938): 155–90, and 30, no. 4 (December 1938): 267–93; quotes on 161, 159, 160. The earlier study of Lieber was Thomas Sargeant Perry, ed., *The Life and Letters of Francis Lieber* (Boston: James R. Osgood and Company, 1882). Its numerous shortcomings are listed in Charles B. Robson, "Papers of Francis Lieber," *Huntington Library Bulletin* 3 (February 1933): 135–55. But even more disparaging is the original draft of Robson's article: "The Francis Lieber Papers in the Huntington Library [Summary Report]," Francis Lieber Papers (H).

13. Dorfman and Tugwell, "Francis Lieber," 172, 174.

14. Francis Lieber, "Anglican and Gallican Liberty," in *Miscellaneous Writings*, II:377, 384.

15. Perry, *Francis Lieber*, 91.

16. TBA, 337.

17. Freidel, *Francis Lieber*, 91.

18. Francis Lieber, translator's preface to *On the Penitentiary System in the United States and Its Application in France*, by Gustave de Beaumont and Alexis de Tocqueville (1833; repr.: Carbondale: Southern Illinois University Press, 1964), 3.

19. Gustave de Beaumont to Francis Lieber, November 16, 1832, Lieber papers (H); first emphasis added.

20. Beaumont to Lieber, November 16, 1832, Lieber papers (H).

21. Quoted in Freidel, *Francis Lieber*, 88.

22. Marie de Tocqueville to Francis Lieber, July 22, 1846, OC, VII:113. See also Marie de Tocqueville to Francis Lieber, December 2, 1844: "Is there no chance of your ever coming to settle in Europe? If you were in Prussia we should see you occasionally, but in America the hope of meeting again more than once during life seems faint" (OC, VII:99.)

23. Beaumont and Tocqueville, *Penitentiary System*, 37.

24. Beaumont and Tocqueville, *Penitentiary System*, 41.

25. David J. Rothman, *The Discovery of the Asylum: Social Order and Disorder in the New Republic* (Boston: Little, Brown, 1971), 81.

26. An excellent discussion of the occasion is in Thorsten Sellin, introduction to *Penitentiary System*, xxxvi–xxxviii.

27. Beaumont and Tocqueville, *Penitentiary System*, 54–60.

28. "Penitentiary System of Pennsylvania," in Beaumont and Tocqueville, *Penitentiary System*, 287.

29. Beaumont and Tocqueville, *Penitentiary System*, xlv.

30. Tocqueville to Beaumont, November 1, 1833, OC, VIII, pt. 1:137.

31. Beaumont to Lieber, August 16, 1841, Lieber Papers (H).

32. Roger Boesche, "Tocqueville and *Le Commerce*: A Newspaper Expressing his Unusual Liberalism," *Journal of the History of Ideas* 44, no. 2 (April–June 1983): 277.

33. See Lieber to Tocqueville, September 20, 1839, in Perry, *Francis Lieber*, 140. Tocqueville assisted many American scholars in becoming corresponding members of the academy. In addition to Lieber (1851), he helped William H. Prescott (1845), George Bancroft (1848), and Edward Everett (1856), as well as the Englishmen Henry Babington Macaulay (1852) and George Grote (1856). Françoise Mélonio, introduction to OC III:17.

34. Lieber to Tocqueville, November 24, 1839, [author's copy], Lieber Papers (H).

35. Freidel, *Lieber*, 213–16.

36. Marie de Tocqueville to Francis Lieber, January 8, 1845, OC, VII:102–3. (Where the OC prints "M. de Tocqueville," the manuscript letter in the Lieber Papers (H), reads "Mr. de Tocqueville.")

37. Jardin, *Tocqueville*, 50.

38. Jardin, *Tocqueville*, 391–92.

39. Lieber to Samuel Ruggles, October 23, 1856, quoted in Louis Martin Sears, "The Human Side of Francis Lieber," *South Atlantic Quarterly* 27, no. 1 (January 1928): 54. Tocqueville had urged Lieber to read the work in the original French rather than wait for a translation; see Tocqueville to Lieber, September 1, 1856, OC, VII:178.

40. Lieber to Tocqueville, September 23, 1853, and September 4, 1854, Lieber Papers (H).

41. Lieber to Tocqueville, September 20, 1839, in Perry, *Lieber*, 140; C. B. Robson, "Francis Lieber's Theories of Society, Government, and Liberty," *Journal of Politics* 4, no. 2 (May 1942): 232.

42. Francis Lieber, *Manual of Political Ethics* (Boston: Little, Brown, 1839), II:521–50; quotes on 523 and 550n3; Lieber to Tocqueville, September 20, 1839, in Perry, *Francis Lieber*, 140.

43. Lieber to Hilliard, November 30, 1839, quoted in Freidel, *Francis Lieber*, 164–65.

44. Francis Lieber, "What I Have Done," copy in the hand of Norman Lieber, c. 1854; Lieber to Tocqueville [author's copy], November 24, 1839, both in Lieber papers (H); Lieber to Daniel Coit Gilman, January 29, 1868, Lieber papers (JHU); Lieber to Charles Sumner, January 25, 1870, quoted in Merle Curti, "Francis Lieber and Nationalism," *Huntington Library Quarterly* 4, no. 3 (April 1941): 263.

45. Lieber to Theodore Dwight Woolsey, May 31, 1869, Lieber Papers (H).

46. Johann Bluntschli, "Francis Lieber," in Lieber, *Miscellaneous Writings* II:13.

47. Sarah A. Leavitt, *From Catharine Beecher to Martha Stewart: A Cultural History of Domestic Advice* (Chapel Hill: University of North Carolina Press, 2002), 10.

48. Catherine [sic] Beecher, *A Treatise on Domestic Economy* (1841; repr. New York: Schocken Books, 1977), 9, 4; Tocqueville excerpts on 5–9, 10–13, 23–24; Kathryn Kish Sklar, "Introduction to the Paperback Edition," in Beecher, *Treatise*, v–xviii; Linda K. Kerber, "Separate Spheres, Female Worlds, Women's Place: The Rhetoric of Women's History," *Journal of American History* 75, no. 1 (June 1988): 10.

49. Jardin, *Tocqueville*, 251; "Catholicism," *Boston Quarterly Review* 4 (July 1841): 320–39.

50. Sklar, "Introduction," vi, xii.

51. *TBA*, 216; "C-SPAN Rolls into Canandaigua," *Canandaigua Messenger*, July 13, 1997, 1; Elizabeth Burchholz Haigh, "New York Antimasons 1826–1833" (Ph.D. diss., University of Rochester, 1980), 295–320; Daniel Feller, *The Jacksonian Promise: America, 1815–1840* (Baltimore, Md.: Johns Hopkins University Press, 1995), 103.

52. Alexis de Tocqueville, *Journey to America*, ed. J. P. Mayer, trans. George Lawrence (Garden City, N.Y.: Anchor, 1971), 13–14.

53. The only extant Spencer correspondence from this period is in the William H. Seward Papers and the Thurlow Weed Papers, both in Rare Books and Special Collections, Rush Rhees Library, University of Rochester, Rochester, New York. None of Spencer's eight letters from the summer of 1831 to the spring of 1832 contains any reference to his French visitors.

54. John C. Spencer, "Preface to the American Edition," in *Democracy in America*, by Alexis de Tocqueville, ed. John C. Spencer (New York: George Dearborn, 1838), i–ix, quote on vi; *North American Review* 47, no. 2 (October 1838): 504; Haigh, "New York Antimasons," 318; John W. Henry Canoll, "The Authorship of 'Democracy in America,'" *Historical Magazine* 8, no. 10 (October 1864): 332–33.

55. Ezra Pound, *The Cantos of Ezra Pound* (New York: New Directions, 1970), Canto LXXXVIII, line 184, p. 583, and line 226, p. 584, Canto LXXXIX, line 89, p. 590, and Canto C, line 98, p. 716; Thomas Hart Benton, *Thirty Years' View, or, A History of the Working of the American Government for Thirty Years, from 1820 to 1850*, 2 vols. (New York: D. Appleton and Company, 1856), I:112; invaluable for approaching the *Cantos* is William Cookson, *A Guide to the Cantos of Ezra Pound* (New York: Persea Books, 1985), esp. 38, 41–42, 89–92, 105–8.

56. Quote is from Alexis de Tocqueville, *Democracy in America*, ed. Phillips Bradley, 2 vols. (New York: Knopf, 1945), I:299; *TBA*, 664.

57. *TBA*, 666; Robert V. Remini, *Andrew Jackson* (New York: Harper Perennial, 1966), 167; Benton, *Thirty Years' View*, I:111–14, 205–8.

58. Benton, *Thirty Years' View*, I:114.

59. Pound, *Cantos*, 583.

CHAPTER THREE

꒞

The American Old Regime

In 1990, the esteemed British Americanist Hugh Brogan let fly a wild surmise that to my knowledge has been completely overlooked by historians, even though, if true, it might be expected to cause a sensation. After a careful review of the foreign correspondence in the newly released seventh volume of the *Oeuvres complètes* of Tocqueville, plus a search of still-unpublished Tocqueville correspondence at Yale's Beinecke Library, Brogan felt confident enough in his interpretation of the evidence to hypothesize that Tocqueville had had an adulterous affair with the sister of Robert E. Lee. Although admitting the absence of direct evidence for such a liaison, he did reach a positive conclusion about a sort of fallback position, namely that Tocqueville had fallen deeply in love with her, and she with him.[1]

This intelligent and beautiful woman was Mrs. Edward Vernon Childe, née Catharine Mildred Lee. Some six years younger than Tocqueville, she was the guiding spirit of a brilliant Franco-American salon that met every Tuesday in her Paris apartments and at which she brought together such outstanding "writers, publicists, and men of the world" as Jean-Jacques Ampère, Prosper Mérimée, and Tocqueville himself.[2] Mr. Childe was a Bostonian of independent means, a Harvard graduate, and a longtime resident of Paris. He wrote a series of letters from that city for a New York newspaper, the *Courier and Enquirer*, between 1845 and 1856.

In a touching "portrait" of Mrs. Childe written to her and at her request, and in a style that, as Brogan coyly put it, "though not [that] of an accepted lover, might be thought to be in that of a man beginning to be in love," Tocqueville had drawn special attention to her firmness of spirit under the trials, great and small, of life, then continued, "as for myself, I imagine that fire . . . may well be one of the elements of your nature; but it is a fire that burns without a flame. Your friends can only suspect its existence; you alone, Madame, can tell us if it has ever been given to anyone to feel its heat." Mrs. Childe's unexpected death from surgery in 1856 at the age of forty-five left˜ Tocqueville inconsolable. After her death, Mr. Childe graciously returned all of the letters that Tocqueville had written to her. They have never been found, and the inescapable inference is that Tocqueville destroyed them. Brogan concluded about this matter, "there can be no doubt that this was the closest of Tocqueville's American friendships."[3]

This is a striking assertion. Can we really maintain that Mrs. Childe was "the closest of Tocqueville's American friendships," closer even than Jared Sparks, Theodore Sedgwick, John C. Spencer, or Francis Lieber, the major sources of information during Tocqueville's American journey, men with whom he had maintained steady correspondence for nearly a quarter of a century? That depends, of course, on what you mean by close. We can safely assume that Tocqueville was not in love with Lieber or Sparks and that whatever degree of intimacy he achieved with Mrs. Childe may well have been unique. But what is surely of overriding importance to the historian is the nature and extent of these people's views on the formation of Tocqueville's own work.

I do not believe Tocqueville had an affair with Mrs. Childe, for several reasons. Nor can I agree even to the watered-down proposition that they were in love. Brogan's evidence is not strong enough to support the inference, and his speculation betrays as well a curious and uncharacteristic deficit of sensitivity and awareness of context.

The issue is, precisely, that context—the spiritual and intellectual state of Alexis de Tocqueville during the first half of the 1850s and the role that American affairs played in affecting his thoughts and concerns. Mrs. Childe was a key informant in this regard, but not, I think, the most important one. This was due to several interacting features of his private life at this stage: partly because Tocqueville was actively soliciting the ideas of a number of older, more experienced sources who were situated in the United States; partly because his mind was focused on the completion of his historical masterpiece, *The Old Regime and the Revolution*; partly because of his failing health; and finally, partly because of his profound distress over the calamity that had yet again befallen France, the calamity of despotism.

The composition of *The Old Regime and the Revolution* was a direct consequence of the turbulence and violent contradictions of the years from 1848 to 1851—that is, of the "mad" February Revolution and the despotic Second Empire that was its upshot and antithesis.[4] Tocqueville's correspondence during the 1850s reveals an abiding despondency, a visceral disgust with the empire that seemed to suffuse every aspect of life. But that despondency and that disgust did not indicate emotional exhaustion or depression. It was rather a feeling of political uselessness, combined with an extreme distaste for the mores of a nation that confirmed Louis Napoleon's coup d'état of December 2, 1851 in a plebiscite with 92 percent of the vote.

These two themes first appeared in a letter to his old English friend, Henry Reeve, the translator of *Democracy in America*, written just one month after the coup. "What should I tell you that you do not know about what is happening in France?" he asked. "When I finally want to speak of our affairs, even to my best friends (and you are among them), a sadness so bitter and so profound seizes me that I have trouble continuing such distressing conversations or correspondence." This is an anguished expression of his cheerlessness and revulsion. Concerning the decline in mores he was equally direct. "Nothing shows two things more clearly: the first, the softening of souls, which the immoral government of Louis Philippe brought about; the second, the dreadful terror into which this violent, but above all mad, Revolution of February has thrown these souls, softened and ready to bear anything with joy and even to assist in anything provided that the phantom of socialism that disturbed their enjoyment by threatening their future would disappear."[5]

But Tocqueville's state of mind in the early 1850s, somber though it was, could hardly be labeled depression, for depression triggers inactivity, and Tocqueville was far from inactive in these years. Indeed, his great intellectual energy was mobilized, in part, to counteract the very bitterness of which he complained to Reeve. For him, in other words, work was a kind of refuge from the Second Empire. After his research in Paris had gotten well under way, he wrote to Gustave de Beaumont: "I do not know if I will extract something interesting and new from this study, which is making progress: I am finding in it, at least, the advantage of forgetting, in surrendering myself to it, the things and the men of our time and of isolating myself, without boredom, from human beings, which appears to me, more and more, the great goal to attain."[6]

Thus, Tocqueville felt revulsion and dismay in these years and combated the malaise with enthusiastic researches on the book he intended to write on the great revolution. But there is a third element to Tocqueville's major preoccupations during his last decade, and that was his health. In March 1850, Tocqueville coughed up blood for the first time: it was the first visible sign of the tuberculosis of which he would die nine years later. He also suffered from pleurisy and from intestinal distresses of various kinds. After the spitting of blood, his physician strongly urged the Tocquevilles to relocate temporarily to drier and sunnier regions during the period of his recovery, so they journeyed to Sorrento, Italy, and took up lodgings in an agreeable house from the roof of which they could take pleasure in a spectacular view of Mount Vesuvius. It was in Sorrento that Tocqueville composed his *Souvenirs*, or recollections of the 1848 revolution and its aftermath.

One way to understand these recollections is to think of them as the way in which Tocqueville worked through and tried to come to terms with the condition of contemporary France in the realm of his feelings or private sentiments.

The dichotomy between feelings and ideas, or sentiment and intellect, is the most consistent and repeated binary opposition in Tocqueville's published works, and it is one that Tocqueville himself deconstructs by means of the concept of *mores*. In the *Democracy*, he had taken great pains to define mores as the inextricable fusion of those putatively separate realms, sentiment and feeling: that indeed was the source of the power of this most crucial concept. By mores, he wrote then, that he referred not only to "the habits of the heart, but also to the various notions that men possess, to the diverse opinions that are current among them, and to the whole range of ideas that shape habits of mind. Thus I use this word to refer to the whole moral and intellectual state of a people" (*DIA* 331). In the *Souvenirs*, Tocqueville said, he was creating "a mirror in which I can enjoy seeing my contemporaries and myself, not a painting for the public to view. . . . I want to express myself honestly in these memoirs, and it is therefore necessary that they be completely secret."[7] These memoirs, in short, were Tocqueville's way of dealing with the empire on the level of sentiment.

Despite its seemingly different subject matter, then, *The Old Regime and the Revolution* is a pendant or companion piece to the *Recollections*. In the *Recollections*, Tocqueville came to terms with his feelings about the new despotic France; in *The Old Regime*, he would mobilize the intellect to come to a public, historical understanding of the coup. Therefore, the two books taken together function on the personal level as the concept of mores does on the social.

The Old Regime and the Revolution is a misleading title, for the book says a great deal about the first named subject and nothing about the second. R. R. Palmer once wrote that in conceiving *The Old Regime*, Tocqueville showed a "tendency toward a kind of infinite regression in the focus of his efforts."[8] This was his way of explaining how the effort to come to grips with Napoleon III's coup ended up being a book about social conditions in pre-Revolutionary

France. Tocqueville first focused his attention on the subject of the first Napoleon because Napoleon's coup of 1799 was the tragedy that his nephew, as Karl Marx put it, farcically imitated as if in a theater. But the consideration of Napoleon I led Tocqueville in turn to the subject of the situation in France before 1799. From there, the regression continued, for it seemed then necessary to examine the great Revolution itself; and from the Revolution, again, back to the situation of France before the Revolution broke out. Here, finally, Tocqueville's regressions could cease, because sixteen years earlier, at the request of his then new friend John Stuart Mill, Tocqueville had produced for Mill's *London and Westminster Review* an essay entitled "The Social and Political Condition of France before and after 1789." This would provide the point of departure and foundation for *The Old Regime*.

During the summer of 1853, the Tocquevilles traveled again, this time to Saint-Cyr, near Tours, where Tocqueville conducted intense research in the provincial archives, aided by a renowned archivist, Charles de Grandmaison. They lived in Saint-Cyr for one year and, in June 1854, relocated again, this time to Bonn, where they resided on the grounds of the university. Tocqueville felt he had to pursue his inquiries in Germany because it was there that feudalism, the system allegedly overthrown by the events of 1789, could be examined most directly. Germany, in a sense, was to feudalism what the New England town was to democracy—a Weberian "ideal type" that reveals the features of the social system in an especially pure form.

It was during this period, when Tocqueville was struggling to understand the new French despotism and was traveling—both for his health and for his project—was conducting research, and was composing his historical masterpiece, that he began to learn about the shocking and distressing new turn of events in the United States. He undertook correspondence and direct conversations with several American friends, and what they had to tell him was in its way as disturbing to him as what had befallen France. For what the news from America portended—especially the news of Senator Stephen Douglas's Kansas-Nebraska bill—was the expansion of an empire of slavery.

One of Tocqueville's leading informants was Francis Lieber. In the spring of 1854, as Tocqueville was trying to learn some German in preparation for his removal to Bonn, Lieber wrote him affectionately, "I wish I was near you to teach you German," and shared his alarm over Douglas's bill, contrasting in conventional terms the wisdom of the Missouri Compromise with "this mischievous Nebraska Bill." Indeed, his letter was written immediately after he had learned of its passage in the Senate (March 4, 1854). "It has passed the Senate and I fear there is no chance of preventing its being passed in the

House of Representatives. It is a wicked and, even with reference to the South, a most unwise law. . . . For the North is now set wholly free with reference to the sad slavery question. There are some men in the South who view things as I do; but we are very few. We shall see great agitation within the next ten years."[9]

Tocqueville had actively solicited Lieber's opinions and advice about American affairs while he was writing *The Old Regime*. In the summer of 1852, he wrote to Lieber at length about his book project, and then concluded by saying, "But that is enough and more than enough about [French] politics. . . . Why do you tell me nothing in your letter of American affairs? Do you believe that the subject has ceased to interest me? Please make good this oversight the next time you write to me."[10] Lieber was not the sort of man who needed to be asked twice to share his opinions, and he provided Tocqueville with his perspective on American developments for the next four or five years.

What was that perspective? It was one marked by Lieber's long residence in the South and by a kind of subservience to Tocqueville which he chafed under, if only slightly, and from time to time.

Two of Tocqueville's leading informants, then—Childe and Lieber—were members of slaveholding families and conservative Unionists. A third was Theodore Sedgwick, a Democratic Unionist, diplomat, and law professor, who, as a young attorney and attaché at the U.S. Embassy in Paris in 1832, had assisted Tocqueville in the composition of the first volume of the *Democracy*. But the correspondence with Sedgwick during the 1850s revolved more around the fortunes of Tocqueville's American investments than around political questions. There were two major exceptions, and they occurred five years apart: the first came when the work for *The Old Regime* was getting under way, the second when the book was finally finished. In the first, Tocqueville wrote in his best direct and passionate fashion about the demagoguery and imperialism that accompanied America's Manifest Destiny. In 1852, an alarmed Tocqueville wrote with as much tact as he could muster for this subject, "You know that I am half an American citizen. That, in some fashion, makes me a citizen of somewhere. In my capacity as a compatriot, I cannot view without apprehension that spirit of conquest, and even of rapine, that is shown among you in the past few years. It is not a sign of good health in a people who already have more territories than they can fill up." Referring to the filibustering expedition against Cuba of Gen. Narciso Lopez in August 1851, he continued, "I must say that I would not foresee without great grief that the nation had embarked in a move against Cuba. . . . This whole affair, if not very prudently managed, could end with you being thrown into the arms of the great nations of Europe; believe it."[11]

But the Kansas issue brought out even deeper expressions of dismay. In his magisterial study of the coming of the Civil War, David Potter reached the following devastating conclusion about the Kansas-Nebraska Act:

> In an era of many futile measures, the Kansas-Nebraska Act approached the apex of futility. No matter how measured, it seems barren of positive results. . . .
>
> One of its most damaging effects was to contaminate the doctrine of popular sovereignty, by employing it as a device for opening free territory to slavery. . . . Before 1854, popular sovereignty may have been perhaps the country's best hope for keeping the territories free and at the same time avoiding sectional disruption.
>
> But when Douglas, with a broad wink to the southerners in Congress, invited them to vote for popular sovereignty as a device for overthrowing the guarantees of freedom north of 36°30', he permanently discredited his own doctrine in the eyes of any potential antislavery supporters.[12]

And after the violence in Kansas and the election of James Buchanan, Tocqueville poured out his fear and dismay. His understanding of the Kansas issue was exactly parallel to that of Potter 115 years later:

> The election of the new President seemed on this side of the ocean, the triumph of the cause of slavery, but perhaps it is not in reality. As for me, who have never been an abolitionist in the ordinary sense of the word, that is to say who never believed it would be possible to destroy slavery in the old States, I am, I avow, violently opposed to the extension of that horrible evil outside of the already excessively great limits where it is today confined. That would seem to me to be one of the greatest crimes that men could commit against the general cause of humanity, and on this point I feel violent political passions.[13]

Here Tocqueville was being both honest and correct in his distinctions. He did not in fact think slavery could be destroyed in the states, but he hated and reviled it. Far more than his American correspondents, Tocqueville viewed the conflict in the United States as a moral struggle over slavery that was intertwined with imperialist conquest, not, as did Lieber and Sedgwick, as a sectional struggle over the integrity of the Union.

Three months after Tocqueville wrote this letter to Sedgwick, Charles Sumner, who was recuperating in Europe after having been caned in the Senate chamber by Preston Brooks in May 1856, called on Tocqueville in Paris and, he wrote in his journal, "found him as usual amiable and interesting, and full of feeling against slavery."[14]

It should be remembered, as many Americans at the time did remember, that Tocqueville was a pioneer French abolitionist and the author of a report on slave emancipation to the Chamber of Deputies that, upon its publication in 1840, had created serious diplomatic headaches for the French consul in New Orleans, who wrote to his superiors in Paris that "it would be impossible . . . to describe to you the impact" of the report in the United States. As Seymour Drescher noted, "Tocqueville's recommendation of immediate, general, and simultaneous emancipation went further than any previous abolitionist proposal in the Chamber."[15]

In 1855, he sent, at the request of Maria Weston Chapman, a "Testimony against Slavery," which she published in her abolitionist paper, the *Liberty Bell*. William Lloyd Garrison picked it up and reprinted it in the *Liberator*. Tocqueville had been put in touch with Chapman by her sister, Elisabeth Laugel, a resident of Paris and also a friend of Harriet Beecher Stowe. Laugel also connected Tocqueville with Stowe, who sent him an inscribed copy of *Uncle Tom's Cabin* in 1856. The "Testimony" is cogent and brief; noteworthy, however, is its moving beyond emancipation itself to a statement of support for equal civil liberties for all.

> [A]s the persevering enemy of despotism everywhere, and under all its forms, I am pained and astonished by the fact that the freest people in the world is, at the present time, almost the only one among civilized and Christian nations which yet maintains personal servitude; and this while serfdom itself is about disappearing, where it has not already disappeared, from the most degraded nations of Europe.
>
> An old and sincere friend of America, I am uneasy at seeing Slavery retard her progress, tarnish her glory, furnish arms to her detractors, compromise the future career of the Union which is the guaranty of her safety and greatness, and point out beforehand to her, to all her enemies, the spot where they are to strike. As a man, too, I am moved by the spectacle of man's degradation by man, and I hope to see the day when the law will grant equal civil liberty to all of the inhabitants of the same empire, as God accords the freedom of the will, without distinction, to the dwellers upon earth.[16]

The Old Regime continued the meditation on the nature of democracy begun twenty years earlier in the *Democracy*. "Some may accuse me of displaying too strong a taste for freedom, which, I am assured, is hardly of concern to anyone in France today," Tocqueville wrote in the foreword to *The Old Regime*. "I ask those who reproach me thus to take into account that in my case this habit is very old. It was almost twenty years ago that, speaking of another society, I wrote almost exactly what I am now about to say." And indeed the rest of the foreword is almost a synopsis of Part IV of the second volume of the *Democracy*. "Liberty alone can effectively combat the natural vices of these kinds of societies [that is, societies in which individuals' ties to 'caste, class, guild, or family' have been nearly severed] and prevent them from sliding down the slippery slope where they find themselves. Only freedom can bring citizens out of the isolation in which the very independence of their circumstances has led them to live."[17]

The intertwined themes of liberty and isolation that Tocqueville here introduces by reference to America constitute the heart of the book, namely the great ninth chapter of Book II, which is entitled "How Such Similar Men Were More Divided Than Ever Before, Separated into Small Groups That Were Estranged from and Indifferent to One Another." "One should read the admirable ninth chapter of Book II of de Tocqueville's *L'Ancien Régime*, which is perhaps the most profound chapter in that profound book," wrote François Furet. "It contains virtually everything."[18]

While Tocqueville was not centrally occupied with American affairs in the 1850s—a time when he was contemplating the despotism of Napoleon III, composing *The Old Regime*, and pondering his mortality—he did keep quite closely informed about American events and was fully aware of the significance of Douglas's Kansas-Nebraska bill. It provoked an antislavery manifesto directed to an American audience, and it honed still further his understanding of the despotic dangers lurking in a democratic society. It is also clear that, while he was dependent on particular sources of information and opinion, Tocqueville reached and espoused very different conclusions from the ones that his American informants, like Lieber and Sedgwick, did. His lifelong intellectual aloofness continued to serve him well into his final decade.

The Old Roman

During 1860s, the imposing figure of Tocqueville continuously landed on the shores of the United States through the medium of publications and translations that came in waves. His authority and prestige remained intact during the decade after his death. Indeed, in the opinion of Charles Eliot Norton early in the 1860s, Tocqueville's reputation was waxing at that time. Tocqueville's continuing presence was due in large part to the undertaking of new translations.

It could be a risky as well as a rewarding task to spread Tocqueville to English-speaking readers. Indeed, Tocqueville's translators constitute a stalwart band of enthusiasts—bold, imaginative, and, one hopes, thick-skinned, for from the middle of the nineteenth century to the present day, they have had to endure harsh criticism, sometimes bordering on insult. Harvey C. Mansfield and Delba Winthrop's 2000 translation of *Democracy in America*, for example, was condemned for somehow bearing the stamp of an "archconservative style," while Mansfield and Winthrop themselves wrote of their own immediate predecessor, George Lawrence, that "when [he] encounters a difficulty in Tocqueville's text, he tends to navigate around it with an approximation or a supposed idiomatic equivalent. Whatever his liking or even enthusiasm for Tocqueville may have been, he proceeds as if this were any job of rendering French into English." But then, Lawrence's translation was necessary, J. P. Mayer wrote in 1966, because two prior attempts to "save a basically *dated* text" of the original English translation had ended in failure. Reviewing Alan S. Kahan's translation of Tocqueville's *The Old Regime and the Revolution* in the *New York Review of Books*, P. N. Furbank (not a Tocqueville translator) adverted to "some sixty . . . errors" or "serious misrenderings" in Kahan's text that were "pointed out to us by Professor Jon Elster of Columbia University," a list that Furbank decided not to pass along to his readers.[19]

Probably most translators feel a compulsion to express some disapprobation of their predecessors, for why else would a new version of a text be called for? In the game of irreverent assessment of forerunners, however, no twentieth- or twenty-first–century academic could match the cheek of the first reviser of an English-language Tocqueville translation, Harvard's Francis Bowen. Bowen wittily managed to express disappointment not only with the command of French exhibited by the previous translator, Henry Reeve, but with Reeve's mastery of English as well. In 1862, Bowen issued a new edition of *Democracy in America*; it was the first since 1838 and the first American translation. In his preface to this edition, which would stand unchallenged for eighty years, Bowen declared that ("to my dismay") he had discovered the current English translation to be "utterly inadequate and untrustworthy" and proceeded to prove his argument with sections of the original French text printed across the page from margin to margin and the relevant portions of the 1835 Reeve translation and Bowen's own version in parallel columns below it, so that it looked like one weak and one strong pillar were holding up the lintel of Tocqueville's prose. This went on for seven pages. As a result of the alterations he made, Bowen concluded, his 1862 edition "might more fitly be called a new translation than an amended one." Or at least that could be said for Volume I, which had been translated in 1835, Bowen continued, because by the time Volume II was published five years later, Reeve's language skills had improved; somehow he "had found time to increase his familiarity with the French language, and even to make some progress in his knowledge of English."[20]

It was a wickedly humorous, yet accurate, remark. Tocqueville's first English translator was barely out of his teens when he sat down to work on the political classic that generations of readers would come to recognize through his rendition. Many years later, Reeve recalled, "I had the good fortune to translate [Democracy in America] into English when I was about one and twenty, and from that time till the date of his death in 1859 I lived in the intimacy of unbroken friendship with Alexis de Tocqueville."[21]

It remains obscure how or why Reeve came to have the offer to produce an English version in the first place, but it was an honor that, at first, he felt he had to refuse. For Reeve happened to be an ardent Tory, and in the tumultuous political atmosphere of England in the era of the Reform Act, that meant entertaining a deep suspicion of popular government. Although he professed to consider Democracy in America to be "a work of first-rate order," he believed the book to contain unqualified approbation of its subject, and so he demurred. "I decline translating it, because I am determined never to write a sentence which I do not believe in my inmost heart," he wrote to his mother on February 25, 1835, scarcely one month after the book had appeared in Paris. "I admire Tocqueville as a philosophical opponent, as a man infinitely valuable to me, because he forces me to furbish all my powers in the great debate which he propounds; but I will not promulgate an erroneous doctrine, nor enter the world with a list of articles in my hand which my hand refuses to subscribe."[22] As the reference to entering the world indicates, Reeve was barely twenty-one years of age—yet even without that phrase one might infer the fact of his youth by the earnestness, the moral certitude, and the callow quality of the passage. In fact, his condescending judgment of the Democracy was rendered before he had actually read the book. Thus began a long tradition of Tocqueville commentary.

But three weeks after this letter, Reeve was invited to dinner with Tocqueville, who, it should be remembered, was still in his twenties himself. It was an event that changed the course of Reeve's life. "On Monday evening I dined with M. de Tocqueville," he wrote to his mother on March 21, 1835. "He is a very agreeable man, and the more I see his book (which I have now nearly finished) the more I like it. My first impression as to its democratic tendency was entirely erroneous. He regards Democracy as the inevitable lot of Europe, and as an evil which we had best prepare to meet, since we cannot escape it. He will be in England in a month, and I shall hope to get him to Hampstead on my return."[23] Thus did Reeve veer from one misinterpretation to another which was its antithesis—from the belief that the *Democracy* expressed a strong predilection for a regime of equality and that its author was a "philosophical opponent" propounding "an erroneous doctrine," to the equally unbalanced position that Tocqueville considered such a regime "an evil" and that Reeve might in fact be able to undertake a translation without grievous damage to his sense of honor.

Tocqueville, as it happened, did finally make it to Hampstead, although not because of any plans made by Reeve. One month after that dinner in Paris, and two months to the day after the publication of *De la démocratie en Amérique*, Tocqueville and Beaumont sailed to England, where they were to sojourn for two months. But Tocqueville fell ill in London and retreated to Hampstead, where he remained for about two weeks, while Mrs. Reeve and her son looked after him. In his correspondence, Tocqueville testified to the strength of the bond that arose between him and Reeve during that interval, and his words fully justified Reeve's claim of intimate friendship.

Tocqueville was not an especially gregarious person. When he did forge friendships, they would be passionate. It does seem that such a deep bond emerged out of Tocqueville's period of recuperation. "I shall never forget Hampstead," Tocqueville wrote Reeve exactly one year later. "I believe I perceive in front of me, you and she in that little house in Hampstead that I visited precisely one year ago. I discover you in your observatory rising philosophically above the smoke of London; and I see below in the salon Madame your mother putting on a good face for her guests. I shall never forget Hampstead. It reconnects me indirectly to a period of my life about which I never wish to lose the memory."[24]

Although direct evidence is lacking on the point, it is clear that it was during those approximately fourteen days that, personally urged by Tocqueville, Reeve managed to discard his Tory scruples and undertake the translation, which was done in its entirety in "that little house in Hampstead" in the space of just a few months. It was finished by the end of the summer.

Tocqueville was better served by Reeve than he and Beaumont had been by Lieber, the Prussian immigrant who had translated their *Système pénitentiaire* two years earlier. But Reeve never abandoned his distrust of democracy, and his version of *Democracy in America* reflects his prejudice. Twenty-five years later, he labeled the idea that Tocqueville looked favorably on democracy "a misconception which has very generally prevailed as to the spirit and design of his principal writings. Because M. de Tocqueville based his literary and political reputation on the study of democracy and democratic institutions, it was hastily inferred that these institutions were the object of his own predilections." In fact, Reeve argued, Tocqueville actually accomplished something more useful and profound, namely, the description of American political society "with perfect impartiality."[25] This theme of Tocqueville's lofty, impartial judgment, along with the imputation of almost supernatural prescience, was coeval with the publication of the *Democracy* itself.

In any case, Francis Bowen had good reasons to be skeptical about the merits of Reeve's translation. Besides drawing attention to the disputed renderings laid out in the two-column display in his preface, Bowen also wished to counter the impression of excessive, almost pure, impartiality that Reeve had tried to project. And, as he signaled by revising the first, more "American" volume of the *Democracy* while leaving the second "philosophical" volume relatively untouched, Bowen also was concerned to draw out the distinctions between the universal and the particular in political life. Tocqueville had himself, unknown to Bowen, chided Reeve for allowing the latter's antidemocratic bias to seep into the translation. Between the appearance of the first and second volumes of the *Democracy*, he told Reeve, "I say these often hard truths about . . . Democratic Societies in general but I say them as friend and not as censor. Just because I am a friend do I dare to say these things. Your translation must maintain my attitude; this I demand not only from the translator, but from the man. It has seemed to me that in the translation of the last book you have, without wanting it, following the instinct of your opinions, very lively colored what was contrary to democracy and rather appeased what could do harm to aristocracy."[26]

Bowen, the irascible "Old Roman," was a linchpin in the line of nineteenth-century moderate conservatives from Jared Sparks through Francis Lieber to E. L. Godkin and Daniel Coit Gilman, for whom Tocqueville served as a touchstone. His revision of the Reeve translation came at a significant moment in Americans' understanding of Tocqueville. Indeed, the years 1851 to 1863 were crucial for Bowen himself. "An aggressive little man with a remarkable talent for giving offense,"[27] Bowen had instigated an extraordinarily bitter controversy in the 1850s by ostentatiously attacking the Hungarian uprising of 1848–1849 and its revered tribune, Louis Kossuth, whose tour of the United States in 1851–1852 was the most triumphal event of its kind during the nineteenth century, excepting only the Marquis de Lafayette's visit in 1824–1825. Mobbed in every city and village and everywhere hailed as the very personification of man's undying thirst for liberty, Kossuth was only the second foreigner invited to address a joint meeting of Congress (Lafayette was the first). After the defeat of the Hungarian forces by the combined armies of Austria and Russia at Arad in 1849, Kossuth's cause was doomed. Tocqueville himself had asked, and not just rhetorically, for he was France's foreign minister at the time, "Is Kossuth's skin worth a general war?"[28] The answer was plain for all to see in Europe, and Kossuth's efforts to raise material support in America ended in bitter disappointment. Sparks wrote to Tocqueville about the affair, "There is not the slightest reason to fear that the United States will meddle with the agitations of Europe. The experiment tried by Kossuth [to turn the State Department against Austria] proved a total failure. The people were ready enough to *sympathize*, but not a voice was raised for action, unless from a few German emigrants and restless agitators."[29] Yet, partly because the Hungarians' cause had been the last to falter of all the revolutions that had erupted in 1848—"the turning-point at which modern history failed to turn," George M. Trevelyan famously remarked[30]—Hungary and Kossuth had to take on the role of symbolizing the doomed, heroic resistance that had exploded everywhere in Europe.

Bowen, however, would have none of it. As the editor of the *North American Review*, he published under his own name a long article portraying the Hungarian uprising not as a struggle by which the Hungarians endeavored to liberate themselves from their Habsburg overlords, but as an internal struggle by which subjugated peoples within the boundaries of the historic Hungarian kingdom sought to overthrow their Magyar oppressors. "The Magyars assumed the position, therefore, of a nation striving to impose or to continue the yoke upon the necks of their own dependents, instead of labouring to throw off a yoke from their own shoulders," he argued. Bowen had once dismissed the literary criticism of his day for being weak-kneed and inoffensive: "We talk what we dare not print," he claimed. This was clearly a shortcoming he was determined to avoid.[31]

Bowen's harsh judgment of the Hungarian revolt was met with vigorous challenges, notably from James Russell Lowell and his sister, Mrs. Mary Lowell Putnam, who published a point-by-point rebuttal in the *Christian Examiner*. It has long been thought that these articles had serious negative repercussions for Bowen. Harvard's faculty had recommended Bowen for the prestigious McLean professorship of history, the chair vacated by Sparks when he, the only previous holder of the chair, was named president of Harvard. But in 1851, Harvard's Board of Overseers, then still a body partly made up of Democratic politicians and subject by the terms of its charter to the Massachusetts General Court, threw out the recommendation and made a different appointment. Recent scholars have not devoted much attention to this episode, but when they do, the customary conclusion is that it was an ignoble violation of academic freedom and retaliation for publicly taking a position that stood contrary to the tide of popular opinion. Daniel Walker Howe, for example, characterized the board's action as "a blatant violation of . . . academic freedom" and "reprisal for his conservative political writings." The appointment to the McLean chair, Howe wrote in a biographical note, "was blocked when certain state office-holders who were then ex-officio members of the Harvard Board of Overseers objected to his outspoken political conservatism (Bowen had denounced the popular Hungarian revolutionary, Louis Kossuth, and had supported the Compromise of 1850)." Bruce Kuklick wrote that Bowen lost the chair for having "denounced the popular Hungarian revolution on historical grounds." A thorough article by Monica Maria Grecu picks up and summarizes the conventional account: "With the support of the teaching faculty he was named to the McLean professorship in history at Harvard but failed to win confirmation by the Board of Overseers. The sticking point was a series of articles in the *North American Review* . . . which supported the Magyar monarchy [*sic*] over Kossuth."[32]

In fact, however, Bowen's attack was not just an expression of a politically unpopular opinion; nor was he a gallant warrior felled in the noble cause of academic freedom (which was a dimly understood ideal in the 1850s, even at Harvard). To the contrary, Bowen's *North American Review* article consisted chiefly of direct translations of articles that had appeared during the previous year in the *Revue des Deux Mondes*. To express it in bluntly modern terms, Bowen was a plagiarist. His article contained neither acknowledgment of sources nor notification that it contained English versions of French originals. Nor is this an anachronistic value judgment on my part. Shortly after the controversy began, a publicist named Robert Carter brought Bowen's sources and the fact of his translations to light in a devastating exposé entitled *The Hungarian Controversy*.[33]

Carter showed that the sum of Bowen's acknowledged "research" into the Hungarian affair consisted of a single reference to a book by Baron Joseph-Marie de Gérando—which, as Putnam had pointed out in the *Christian Examiner*, had been published in 1848, and thus contained no new information about events after 1847—plus two articles in the *Revue des Deux Mondes*, a journal "notorious for its anti-republican tendencies," which had been written by authors who were noteworthy as "royalists, apologists for Austria, and admirers of Haynau [the Austrian general who defeated the Hungarian forces] and Metternich."

Carter furnished several startling examples of Bowen's plagiarism. Bowen's extended section on the Hungarian liberal Count István Széchenyi, for example, was "perhaps the best and most striking passage of the article," Carter wrote. "If original with Mr. Bowen, it would have deserved the credit it has received as the result of considerable research. It is in fact, however, entirely translated [from the *Revue des Deux Mondes*] without the slightest acknowledgement. Yet Mr. Bowen prints it as altogether his own production. He does not give the least intimation that he is indebted in its composition to any one, but offers it as the result of his own researches upon Hungarian history." Then, anticipating the visual-rhetorical strategy that Bowen himself would deploy against poor Henry Reeve a decade later, Carter printed literal English translations of passages from the pertinent *Revue des Deux Mondes* articles followed by Bowen's text. The conclusion was irresistible: Bowen had taken the passages wholesale from the article in question. Carter then showed clearly that "of the sixty pages of that article, at least fifty are taken directly from the *Revue des Deux Mondes*" with "no acknowledgement whatever." Furthermore, Bowen actually omitted from his *North American Review* article portions of the more balanced French originals that had actually been favorable to the Hungarians. Carter's summary, in conjunction with the evidence in Putnam's *Christian Examiner* rebuttal, was irrefutable: "It is not merely 'information' that Mr. Bowen has derived from the *Revue*; he has taken from it his narrative, by literal translation or by an easy abridgment; he has taken from it nine-tenths of his facts; he has taken from it his rhetoric, the very ornaments of his style."[34]

The notion that Bowen was unduly victimized in this matter is further undermined by the fact that, almost as soon as his misconduct surfaced, he was offered a plum as great in prestige as the McLean chair that had been snatched from his grasp in 1851. The Harvard Board of Overseers named Bowen to the Alford professorship in natural religion, moral philosophy, and civil polity. This chair, so central to the university's mission, had just been vacated by James Walker when he was named by those same overseers to succeed Sparks as president of Harvard. Bowen would occupy this enormously powerful position from 1853 until 1889, years in which he was instrumental in training perhaps the most influential generation of philosophers America has ever produced. Among his students were Charles S. Peirce, Chauncey Wright, and William James, all of them originators of the famed

Metaphysical Club and two of them, Peirce and James, the progenitors of pragmatism. They left the naive empiricism of Francis Bowen far behind, and yet, in several ways, Bowen's stamp appears on such foundational works of pragmatism as Peirce's "How to Make Our Ideas Clear." In Bruce Kuklick's judgment, that great essay's "attack on *a priori* obscurantism surely derived from Bowen's contempt for verbal, 'metaphysical,' reasoning."[35]

The most intriguing angle on the whole Magyar controversy arises from Carter's claim that Bowen "has been appointed to the [McLean] Professorship of History in Harvard University on account of the historical merit of that article." This statement, while quite startling at first, gains credibility upon reflection, because, first of all, it fits the chronology of events much better than the received version of the episode. Bowen did not receive the offer of the McLean chair in 1853, as Howe maintained, but in 1851, and took the Alford professorship after things had calmed down a bit in 1853. But more significantly, Carter's assertion furnishes a more credible answer to the obvious question of why the Board of Overseers would violate a man's academic freedom and rescind a professorship on the basis of his allegedly unsound political opinions, then turn around and offer him another chair of equal stature just a little over a year later. It seems extremely likely, therefore, that the story of Bowen's adventures with the Harvard board is the opposite of the one that has gained scholarly currency. Bowen, I would argue, did not *lose* the McLean professorship because of the impressive anti-Magyar articles, but rather gained it. However, when the exposés by Carter and Putnam appeared, the board had to retract its offer. After all, the professorship was in history. It would be very difficult to give an appointment in that field to someone who had faked his research and then published it in the journal he edited himself. A professorship had been promised, however, and a short time later Bowen could be offered the polymathic Alford chair, for which serious historical research was not a qualification.

Ironically, the Alford chair had been offered to Sparks many years earlier, but after agonizing vacillation, Sparks had rejected the offer. Sparks worried about the Alford chair because, as he wrote in his journal on June 16, 1836, "This professorship includes moral philosophy, metaphysics, and natural theology. Political economy and civil polity are also brought into the same department." It was, in short, a mishmash of vaguely politically correct fields of study that as yet were undifferentiated into separate disciplines. The establishment of the McLean professorship came just in time for Sparks; it was a straightforward chair in American history, the first in any university.[36]

Bowen's new professorship, then, came with a workload sufficient for an entire modern liberal arts college. Natural (in contrast to revealed) religion was understood to encompass all evidences of God's existence and works that are attainable by the unaided reason. Moral philosophy taught the means of discerning forms of right behavior. Finally, civil polity took in roughly what the social sciences investigate in the modern university.

Soon after assuming his new position, Bowen turned to the task of producing a new, comprehensive text on political economy. The world at large did not urgently need another 550-page boulder of an economics treatise, Bowen admitted, but the United States did. Echoing the title of Beaumont and Tocqueville's study of America's penitentiaries, Bowen called his book *Principles of Political Economy Applied to the Condition, the Resources, and the Institutions of the American People*, and it was a major effort to sort out the particular, unique features of American society, markets, inputs, demand, supply, finance, currency, and trade from the universal principles that were said to determine all economic behavior. *Principles of Political Economy* was published in 1856, adopted at Harvard, Episcopalian Trinity College in Hartford, Connecticut, and the University of Pennsylvania, and it went through five editions in the next twelve years.

Bowen employed a line of argument strikingly similar to Karl Marx's in one respect at least. He derided the universalist pretensions of the field and maintained that the so-called science of political economy originated in order to advance particular interests. Though he professed to remain loyal to the idea that political economy could make universal claims, the arguments he advanced subverted such professions in every important example. "These universal principles are . . . little more than truisms," he wrote. Political economy, "having been suggested by the peculiar circumstances and conditions of one country [Great Britain], relating almost exclusively to the experience of one nation, and deriving, in truth, most of its utility from this very fact, . . . is at least partially inapplicable and unsound in every other case." Indeed, as traditionally taught and understood, political economy was "adapted to the physical condition and industrial pursuits of an insular people."

Bowen differed from Marx, of course, as to the all-important question of the class origin of this bourgeois mythology. Marx viewed classical political economy as little more than a fable of class dominance justifying the rise and flourishing of a band of parasites; for Bowen, the English social structure was so peculiarly that of "an insular people" that it had little relevance to American conditions. In short, both Marx and Bowen unmasked economics as an ideology. For Marx, it served class, and for Bowen, national interests. Consequently, Bowen's announced goal in the *Principles* was "to lay the foundations at least, leaving it for others to raise the superstructure, of an American system of Political Economy."[37]

In his magisterial *The Economic Mind in American Civilization*, Joseph Dorfman included Bowen among a small band of "cautious protectionists," men who, while accepting the abstract principles of Adam Smith and David Ricardo, argued that those principles, when applied to particular cases, needed to be modified in small ways. But this is to understate the extent to which Bowen departed from the universalist orthodoxy of the newly developing discipline. Bowen's aim was to produce a study of political economy suitable to America in an industrializing age. In his *Principles*, he nearly succeeded in doing for the United States what John Stuart Mill had done for Britain in his own 1848 *Principles of Political Economy*. Bowen's book, as Daniel Walker Howe noted, was "a statement of faith in the potentialities of industrial America."[38]

The principal way in which American and English economic and social states differed (and thus undermined political economy's claims to being a universally valid science) was in the comparative equality of wealth distribution in the United States. An epigram on Bowen's title page came from the Scottish economist Samuel Laing: "It is not that a Duke has 50,000 *l.* a year, but that a thousand fathers of families have 50 *l.* a year, that is true national wealth and well-being." Bowen, in his dependably witty—or caustic— manner, turned this apothegm against its author by, first, opening his book with a critique of Laing's principles and, second, showing that the truth of Laing's observation was pertinent not in an aristocratic nation where dukes can amass enough property to sustain a thousand families, but in a republic where dukes cannot exist in the first place and where property distribution proceeds according to laws that are the complete reversal of the English inheritance system.

"I know of no other country where the love of money occupies as great a place in the hearts of men or where people are more deeply contemptuous of the theory of permanent equality of wealth," Tocqueville wrote in 1835 (*DIA* 57). And in the second volume he observed: "It is strange to witness the fervent ardor that Americans bring to the pursuit of well-being and to see how tormented they always seem by a vague fear of not having chosen the shortest way of getting there" (*DIA* 625).[39] More than merely convenient quotes, these remarks together constitute a synopsis of Bowen's major argument in his economics textbook. Americans' unbounded pursuit of wealth and the rapid changes of fortune that resulted meant that some of the most urgent questions of English political economy—such as whether consumers' buying power and increased desire to consume might lag behind heightened efficiency in the system of production—were pushed to the margins of American economic thought.

The supposed volatility of the American class structure was accompanied by a dynamic, ever-shifting equality of property distribution, Bowen held. In other words, property ownership was comparatively equalized but unstable. The key to this dynamic equilibrium was not radical utopian fantasies or "vicious agrarian schemes" but the absence of primogeniture and entail, the bedrock of all aristocratic inheritance codes. When property came to be divided among all children, rather than passed directly to firstborn males, the likelihood that the current structure of wealth disparities would endure was drastically diminished.[40]

In the larger context of the argument of Bowen's book, this was no mere ancillary fact by which the brighter students of economics might be separated from the plodders. To Bowen, it was the very groundwork of the nation's welfare. "These are grave questions [about the division of estates]," he maintained, "and on the answers to them, more, we had almost said, than on all other causes united, the form of government and the welfare of the people, the whole political and social framework of society, in every country must ultimately depend." Almost more important than all other causes of social welfare and political structure *combined* was estate law. And at precisely this point, Bowen drew on Tocqueville explicitly for the only time in his book (although Tocqueville is an implicit, hovering presence throughout). Bowen reproduced a long quotation from *Democracy in America* in which Tocqueville vastly overstated the effects of inheritance laws, just as Bowen would do twenty years later. "Laws of inheritance," Tocqueville wrote in 1835, "ought . . . to be placed at the head of all political institutions, for, while political laws are only the symbols of a nation's condition, those which determine the descent of property exercise an extraordinary influence over its social state." According to Bowen, such laws even led to the European revolutions of 1830 and 1848.[41]

Bowen's general authorial strategy in the *Principles* was to present, in each chapter, the state of economic theory on the subject of that chapter as expressed by the classical exponents, chiefly Adam Smith, David Ricardo, and Thomas Malthus; then to critique that theory on empirical grounds, drawing his evidence from American examples; and, finally, to offer a new perspective on the subject that explicitly refuted the claims to universal validity made by his British predecessors.[42] But many of Bowen's arguments had been anticipated, and certainly at least some of them were derived, from a reading of Tocqueville. Tocqueville's own work as a political economist has been underappreciated. He possessed a sophisticated technical knowledge of political economy, which he put to use in several notable instances. He was a close friend of the great economists John Stuart Mill and Nassau William Senior and displayed a thorough knowledge of their work, as well as that of Smith, Ricardo, Malthus, J.-B. Say, and many others. His analysis of the political and economic costs of slave emancipation in the French colonies, for instance, which he completed in 1839 for a committee of the Chamber of Deputies—along with other writings on this volatile subject—were primarily economics treatises that treated moral considerations only secondarily.[43]

In chapters 5, 6, and 7 of Part III in the 1840 volume of *Democracy in America*, Tocqueville had laid out in concentrated form an American economic theory of his own. It was based on the twin social forces of equality and mobility. In chapter 6, for example, Tocqueville succinctly pointed out the effect of these forces of mobility and equality on rents. "In the Middle Ages," he wrote, "people . . . believed in the immortality of families. Conditions seemed fixed forever"; but "In centuries of equality the human mind takes on a different cast. It is easy to imagine that nothing stays put. The mind is possessed by the idea of instability. Given this attitude, both landlord and tenant feel a kind of instinctive horror for long-term obligations" (*DIA* 681). The economic ties between tenant and landlord were weakened at both ends; rents rose as the duration of leases was shortened.

A similar dynamic could be observed in the case of workers' wages. "One of the general laws governing democratic societies is that wages will slowly and gradually increase," Tocqueville asserted (*DIA* 683). And it was the restlessness of workers that caused this very phenomenon: "For when the entire society is on the move, it is difficult to keep one class fixed in its place." (*DIA* 684). Bowen noted how "the restless, migratory spirit, and the want of local attachments . . . have so often attracted the attention of foreign visitors," although he neglected to name any. His arguments concerning wages, however, echo those of Tocqueville, not Ricardo. "The peculiar mobility of society, the ease and frequency of the interchange of social position, which is one of the characteristic features of American life, . . . keeps down the number of laborers for hire, in spite of the rapid increase of the population, and it keeps up the rate of wages, or at least prevents it from falling so rapidly as it would otherwise do."[44]

Bowen, then, did not wait until 1862 before discovering—to his dismay—

the manifold shortcomings of Reeve's mastery of French and English in the latter's *Democracy* translation. His own economics text reveals a close familiarity with some of Tocqueville's most important economic arguments.

The year 1859 was a turning point in Bowen's academic career, as it presented him with the grimmest of all fates, an adversary whom he could neither defeat nor leave alone. That adversary was Charles Darwin. Bowen's academic field was natural religion; Darwin proposed to eliminate it. Darwin's *Origin of Species* was published in December 1859, and in a matter of months Bowen had attacked Darwin's science on the ground that it negated, with insufficient empirical evidence, the philosophical argument from design for the existence of God. Darwin's hypothesis, Bowen immediately saw, left the cosmos devoid of "all proof of the incessant creative action of a designing mind, by reducing it to a blind mechanical process."[45]

This was but the first in a series of condemnations as a result of which, over the years, Bowen would lose much of his stature as a philosopher. "Bowen's reputation as a philosopher did not survive the 1860s," maintained Kuklick.[46] Yet, as a teacher, translator, critic, and economist, Bowen did continue to wield considerable influence, in spite of the irresistible flood tide of Darwinism.

Eighteen fifty-nine was also the year of Tocqueville's death. His passing gave rise to a stream of articles in the American press. They were respectful, even reverent, reminiscences of the great analyst of democratic culture. Yet, Tocqueville, in 1860, did not need to be introduced to Americans—even to younger American intellectuals who came of age after the *Democracy* had been published, read, and digested. Tocqueville was familiar both because of the *Democracy* and because, just a few years before his death, he had published a second masterpiece, *The Old Regime and the Revolution*.

But in addition to Tocqueville's death and the publication of *The Old Regime*, several other events had converged by 1861 to draw Bowen's attention to Tocqueville and the *Democracy*. Most prominent, of course, was the Civil War, which raised in the most desperately urgent and concrete terms the question that Tocqueville had asked three decades earlier. He knew that the most arresting feature of the whole American democratic enterprise was its sheer endurance. It was not the origins but the continuity of American democracy that needed explaining, Tocqueville wrote. In one of the longest and yet most concentrated of his chapters, Tocqueville attributed "the perpetuation of democratic institutions in the United States" to three causes: circumstances, laws, and habits and mores. These he listed in reverse order of importance: "Laws do more to maintain a democratic republic in the

United States than physical causes do, and mores do more than laws" (*DIA* 302). Indeed, the demonstration of this argument he considered his "principal goal" (*DIA* 356). Then, he let loose the torrent of fears and speculations that concluded the first volume—the famous chapter on "the three races" with its dark tone and tragic conjectures.

These chapters were recalled to the minds of Northern intellectuals in the months leading up to the war and in the war's early phase. But, in addition to the coming of the conflict itself, Tocqueville's death, and the publication of *The Old Regime*, Mme. de Tocqueville's decision to publish an edition of some of her husband's previously uncollected works also fed the 1860s Tocqueville resurgence. The two volumes, edited by her and Beaumont, were published by Michel Lévy in 1861 and immediately translated into English.

Therefore, Bowen's decision to revise the English translation that had been in circulation for twenty-seven years and reissued under various titles in over twenty editions, appears, in this larger view, to have been as much a matter of self-promotion and publisher's fees as of scholarly scrupulosity. In 1862, he was, like his successors a century later, riding a Tocqueville wave.

Bowen remained at Harvard as Alford professor for twenty-seven years after publishing the revised translation. He produced three major philosophical studies, including what Kuklick ironically called "the finest history of modern philosophy produced by a Harvard scholar," as well as dozens of well-crafted critical essays. He died in 1890, six months after his retirement. Bowen's antipathy to Darwin's developmental biology diminished his reputation and relegated him to a secondary rank among nineteenth-century intellectuals—despite the more respectful attention he has received from modern historians. "The contempt shown him by posterity epitomizes the treatment accorded to theorizing that could not meet the challenge of Darwinism," Kuklick concluded.[47] At the start of the twenty-first century, Bowen was best known as the reviser and cotranslator with Reeve of Tocqueville's *Democracy*.

Tocqueville's lifelong preoccupation with France's recurrent loss of liberty led him down a long and difficult trail of historical inquiry, taking him to the decades preceding the French Revolution. Earlier in this chapter I noted R. R. Palmer's opinion that Tocqueville showed a "tendency toward a kind of infinite regression in the focus of his efforts" in the 1850s. Tocqueville had been shocked by the coup d'état of Louis Bonaparte on December 2, 1851, which ended the short-lived Second Republic. He had served with distinction as foreign minister of France under Bonaparte when the latter was president of that republic, in 1849. Along with some fifty deputies who protested the shameful coup, Tocqueville was removed from Paris to Vincennes in a prison carriage, and he remained in jail until December 4. He reacted to this injury with a grave dignity. Very shortly afterwards, he composed a disdainful account of the coup and had it smuggled out of France by Harriet Grote, who in turn, delivered it immediately into the familiar and trustworthy hands of Reeve. Reeve translated it and saw to its publication in the *Times* on December 11, 1851. "The coup d'état of December 2 put an end to a period of his life that had begun almost thirteen years before," André Jardin wrote. "He never forgave the man who had brought this about for the affront to representative government and the consequent loss of civil liberties."[48]

Forced once again to ponder the loss of freedom (always a more salient theme in his work than its pursuit, Alan Kahan has pointed out[49]), Tocqueville began to consider the origins of Napoleon III's despotism. While sojourning in Sorrento in an effort to improve his health, he wrote most of the *Souvenirs,* or recollections of the 1848 revolution and its aftermath. Not published until 1893, the *Souvenirs,* one of the great memoirs of nineteenth-century European literature, was an intensely private, even secret, account of his reactions to the disaster. In the *Souvenirs,* Tocqueville gazed at himself observing past events. But he wished also to produce a public, historical view of the calamity. And, as an author who sought to isolate what he called "the point of departure" of modern France and America, he soon followed his thought back to Napoleon Bonaparte, who had established the despotic regime of the Empire, behind Napoleon to the great Revolution itself, which had made possible his emergence, behind the Revolution to the causes of the prior system's total collapse, behind that system. . . . But he did not have to pursue those fleeing, regressing thoughts any further into the past, for he already had to hand an account of French society immediately prior to the Revolution. It was an old essay he had written in 1836 at the request of his (then) closest English friend, John Stuart Mill. Entitled "The Social and Political Condition of France before and after 1789," it contained already the thesis of *The Old Regime,* namely that the changes to the French polity and society that were universally attributed to the blood and smoke of the Revolution, actually were well along toward fulfillment long before 1789. "All that the Revolution did would have been done, I have no doubt, without it." Mill translated the essay himself and published it in his new journal, the *London and Westminster Review,* in April 1836.[50]

With this essay, Tocqueville had a foundation and a plan of research. He had substantially completed *The Old Regime* by February of 1856. Publication was delayed briefly while he fumbled about for a title—his original idea was to call it "La Révolution"—and because of his father's unexpected death, but it was published in June.

Once again Reeve was chosen as the first translator. But *The Old Regime* would not, like the first *Democracy* volume, have to wait for nearly three decades before receiving a separate American treatment. In the early autumn of 1856, Harper and Row brought out in New York City an exemplary translation by John Bonner. Ninety-nine years later, after Bonner's edition had been out of print for decades—there was only one American edition of the work—Stuart Gilbert produced a translation of the major portion of Tocqueville's text for Anchor Books. (He retained Bonner's translation of the notes, which are extensive.) As a translation, the Gilbert version was a step backwards—although simply having the work in print as a cheap paperback, as it remained for fifty years, was surely a useful service in itself. Gilbert was a well-known figure in literary circles in both America and Europe. His most famous book was the indispensable *James Joyce's Ulysses*, a combination user's guide, handbook, and consistently intelligent interpretation of modernism's greatest classic. Gilbert also translated *Ulysses* into French. But he seemed to have more difficulty working in the other direction, from French into English, as his Tocqueville translation contains frequent infelicities.

Bonner's version was not the only one available in English. As noted previously, Tocqueville first turned to Reeve when *The Old Regime* was completed. The intimate friend from the Hampstead spring of 1835, the man to whom the coup account was entrusted in 1851, was also in close contact with Tocqueville as *The Old Regime* was going into production. In fact, Reeve translated it from the proofs, before Tocqueville had even come to a final decision about the book's title. Consequently, it appeared in London under the title *On the State of Society in France before the Revolution of 1789, and on the Causes Which Led to That Event.* Bonner did not get his hands on the French original until it was available in the bookshops, on June 17, 1856.

The first American notice of the publication of Tocqueville's second masterpiece came as early as October 1856, in an editorial note in *Putnam's Monthly Magazine*. The editor instantly made the connection between Tocqueville's American and French preoccupations. "In spite of the many errors of doctrine and fact" that mar *Democracy in America*, he wrote, it nevertheless remains "altogether the best criticism that was ever made of us and our institutions." Now, in his new book, Tocqueville "endeavors to perform a similar service for French society" of the eighteenth century to the one that he had bestowed on nineteenth-century America. The editor (probably chief editor Charles F. Briggs) also astutely singled out the book's unique qualities, namely, its extensive original research in provincial archives and its theme of relentless centralization on the part of the monarchy.[51]

Only one month later, *Putman's* devoted a full feature article to *The Old Regime* in which, again, appreciation was mixed with analysis; but this time, the reviewer revealed a much clearer bias. The article, in fact, introduced all the major themes in the American understanding of *The Old Regime* during the brief period when attention was directed toward it. The main theme of the article was that the United States served as the focal point of Tocqueville's life and ideas, that he believed his own fatherland could best be comprehended by comparison with America, and that this was true to such a degree that French politics and government might best be understood by the extent to which they conformed to or deviated from an American prototype. The author of the article was almost certainly George W. Curtis (I will refer to the author as Curtis in what follows).[52] "Ask a legitimist in France what his notion is of the true organization of power, and he will sketch you out a scheme something like the absolute monarchy of Louis XIV.; and ask a democrat, and he will begin to glorify Robespierre or Ledru Rollin; yet they are all fundamentally the same," Curtis contended. But with Tocqueville, he wrote, we see a unique difference: "his study of our American townships, combined with his own good sense has taught him the value of local self-government."[53]

The portrayal of Tocqueville in the United States in 1856 was therefore an inverted image of the Tocqueville that has been painstakingly assembled by twentieth-century scholarship; that is, Tocqueville is presented by leading current scholars (most notably Roger Boesche) as a man fully absorbed by his own generation and by France and passionately concerned to address questions of direct relevance to his own time.[54] "History for Tocqueville was a necessary detour on the way to understanding the present. Erudition had little place in it," wrote Françoise Mélonio and François Furet, the twentieth century's leading experts on *The Old Regime*.[55] In contrast to this profoundly situated intellectual driven to understand his nation's current predicament, *Putnam's* presented Tocqueville as an almost antiquarian crypto-American whose political principles were grounded in the traditions of New England towns.

Curtis actually faulted Tocqueville, whose modern fame as a historian rests so largely on the sheer originality of the thesis he propounded in *The Old Regime*, for producing a work not "so entirely novel, in its contents, as the author asserts and even boasts." Although his conclusions are presented as fresh discoveries, "in this country, at least, they have long been familiar to us" (473).

Curtis classified Tocqueville in what he termed "the legitimate school of historical philosophers." Unlike the "rhetorical theologians (who can scarcely be called philosophers)"—persons for whom the French Revolution represented a mass outbreak of human perversion; or on the other hand those who minimized the force of human free will and could find in the Revolution only some sort of "inevitable and mysterious destiny," Tocqueville adhered to the belief that human beings shape the very forces that in turn come to seem like instruments of impersonal destiny to them. Yet, according to Curtis, Tocqueville still managed to overstate the extent to which the Revolution came as a shock, a visitation out of nowhere. Actually, although the aristocracy proved to be "quite blind about gathering developments, both the sovereigns of neighboring countries, on the one hand, and, on the other, the neglected masses within France itself, showed a clear presentiment" about the coming upheaval (473, 474).

Moreover, Tocqueville failed to reach deep enough into the past in his effort to draw out the origins of the Revolution, Curtis argued. Without knowing about Tocqueville's "tendency toward a kind of infinite regression," Curtis in effect found fault with the fact that Tocqueville's 1836 essay provided him with the creative point of departure that he needed to get his project moving, and he expressed disappointment that Tocqueville's thoughts had not regressed still more. "We should at least begin with the ministry of Richelieu, if not, indeed, with the triumph of modern monarchy over feudalism in the fifteenth century" (475).

Curtis reserved the main force of his critique, however, for a point that is of little interest to modern historians, namely the supposed growth of free political institutions in Britain during and after the seventeenth century, in contrast to the corruption, despotism, and anarchy to which the rest of Europe fell prey after the withering away of feudalism. "England alone, after rocking in the tempests of civil commotion for a while"—rather a soothing trope for the English Civil War and Glorious Revolution—"attained to a really secure, stable, and free constitution." Tocqueville's error was to adopt an excessively class-oriented approach to the problem. Like other "aristocratic writers," Tocqueville pointed to a single variable in his attempt to explain these disparities between England and the continent with respect to freedom and despotism, namely "the greater or less destruction in each [country] of the ancient nobility." Tocqueville's chief purpose "is, to show that despotism is an unavoidable outgrowth of those societies in which the aristocracies have been swept away" (476).

But this explanation is inadequate to the task, Curtis insisted. Tocqueville's scenario "ascribe[s] to the services of a class, results which properly belong to popular institutions." It is, rather, to England's "parliaments, its courts, and its local meetings, as *free assemblies in which the popular heart can find some expression for itself*" that the English-Continental divergence must be ascribed. According to this interpretation, Tocqueville even went so far as to advocate an aristocratic restoration. "The inference" from this reading of *The Old Regime* is "that to restore the liberties of France, something like the old aristocracy should be restored" (476).

At this point, Curtis's argument swerved from the path of simple misunderstanding to that of major error. Because Tocqueville argued that the destruction of an aristocracy eliminated certain brakes and parameters to despotic, centralizing, kingly authority in France, Curtis believed he had therefore reached the conclusion that the aristocracy ought to be restored in order to protect or advance the cause of liberty.[56] The *Putnam's* article, published as the magazine was going under, seems calculated to postulate a contrast between England, in its role as a "mother country" replete with free popular and representative institutions, with despotic European monarchies.

It was, then, no great benefit to the appreciation of Tocqueville among American intellectuals that *The Old Regime* came to public notice in the venue and at the time it did. *Putnam's* had been launched in 1853 as an upper-middlebrow journal with heavy paper, excellent printing, and respected authors. It pursued a rigorous policy of author anonymity, however, and was culturally nationalistic in tone. Moreover, it was about to face grim competition from a middle-middlebrow magazine with sparkling writing and an abundance of realistic illustrations, published only a few blocks away in the same city: *Harper's Weekly*. *Harper's* was on the verge of being launched when Curtis's *Old Regime* article appeared; the first issue was still a couple of months away. But the Harper brothers were also the publishers of the other leading monthly, *Harper's New Monthly Magazine*, which had been a going concern since 1850 and which the upstart G. P. Putnam had challenged in 1853 by starting his own monthly.

To the later observer, two items bob to the surface of the turbulent crosscurrents that flowed between *Putnam's*, *Harper's*, and *The Old Regime*: first, the fact that *The Old Regime* was published by the firm of Harper and Brothers; second, the fact that the man who, for all practical purposes, would serve as the editor of the new magazine published by the Harper's firm was also the translator of *The Old Regime*, John Bonner.[57]

Events, interests, and political and economic calculations that were only tangentially related to the contents of the book thus affected Americans' reception and comprehension of *The Old Regime*. *Putnam's* "resolutely American" editorial policy[58] stood in conscious contrast with *Harper's Monthly's* Europe-oriented articles on cultural affairs, and it consequently portrayed *The Old Regime's* author as a nostalgic aristocrat in need of a good history lesson.

The next serious, extended notice of *The Old Regime* came from Philadelphia. Rather than serving to correct any distortions that readers might have picked up from New York sources, this long article in the Rev. Charles Hodge's *Biblical Repertory and Princeton Review* merely added to the confusion. It not only twisted Tocqueville's ideas into unrecognizable shapes, but it used *The Old Regime* as a point of contrast with the ideas of the political scientist whom the author considered the real genius of nineteenth-century political thought, Francis Lieber.

Written by Samuel Tyler, the *Princeton Review* article is an early example of the Teutonic thesis—that mythic construct so widespread in late-nineteenth-century historical circles according to which the modern regimes of civil liberties had their point of departure in the misty German forests of late antiquity. In the American variant of this theory, the Saxons held pride of place among all Teutons, at least in respect to nurturing embryonic New England townships. "The Teutonic spirit was more fully exemplified by the Saxons in England than by any other family of the race," wrote Tyler. "The great contest in modern European politics has been between the law as an independent organism, and the will of the Prince. The Teutonic spirit has, as its chief political aim, striven to organize justice in such a way as to make the law supreme. This aim is the grand *epos* [epic poem] of English history." This is as clear a brief statement of the Teutonic idea as one could ever hope to find in the 1850s.[59]

Tyler's article set Tocqueville's *The Old Regime* up against Lieber's major work of the 1850s, *Civil Liberty and Self-Government*, in order to stress certain areas of complementarity between the two. In Tyler's view, Lieber's *Civil Liberty* articulated certain principles of modern political theory for which Tocqueville then provided, albeit to only a limited extent, a measure of empirical verification. "There is not a political idea much less a principle of political science propounded by De Tocqueville which Lieber had not before announced in his 'Civil Liberty.'" Thus, Tocqueville's book "at most, can only be considered a supplement to [Civil Liberty]. It merely exhibits, with great force it is true, the evidences of the means by which institutional local government was overthrown in France" (627).

The significance of this contrast lies in the way in which the article echoes the *Putnam's* piece of two years earlier. Like his predecessor Curtis, Tyler faulted Tocqueville for not having regressed sufficiently in his historical thinking: "he does not look back far enough into history, nor deep enough into the foundations of European institutions" (629). But seeing just how far back Tyler would have had Tocqueville look makes it clear that he was not interested in discussing the book that Tocqueville actually wrote. The point of departure that Tocqueville should have selected for interpreting the French Revolution, Tyler thought, was the fall of the Roman Empire. Only from such a standpoint straddling the boundary of the ancient and the medieval epochs might one directly observe the process by which the contrasting legal traditions of the Romans and the Saxons developed. For Tyler, that contrast of tradition determined almost all of subsequent European political history up to and including the French Revolution. Tocqueville had provided a useful evidentiary base for understanding the advance of administrative and political centralization, but he stopped, in his backward march through history, at too modern a moment. What he thought would make a useful starting point for his study of the old regime was actually a culminating point of the Roman legal system, an institution that, as the empire collapsed, had been tragically bequeathed to the hapless Gauls. The Revolution and its aftermath thus exhibited "the fickle old Gallic race returned to the theater of political action, after an unprofitable tutelage of many centuries" (633). The conclusion to which this farcical ethnography led would have been anticipated by the *Princeton Review* reader many pages before Tyler got around to stating it. It is this: just as the Saxons of England knew themselves to be "the most Teutonic of Teutons" (634) and "the freest family of the Teutons" (631), so do the Americans "realize in their national consciousness, that they are the great Anglican tribe struggling to act out, on a still nobler theater, the *epos* of freedom" (642).

About twenty-five years after Tyler's essay, the Tocqueville scholar and pioneer Johns Hopkins historian Herbert Baxter Adams, transported by the Teutonic theory, which had by that time been refined and crystallized by E. A. Freeman and others, wrote of the towns of New England, "In such [German] forests liberty was nurtured. Here dwelt the people Rome never could conquer. In these wild retreats the ancient Teutons met in council upon tribal matters of war and peace. . . . Here were planted the seeds of Parliament or Self-government, of Commons and Congresses." Of the Saxon incursions on Britain, Adams boldly claimed that when those Teutonic pillagers arrived, they brought "with them a knowledge of self-government. . . . Magna Carta and the Bill of Rights are only the development of those germs of liberty first planted in the communal customs of our Saxon forefathers."[60] Little had changed since Tyler's day, it would seem, but the thesis was about to undergo a transformation when it became reconnected, as it were, to its systematic philosophical formulation by Tocqueville's friend and intellectual adversary, Count Arthur de Gobineau, "the father of racist ideology."[61]

While Curtis had advocated using the decline of feudalism as the starting point for an inquiry into the French Revolution, then, Tyler emphasized starting with feudalism's origin. Looking back on these early attempts to comprehend *The Old Regime*, we are astonished at the scholarly and philosophical chasm separating Tocqueville and the American journalists. To them, studying ancient history meant reading Tacitus, while for Tocqueville, who was just emerging from years in the archives deciphering, collating, connecting, and adjudicating discrepancies between the primary sources, history meant something close to a Rankean effort to express what really happened in the past. Modern historians, placing their awe to one side, could recognize in Tocqueville a fellow professional, while Curtis and Tyler, who criticized Tocqueville for what they saw as a certain shallowness, an insufficient commitment to understanding the *longue durée*, and a lax willingness to begin with a convenient starting point rather than deep structures, appear to us as complacent amateurs far out of their intellectual depth. There is this additional paradox: while the journalist-critics such as Curtis and Tyler yearned to grasp a full knowledge of the far past and could only come up with undergraduate generalizations about feudalism and the German forests, the historian, Tocqueville, held out only the modest hope that he might attain a partial knowledge of events that had occurred less than a century before he wrote, and then only because he yearned to grasp the significance of the present moment.

Tocqueville's *The Old Regime*, then, was published at a moment in American intellectual history that was least auspicious for a sympathetic reception or accurate comprehension of its contents. The origins of the French Revolution had little resonance in the American debates of the 1850s. The fear that pervaded Tyler's and, to a lesser extent, Curtis's essays was that of national disintegration, not administrative centralization. Tyler's article, in fact, was little more than a coded defense of the Union, wherein he tried to demonstrate that the most basic constitutional principles—from habeas corpus to trial by jury to separation of powers—are not merely grounded in the labor and ideas of eighteenth-century founding fathers but have their roots in the farthest reaches of recorded time. That is what he meant by presenting "the democratic spirit . . . applied to a pure republic" as the American epos of freedom (641–42).

The political romance of Teutonic liberty in the ancient German wilderness eventually developed into a monstrous fable of racial superiority and a warrant for imperial expansion. But like all fables, it had a dynamic history, not a static existence. The writers of the 1850s who used it as a point of contrast with Tocqueville's narrative of the onset of revolution were doing so in order to defend what was then a liberal and inclusive social order. In the political allegory they constructed, the adversary of such a free and open system as obtained in the nonslaveholding, democratic North was a fundamentally "feudal" Southern social order based on forced labor that was seeking to overturn civil liberties and an ancient constitutional structure. Therefore, Tyler's argument exemplified Teutonism as a form of unionism, not racism.

When civil war did come, very shortly after Tocqueville's death, it was the *Democracy* rather than *The Old Regime* that provided American intellectuals with direct and immediate insights into the contemporary crisis. *Democracy in America* was ethnographic, concrete, and descriptive—especially Volume I, which had been reprinted more often than Volume II or the *Democracy* as a whole and had been adopted as required reading by schools and colleges. The *Democracy* was praised and welcomed for the alleged reliability of its discussion of American politics and society. For example, the *American Whig Review* welcomed an 1851 reprint of Volume I as "a most judicious textbook." A. S. Barnes, the publisher of the reprint, had intended to piece together an abridged version of the complete two-volume work, "but finding that to condense would be to destroy, inasmuch as our author's opinions and illustrations are so admirable on every branch of the subject he touches," he decided to jettison Volume II. The result, the *Review* concluded, was "a complete and succinct essay on the institutions of our country."[62]

The Old Regime, by contrast, could be made relevant only through the lens of allegory; readers could apply its lessons to the perilous present only after critics had tutored them on the respective historical roles that the major characters in the book were assigned to play. Furthermore, those characters themselves were seldom real individuals but rather collective entities or abstractions—such as the aristocracy, the *intendants*, the monarchy, or centralization.

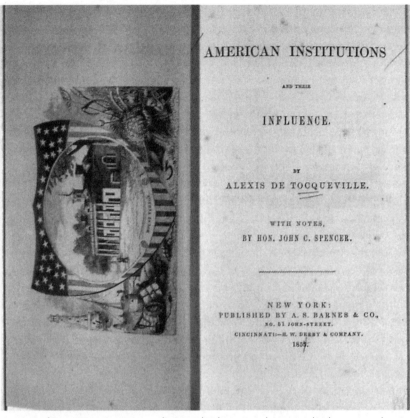

AMERICAN INSTITUTIONS

AND THEIR

INFLUENCE.

BY

ALEXIS DE TOCQUEVILLE.

WITH NOTES,
BY HON. JOHN C. SPENCER.

NEW YORK:
PUBLISHED BY A. S. BARNES & CO.,
NO. 51 JOHN-STREET.
CINCINNATI:—H. W. DERBY & COMPANY.
1855.

Reprints of Democracy in America *eliminated Volume II and presented Volume I as a descriptive account of American institutions. Publishers cavalierly changed the title to reflect this market. The frontispieces of such reprints always contained references to Washington, either by portrait or by landscapes of Mount Vernon.*

Thus, no reviser would follow Bonner as Bowen had followed Reeve.

One other extended essay on *The Old Regime* was published during this period. It appeared in the journal that one would have expected to respond to the book immediately upon its appearance, the *North American Review*. But it was a full five years after its publication that E. L. Godkin got around to discussing *The Old Regime*, and, like those of Tyler and Curtis, his article expressed much more about his own anxieties in 1861 than Tocqueville's in the 1850s. The essay, in fact, focused more on Edmund Burke than on Tocqueville, and, indeed, Godkin deployed *The Old Regime* chiefly as a springboard to purvey his ideas about Burke. This is the earliest comparison of the two writers that I am aware of. In the second half of the twentieth century, such comparisons would appear more frequently—from, for example, conservatives such as Russell Kirk and Ross J. S. Hoffman in the 1950s and neoconservatives like Bruce Frohnen in the 1990s. None of these twentieth-century comparisons, however, revealed any awareness of Godkin's earlier work.[63]

Like the essays of the 1850s on *The Old Regime,* Godkin's is another text brimming with unstated implication. The thrust of Godkin's argument is that apparent divergences of fact and interpretation between Tocqueville's *The Old Regime* and Burke's *Reflections on the Revolution in France* are mere illusions, despite Tocqueville's repeated assertions to the contrary. "The points [of disagreement] on which De Tocqueville insists are not important discrepancies, and, further . . . scarce any such are to be found between him and Burke from first to last."[64]

Godkin's interpretation on this issue is distinctly at odds with current scholarly opinion. As the editor of the most recent critical edition of *Reflections on the Revolution in France* notes, *The Old Regime* "was partly written to refute Burke's *Reflections.*"[65] *The Old Regime* is notable for its passages in which Tocqueville attempted to place himself at a distance from his Anglo-Irish predecessor. Indeed, establishing such a distance was intrinsic to his purpose. As Robert T. Gannett Jr. demonstrated beyond a doubt, although Tocqueville and Burke shared "broad areas of congruence" in their analyses of the Revolution, Burke's chief role in *The Old Regime* was to serve as a foil for the exposition of Tocqueville's own views. "[Tocqueville] refers to Burke by name eleven times in eight passages within the body of his text . . . and includes six quotations from five of his works. On each occasion, he introduces Burke to argue against him, either explicitly or implicitly."[66] Tocqueville's aim was not to denounce and deplore the Revolution; it was to reveal how its major achievements, good or evil, were already in the process of being accomplished through the slower-moving action of political, intellectual, and social forces that were well underway since the late stages of the reign of Louis XIV.

Godkin, however, papered over those differences by attributing them to simple errors of interpretation on Tocqueville's part: "De Tocqueville misconceived Burke," he flatly claimed (395). His misconception consisted principally of a category mistake: Tocqueville took Burke's arguments to be philosophical in nature, and thus he applied philosophical criteria to evaluate them, but Burke's arguments were political, and in political discourse "the writer . . . appears not as an investigator, but as an advocate" (395). In other words, rigorous standards of logic and argumentation do not have to be applied to political texts because a kind of adversarial discount has already been applied to those intellectual goods by the informed reader. This distinction is torturous enough by itself, but it has the additional weakness of misconceiving Tocqueville, who knew perfectly well how to read Burke. The purpose of this line of argument became clearer as the article proceeded along its stately Godkinian path. Godkin wished to use Tocqueville's esteemed reputation in order to vindicate Burke's horrible depiction of the French Revolution and to apply the abundant lessons contained in that picture to the current crisis in the United States. Obviously, an essay about Burke's *Reflections*, which had been published in 1790, would have been out of place in a journal devoted primarily to the criticism of current books. But the coming of the Civil War, in conjunction with Tocqueville's recently published *The Old Regime*, provided a convenient pretext for writing about the subject that Godkin really wanted to address: Burke on the French Revolution.

Godkin's opening tactic was therefore to present Tocqueville as both deeply respected, yet not too well known, in the United States. Just a few months after Godkin's essay appeared, the *New York Times* asserted: "it is not necessary to introduce De Tocqueville to the American reader. His name is probably more familiar here than in Europe," and referred to *Democracy in America* as a book "known to every school boy." Charles Eliot Norton declared in November 1861 that Tocqueville's "reputation and the weight of his authority are continually increasing."[67] Yet Godkin, in that same autumn of 1861, opened his article with the dissenting claim that Tocqueville's "works deserve to be better known than they yet are to Americans" (391). By taking on the role of a well-informed teacher who could supply the antidote to this intellectual deficiency, Godkin could expound the ideas of Tocqueville, then advance to his discussion of Burke.

The Old Regime's chief virtue, in Godkin's estimation, was its patient accretion of facts, its gathering up of a treasury of empirical verification that, combined with Tocqueville's magisterial tone and absence of a need to show off his achievement, produced a historical account of solid reliability. In an arresting image, Godkin wrote that Tocqueville's work "is like specie in sealed packages. We have only to count the parcels, without being obliged to number and test their contents" (392). The sum of those parcels was an account of France that, Godkin said, confirmed the portrayal in Charles Dickens's *A Tale of Two Cities* (a very topical reference, for *A Tale of Two Cities* had been published just two years earlier, in 1859).

Turning next to the "discrepancies" between Tocqueville and Burke, which Godkin would take it upon himself to reconcile, there were three. First, on the level of fact, Tocqueville was simply correct, and Burke mistaken, on the condition of the lowest classes before the Revolution. They suffered much more oppression than Burke had known or acknowledged. Godkin thus conceded the advantage to Tocqueville on a terrain that Godkin could later occupy in order to demonstrate the overall veracity of Burke's account. By conceding Tocqueville to be the superior historian or master of the facts, Godkin could adduce Tocqueville's account as factual support for Burke's conclusions.

Second, as to interpretation, Tocqueville made two mistakes. At the outset Tocqueville criticized Burke for his prediction that the Revolution would annihilate France. Burke's opinion, however, Godkin thought, constituted a deduction based on the data of an ongoing current event, not a solid prediction of the future. "But for the astounding victories of [Napoleon, which came years after Burke wrote], it may well be questioned how long France could have avoided the fate of Poland. The tendency of the Revolution was, as Burke 'inferred,' to destroy France; the advent of a military despot, in the providence of God, saved her from its natural effect" (395). Tocqueville's second misinterpretation of Burke was similar to the first. Burke had bemoaned the failure of the French to preserve the ancient common law; Tocqueville charged Burke with blindness to the Revolution's aim, which was in fact the destruction of that law.

Yet, even though Tocqueville "is constantly charging Burke with some misrepresentation" (394), we can dismiss those charges and release Burke from custody, Godkin wrote, because the charges are all based on misconceptions anyway. Read correctly, one can see that there are very few points on which Tocqueville and Burke disagree. The two authors almost read as if they compiled a single book together. Indeed, "had De Tocqueville completed his design"—had he lived to write the promised second volume of his history, which would have told the story of the Revolutionary era itself—"his work would undoubtedly have been more nearly parallel to the writings of Burke" (396).

Godkin allotted more space to his interpretation of Burke than to the work of the writer to whom his essay was purportedly devoted. In brief, he contended that Burke, contrary the charges of his critics, did not condemn all revolutions as a matter of general principle but only the French Revolution, a specific instance. Such a distinction was crucial because it exempted the American version of revolution from Burke's ruthless broadsides. "Some revolutions have been blessings to the race. . . . A writer may with perfect consistency condemn the revolution of 1789 and extol that of 1776" (399–400). The French Revolution had been an evil to France and Europe chiefly because its sole aim was to destroy. Moreover, it was "intrinsically wrong" (402), immoral and erroneous at its root, not merely wrong because it got out of hand or because its leading actors twisted a fundamentally just objective by their extreme and unjust behavior. That is because its driving theoretical justification, "the theory of government known as the 'rights of man,' is utterly false." Godkin contended that "Abstract reasoning can never determine matters of fact," such as the contingent and time-bound question of how to erect political arrangements suitable to a given social order (402). And finally, the Revolution was wrong because it placed arbitrary power in the hands of an ungovernable mob.

Three great lessons were to be derived from a study of the Revolution as viewed through this Burkean lens. "The first is the necessity of religion to the security of nations." Indeed, "even a corrupt form of religion is better than infidelity" (413). Second, "arbitrary power is not good for man, either for the individual or the race" (413–14). The revolutionists had stripped arbitrary rule from the hands of an individual, King Louis XVI, and they thought that they were advancing the cause of liberty and the rights of man by then vesting it instead in the people. "Their great error was in failing to see that it might be evil in the hands of the multitude" (415). The result was, tragically, the destruction of an entire social system of ancient and honorable mutuality that was, after all, capable of gradual improvement. Finally, Godkin wrote, political societies must seek such incremental reform over violent change. The revolution, however, "sought rather to reconstruct than to amend" (416).

So much for the Revolution's value as a teacher. Such "lessons" were, for Godkin, the main reason for turning to Burke. But Godkin became hopelessly entangled in contradictions as he attempted to blend Burke with Tocqueville. For him, the force of Burke's *Reflections* lay not where most readers had located it—in its magnificent mastery of rhetorical devices—but where they forgot to look—in its deployment of compelling, "resistless" logic. Burke's brilliant prose, Godkin argued, actually hindered proper comprehension of his views. "It is certainly unfortunate . . . that this treatise was made so magnificent." Indeed, Burke unwisely "wreathed his sword in flowers so as to destroy its power." For the power of the *Reflections* resides not in its eloquence but in its "irresistible refutation of the system it attacks." Thus, "he who would read the work with profit should often turn back and, *disre-*

garding all the beauties of the style, draw out a continuous abstraction of the argument it unfolds" (397, emphasis added). This is a difficult argument to accept for anyone who has read the *Reflections* with care. J. C. D. Clark, in his definitive 2001 edition, stated flatly that "Burke's *Reflections* was a work of practical political rhetoric, not of abstract, systematic analysis"—the antithesis of what Godkin would have his readers suppose.[68]

The ultimate sanction and support for Burke's position, then, was its logical coherence, not its discursive grace. And therein lay the contradiction in Godkin's line of argument. The supposed shortcoming of Tocqueville's attempts to construe Burke came from Tocqueville's having employed clear and distinct "philosophical" and logical criteria to evaluate arguments that were nonphilosophical in nature—arguments to which such strict logical standards were misapplied. In other words, the supposed merits of Burke's *Reflections* were held to lie precisely in the realm of which Godkin denied the relevance when applied to Tocqueville—the realm of logical coherence and philosophical rigor.

In sum, then, Godkin attempted to use the prestige of Tocqueville's name to support the contentions of Burke. Tocqueville's numerous and explicit divergences from Burke constituted a potential difficulty, however. Godkin responded to the challenge by dismissing the disagreements as illusory while underlining areas where their ideas conformed. At the same time, he cast Tocqueville in a sort of historical supporting role whereby he could provide evidentiary support for the arguments, at once philosophical and political, of the great parliamentarian. In reality, this argument held, Tocqueville can be assimilated to Burke.

Such a rhetorical tactic would continue to be evident in works about Tocqueville by later writers who explicitly tried to claim him as an ally in the cause of American conservatism.

What finally were the reasons for Godkin's tortured logic and willful distortions of Tocqueville's thought? Although Tocqueville could provide a useful entrée to a discussion of Burke, other thinkers or recent books might have proven more serviceable for that purpose in 1861. Nor was Tocqueville's honored reputation in itself a sufficient reason. It was, I believe, Tocqueville in his role as special European friend of America who was essential to Godkin's purpose; and this famously prescient and disinterested European observer had recently produced a distinguished work on the most destructive upheaval in European history, as well. Godkin's choice of Tocqueville as entrée to Burke came just as the Civil War erupted in our own country. That conflict seemed redolent of the dangers of the French Revolution—if not (in

1861) in its massacres and mob action, then in its radical, fanatical drive to overthrow an effective constitutional system that was amenable to moderate change. Reading Burke as Godkin would interpret him "is of the utmost importance in our own time and country," Godkin wrote. "It is to be wished that its sentiments were much more generally diffused among us; for, rightly understood, it is a bright beacon placed over that lee-shore of democracy toward which many causes combine to urge our American Republic" (397). He turned to Burke, via Tocqueville, in order to confront and work through his apprehensions about the present and future condition of America.

In 1959, at the Tocqueville Centenary Conference organized by John Lukacs at Chestnut Hill College, the conservative Catholic historian Ross J. S. Hoffman read a paper on Tocqueville and Burke in which he freely admitted that he could find no direct evidence that Burke's political philosophy had had any influence on Tocqueville's own writings. But he was nevertheless intrigued, he said, by what he called "some morphological resemblances" between the two.[69] Morphology—the study of form or structure, separate from function—is a judicious and revealing trope for this argument. Hoffman meant that there was a congruence of spirit between the two thinkers that transcended the specific content of their respective writings. Whether this claim is true or not—and I do not find it convincing—Hoffman's claim was honestly advanced.

A close, unbiased, scholarly study of the exact uses made by Tocqueville of Burke, whom Tocqueville probably read between February and June of 1853 in preparation for The Old Regime, would not be published until 2003. In this brilliant work of exhumation and exegesis, Robert T. Gannett Jr. showed how despite his admiration for Burke's insights into the Revolution's course, Tocqueville found Burke's work fundamentally unsound. As Tocqueville wrote, he found Burke's narrative "filled with true touches, but very false on the whole."[70]

There is, however, an additional, more ironic type of morphological resemblance at work in the Tocqueville-Burke discourse. Twentieth- and twenty-first-century conservative commentators seem not to have read Godkin's work, but on this subject at least, there is a distinct resemblance between what Godkin wrote in 1861 and more recent output. When points of contention between Burke and Tocqueville were elided, and the latter was touted as a sort of corroborating witness and philosophical endorser of Burke, the distinctions between the two men became blurred to the point where their identities merged.

Of all the notable passages in Burke's Reflections, none is more famous than the one containing his remark about "the little platoon." Early in the work, Burke expressed his shock and dismay over members of the aristocracy in France, who in their "personal pride and arrogance," betrayed that portion of the social order to which they belonged, instead of acting with courage, dignity, and charity within it. An abstract, generalized affection for mankind could never substitute for such devotion to one's "platoon," Burke said, and, in fact, that little portion of society is itself the modest starting point from which a love for mankind must have its beginning.

Alexander Pope provided the perfect eighteenth-century definition of wit as "what oft was thought, but ne'er so well expressed" ("An Essay on Criticism," 198). In his metaphor of the platoon, Burke offered an indelible illustration of Pope's criterion. He gave an ideal form of expression to what was a rather commonplace idea in the eighteenth century: that persons are connected in a great chain of interdependence, and that therefore sentiments of benevolence must arise out of one's immediate circumstances, only from there to move outward and encompass an ever wider scope. Here is the passage in Burke:

> Turbulent, discontented men of quality, in proportion as they are puffed up with personal pride and arrogance, generally despise their own order. One of the first symptoms they discover of a selfish and mischievous ambition, is a profligate disregard of a dignity which they partake with others. To be attached to the subdivision, to love the little platoon we belong to in society, is the first principle (the germ as it were) of public affections. It is the first link in the series by which we proceed towards a love to our country and to mankind.[71]

In 2003, the journalist Nicholas Lemann inquired of the self-described conservative revolutionary Karl Rove, who was serving as chief political adviser to President George W. Bush, what Rove thought about Tocqueville. "Tocqueville all the way!" came Rove's enthusiastic response. "I think Tocqueville values the little battalions for the sake of being little battalions."[72] It would be hard to find a clearer illustration of assimilating Tocqueville to Burke than this. It is a quibble to point out that Rove expanded Burke's military unit from platoon to battalion strength in his remark; what really matters is the attribution of this clichéd Burkean conception to Tocqueville. Karl Rove's inadvertent identity switch had its origin in the mid-nineteenth century.

Notes

1. Hugh Brogan, "Alexis de Tocqueville and the Coming of the American Civil War," in *American Studies: Essays in Honour of Marcus Cunliffe*, ed. Brian Holden Reid

and John White (New York: St. Martin's, 1990), 83–104; OC, VII, *passim*, see especially, 154–204 and 249–51.

2. OC, VII:154n74–1.

3. Brogan, "Tocqueville and the Civil War," 88–89; "Portrait de Mme Childe née Lee," OC, VII:250.

4. However, the plan of writing about the Revolution first took shape in December 1850; see Jardin, *Tocqueville*, 482; see also Françoise Mélonio and François Furet, introduction to OR, I:1–12.

5. Tocqueville to Henry Reeve, January 9, 1852, *Letters*, 285, 286.

6. Tocqueville to Gustave de Beaumont, April 8, 1853, *Letters*, 291.

7. R, 3–4. Of course, they could never be "completely secret," and there is a disingenuous element in both the declaration and the memoirs themselves. See L. E. Shiner, *The Secret Mirror: Literary Form and History in Tocqueville's Recollections* (Ithaca, N.Y.: Cornell University Press, 1988), esp. 13–39.

8. R. R. Palmer, "Two Preliminary Notes," *The Two Tocquevilles, Father and Son: Hervé and Alexis de Tocqueville and the Coming of the French Revolution*, ed. and trans. R. R. Palmer (Princeton, N.J.: Princeton University Press, 1987), 148.

9. Francis Lieber to Alexis de Tocqueville, March 12, 1854 (facsimile), Lieber papers (H).

10. OC, VII:145.

11. Tocqueville to Theodore Sedgwick, December 4, 1852, OC, VII:146, 147.

12. David M. Potter, *The Impending Crisis, 1848–1861*, completed and edited by Don E. Fehrenbacher (New York: Harper and Row, 1976), 173–74.

13. Tocqueville to Theodore Sedgwick, January 10, 1857, OC, VII:189–90.

14. Edward L. Pierce, *Memoir and Letters of Charles Sumner*, 4 vols. (Boston: Roberts Brothers, 1877–1894), III:535.

15. Alexis de Tocqueville, "Report on Abolition," TBSR, 98–99n1.

16. OC, VII:164 and 163–64n1.

17. OR, 87–88.

18. OR, 152–63; François Furet, *Revolutionary France, 1770–1880*, trans. Antonia Nevill (Oxford: Blackwell, 1992), 9.

19. Caleb Crain, "Tocqueville for Neocons," *New York Times Book Review*, January 14, 2001, 11; see also James Q. Wilson to the editors, *New York Times Book Review*, February 4, 2001, 2; Harvey C. Mansfield and Delba Winthrop, "Translating Tocqueville's *Democracy in America*," *La Revue Tocqueville/The Tocqueville Review* 21:1 (2000): 154; J. P. Mayer, foreword to *Democracy in America*, by Alexis de Tocqueville, ed. J. P. Mayer, trans. George Lawrence (New York: Harper and Row, 1966), vii; P. N. Furbank, "Tocqueville's Lament," *New York Review of Books* 46, no. 6 (April 8, 1999): 48.

20. Francis Bowen, "Preface of the American Editor" to *Democracy in America*, by Alexis de Tocqueville, trans. Henry Reeve (Cambridge, Mass.: Sever and Francis, 1862), vi, xiii.

21. Henry Reeve, *Royal and Republican France*, 2 vols. (London: Longmans, Green, and Co., 1872), II:79n1.

22. John Knox Laughton, *Memoirs of the Life and Correspondence of Henry Reeve*, C. B., D. C. L., 2 vols. (London: Longmans, Green and Co., 1898), I:42–43.

23. Laughton, *Henry Reeve*, I:45.

24. Laughton, *Henry Reeve*, I:50, 65; Jardin, *Tocqueville*, 233; Seymour Drescher, *Tocqueville and England* (Cambridge, Mass.: Harvard University Press, 1964), 54–55; Tocqueville to Henry Reeve, April 17, 1836, OC, VI, pt. 1, 30.

25. Reeve, *Royal and Republican France*, II:84–85.

26. Tocqueville to Reeve, September 15, 1839, OC, VI, Pt. 1, 48.

27. Daniel Walker Howe, *The Unitarian Conscience: Harvard Moral Philosophy, 1805–1861* (Cambridge, Mass.: Harvard University Press, 1970), 309.

28. R, 324. Tocqueville was foreign minister at the time of the collapse of the Hungarian revolt and Kossuth's flight into exile, matters he discusses on pp. 314–27.

29. Jared Sparks to Tocqueville, June 13, 1853, in Herbert Baxter Adams, *The Life and Writings of Jared Sparks*, 2 vols. (1893; repr. New York: Books for Libraries Press, 1970), II:43.

30. George M. Trevelyan, *British History in the Nineteenth Century and After* (London: Longmans, Green, 1937), 292.

31. Francis Bowen, "The War of Races in Hungary," *North American Review* 70, no. 1 (January, 1850): 80; Monica Maria Grecu, "Francis Bowen," in *American Literary Critics and Scholars*, vol. 59 of *Dictionary of Literary Biography*, ed. John W. Rathbun and Monica M. Grecu (Detroit, Mich.: Gale, 1987), 25.

32. Howe, *Unitarian Conscience*, 267, 309–10; Bruce Kuklick, *The Rise of American Philosophy: Cambridge, Massachusetts, 1860–1930* (New Haven, Conn.: Yale University Press, 1977), 29; Grecu, "Bowen," 22.

33. Robert Carter, *The Hungarian Controversy: An Exposure of the Falsifications and Perversions of the Slanderers of Hungary* (Boston: Redding and Co., 1852). John H. Komlos also referred to Carter's charges in a meticulous but virtually unnoticed monograph, *Louis Kossuth in America, 1851–1852* (Buffalo, N.Y.: East European Institute, 1973), 36–38.

34. Carter, *Hungarian Controversy*, 3, 4, 6.

35. Kuklick, *Rise of American Philosophy*, 121, see also, 47–54; Max Fisch, "American Pragmatism before and after 1898," in *American Philosophy from Edwards to Quine*, ed. Robert W. Shahan and Kenneth R. Merrill (Norman: University of Oklahoma Press, 1977), 78–110; Louis Menand, *The Metaphysical Club* (New York: Farrar, Straus & Giroux, 2001).

36. Adams, *Sparks and Tocqueville*, II:365–66.

37. Francis Bowen, *The Principles of Political Economy Applied to the Condition, the Resources, and the Institutions of the American People*, 3rd ed. (Boston: Little, Brown, 1863), vi–vii.

38. Joseph Dorfman, *The Economic Mind in American Civilization, 1606–1865*, 2 vols. (New York: Viking, 1946), II:826–43; Howe, *Unitarian Conscience*, 231.

39. This observation, or "witness," occurs in the chapter entitled "Why Americans Seem So Restless in the Midst of Their Well-Being," another key element of Bowen's economics.

40. "Vicious agrarian schemes" is Dorfman's term: *Economic Mind*, II:839.

41. Bowen, *Principles of Political Economy*, 502–4. The Tocqueville quote appears in *DIA*, 54–55.

42. For an especially clear example, see Bowen, *Principles of Political Economy*, 164–93, on the theory of rent.

43. Matthew Mancini, "Political Economy and Cultural Theory in Tocqueville's Abolitionism," *Slavery and Abolition* 10, no. 2 (September 1989): 151–71; Michael Drolet, "Democracy and Political Economy: Tocqueville's Thoughts on J.-B. Say and T. R. Malthus," *History of European Ideas* 29, no. 2 (June 2003): 159–81.

44. Bowen, *Principles of Political Economy*, 201.

45. Bowen quoted in Howe, *Unitarian Conscience*, 41.

46. Kuklick, *Rise of American Philosophy*, 30.

47. Kuklick, *Rise of American Philosophy*, 33, 28.

48. R. R. Palmer, "Two Preliminary Notes," 148; Jardin, *Tocqueville*, 461.

49. Alan Kahan, "Tocqueville's Two Revolutions," *Journal of the History of Ideas* 46, no. 4 (October 1985): 592.

50. Alexis de Tocqueville, "On the Social and Political Condition of France," *London and Westminster Review* 25, no. 1 (April 1836): 137–69; Jardin, *Tocqueville*, 246–48; Mélonio and Furet, "Introduction," I:3–7.

51. "Editorial Notes—Literature," *Putnam's Monthly Magazine* 8 (October 1856): 471; on *Putnam's Monthly* see Frank Luther Mott, *A History of American Magazines, 1850–1865* (Cambridge, Mass.: Harvard University Press, 1938), 419–31.

52. See Mott, *History of American Magazines, 1850–1865*, 424.

53. "De Tocqueville on the Causes of the French Revolution," *Putnam's Monthly Magazine* 8 (November 1856): 471. Subsequent page references appear in parentheses in the following paragraphs.

54. See, especially, Roger Boesche, *The Strange Liberalism of Alexis de Tocqueville* (Ithaca, N.Y.: Cornell University Press, 1987); Hugh Brogan, *Tocqueville* (London: Fontana, 1973).

55. Furet and Mélonio, "Introduction," I:4.

56. Sheldon S. Wolin came, albeit via a very different route, close to the same position in 2001; see Wolin, *Tocqueville between Two Worlds: The Making of a Political and Theoretical Life* (Princeton, N.J.: Princeton University Press, 2001), esp. 450–55; and Seymour Drescher, "Who Needs *Ancienneté*? Tocqueville on Aristocracy and Modernity," *History of Political Thought* 24, no. 4 (Winter 2003): 624–46.

57. The first person appointed editor of *Harper's Weekly* never fully took over his responsibilities because he was named ambassador to The Hague in 1857, then U.S. Attorney for the Southern District of New York one year later. This editor, lawyer, and diplomat was Theodore Sedgwick, who over twenty years earlier had provided indispensable assistance to Tocqueville in Paris as Tocqueville was laboring on the first *Democracy*. Bonner was officially named editor in 1858 and remained in the position until 1863. J. Henry Harper, *The House of Harper: A Century of Publishing in Franklin Square* (New York:

Harper and Brothers, 1912), 132–33, 222; Mott, *History of American Magazines, 1850–1865*, 469–70.

58. Mott, *History of American Magazines, 1850–1865*, 420.

59. [S. Tyler], "De Tocqueville and Lieber, as Writers on Political Science," *Biblical Repertory and Princeton Review* 7, no. 4 (October 1858): 629, 630. Subsequent page references appear in parentheses.

60. Herbert Baxter Adams, "The Germanic Origins of the New England Towns," *Johns Hopkins University Studies in Historical and Political Science* (Baltimore, Md.: Johns Hopkins University Press, 1882), 13, 23.

61. Michael D. Biddiss, *The Father of Racist Ideology: The Social and Political Thought of Count Gobineau* (New York: Weybright and Talley, 1970), 147–50.

62. "Critical Notices," *American Whig Review* 13 (April 1851): 382.

63. Russell Kirk, *The Conservative Mind: From Burke to Eliot*, 6th rev. ed. (South Bend, Ind.: Gateway, 1978), esp. 161–95; Ross J. S. Hoffman, "Tocqueville and Burke," *The Burke Newsletter* 2 (1961): 44–47; Bruce Frohnen, *Virtue and the Promise of Conservatism: The Legacy of Burke and Tocqueville* (Lawrence: University Press of Kansas, 1993).

64. [E. L. Godkin], "De Tocqueville on the French Revolution," *North American Review* 93, no. 2 (October 1861): 396. Subsequent references appear in parentheses in the text.

65. J. C. D. Clark, introduction to *Reflections on the Revolution in France*, by Edmund Burke, ed. J. C. D. Clark (Stanford, Calif.: Stanford University Press, 2001), 78.

66. Robert T. Gannett Jr., *Tocqueville Unveiled: The Historian and His Sources for The Old Regime and the Revolution* (Chicago: University of Chicago Press, 2003), 77, 70.

67. *New York Times*, July 4, 1862, 2; Norton, "Alexis de Tocqueville," 552.

68. Clark, "Introduction," 85.

69. Hoffman, "Tocqueville and Burke," 44. Hoffman delivered the paper at the "Tocqueville Centenary" conference at Chestnut Hill College, Philadelphia, Pennsylvania, April 14, 1959. I am grateful to the archivist of Chestnut Hill College, Dr. Lorraine Coons, for providing the conference program to me.

70. Gannett, *Tocqueville Unveiled*, 187n31, 62; on Burke and Tocqueville, see especially 39–56.

71. Burke, *Reflections*, 201–2.

72. Nicholas Lemann, "The Controller," *New Yorker* 79, no. 11 (May 12, 2003): 82.

CHAPTER FOUR

The Myth of Oblivion

In 1857, Tocqueville wrote to his nephew Hubert, whom he treated almost like a son, "Everything that is specific is always more or less doubtful." This is an unexpected sentiment coming from the pen of a historian. Richard Herr interpreted it to mean that it was the ideas, opinions, beliefs, and mental habits of men and women that are the primary forces behind social and political change. As Tocqueville explained further in that same letter, only "the movement of ideas and passions" can be considered "absolutely sure in history."[1] Not the specific datum of one historical event but the mental and moral universe in which it occurs and is interpreted: that is the historian's rightful subject.

In a similar manner, William James wrote that "*all perception is acquired perception*"—roughly, that the investigator sees what his mind has prepared him to see.[2] It may sometimes happen, even among historians, that certain mental habits of perception can become ingrained. When that occurs, the data produced by events of the past will fail to be adequately recognized, let alone understood and endowed with due significance. To take one well-known example: everyone could see that the American Civil War destroyed a dying, paternalistic, quasifeudal way of life, that slavery was a wasteful, inefficient, and unprofitable labor system that could not have survived another two generations, that the war itself was fought in any case not for slavery but for the cause of states' rights, and that the South in particular fought with conspicuous gallantry on the field of battle. Such "truths" as these governed the enormous historiography of the Civil War for a hundred years. The trouble is, all of those statements have been subjected to devastating assaults, and no current historian could maintain such positions and expect a respectful hearing.[3]

Such mystifying truths occurred in the Tocqueville scholarship, as well. In the first part of this chapter, I wish briefly to interrupt the chronological narrative and broaden the perspective by adding a consideration of some of the late-twentieth-century literature on Tocqueville's American reputation. I will show how the context of American intellectual culture and the social location of Tocqueville commentators made Tocqueville a far more important figure after 1865 than scholars have allowed, especially scholars who adopt the method of counting articles as a proxy indicator of intellectual influence.

Curiously, given Tocqueville's stature and acknowledged, continuing relevance, it became an unshakeable tradition, a kind of folklore amongst the specialists, that the reputation that Tocqueville enjoyed at the end of the twentieth century was an inconceivable phenomenon from the perspective of the end of the nineteenth, or even a generation before that. To read the commentary on the issue of Tocqueville's status and influence (and the commentary is quite thin and scattered) is to watch helplessly as a pitiful spectacle unfolds: that of a great man, once famous, honored and illustrious, sinking, sinking ever deeper into the waters of oblivion, being lost, erased, silenced to the point where even well-educated men and women could hardly identify his name. This drowning was believed to have occurred around the time of the Civil War; yet, many years later a wondrous resuscitation occurred that, *mirabile dictu*, coincided with the worldwide struggle against fascist and Nazi tyranny. Many historians could not resist the impulse—after all, for historians it is more like a reflex action—to weave a dense fabric of causation out of these slender threads of correlation. And so, a narrative developed in which Tocqueville became a kind of Sleeping Beauty, who had been awakened by the caressing promise of a more democratic future, a future that could only be realized after the destruction of the Axis powers. Of course, there was evidence to hand that could be employed to construct this story. Historians did not need to fabricate material in order to build this narrative, but they did need to exaggerate, to make too much of good quotes that reinforced a neat correlation.

The Second World War itself was bookended by two mighty Tocquevillean works that are central to all Americanists' understanding of American culture since the age of Jackson. In the months leading up to Hitler's invasion of Poland, Oxford University Press published George Wilson Pierson's *Tocqueville and Beaumont in America*, while three weeks before the surrender of the Nazis, Alfred A. Knopf brought out the Phillips Bradley edition of

Democracy in America. It seemed indeed that a new age of Tocqueville was dawning, ninety years after the philosopher-statesman's death.

This post–World War II upsurge in interest in Tocqueville was variously referred to as a rebirth, a return, a vogue or fashion, or a rise in stock price. In 1951, Oxford University's Max Beloff formulated the metaphor that would often recur in ensuing decades when, in an essay about J. P. Mayer's first volume in the French National Commission's complete works, he wrote, "If political philosophers were quoted on 'change [the London Stock Exchange] instead of in the class-room, the last few years would have seen a steady rise in the price of Tocqueville," and he sardonically complimented Mayer for having undertaken "an intelligent investment . . . in the fortunes of Tocqueville's reputation at a comparatively early stage in the boom."[4] Beginning in the 1960s, a few historians would look back at this "boom," and at the relative slump in value that had preceded it, and they proceeded to draw conclusions that far outran their data. In order to support the thesis that a Tocqueville boom was in progress, many historians not only noted the increase in attention Tocqueville started to receive after the war, but also portrayed the prewar era as a sort of empty slate, the better to dramatize the novelty of the more recent situation.

The first scholar to consider the supposed gap between 1950s and 1960s Tocqueville scholarship and the period before the war was also the most precise and circumspect: Seymour Drescher. An appendix to his invaluable *Tocqueville and Beaumont on Social Reform* (1968) contained a clever, effective visual display in the form of a table and simple bar graph indicating that 44 percent of all Tocqueville scholarship had appeared between 1950 and 1969. No commentary accompanied the table and graph, however.[5] Drescher would soon establish a reputation as a quantitative historian of formidable talent, but this early foray into cliometrics, while visually arresting, was lacking in several important qualifying explanations and supporting information. Nevertheless, it seemed to depict a phoenixlike Tocqueville rising from the ashes of neglect and ignorance.

Along with Lynn L. Marshall, Drescher published in that same year, 1968, what served in effect as the commentary to accompany that table and graph in the form of an article in the *Journal of American History*. Marshall and Drescher focused only on American historians and only on one of Tocqueville's works, the *Democracy*, in the article, but their assertions dovetailed with Drescher's graphic. Pointing out that "the present Tocqueville vogue dates only from the very recent past," Marshall and Drescher noted that, while sociologists had found Tocqueville's emphasis on associations to be attractive, they traditionally had demonstrated little curiosity about the past, while the historians, on the other hand, had not paid much attention to issues of social organization.

Concerning the issue of Tocqueville as vogue or fashion, Marshall and Drescher gave a precise date as to its appearance: "Tocqueville became a fashionable source after the publication in 1938 of George Wilson Pierson's *Tocqueville and Beaumont in America*." For Marshall and Drescher, then, "the very recent past" meant thirty years before they wrote, or one generation. Prior to their intellectual parents' generation, there were, in their view, virtually no American scholars who paid any attention to Tocqueville whatsoever. "In what might be called the pre-Pierson years," they wrote, "*only an occasional seminal European political scientist or sociologist*, for example Moises Ostrogorski, recognized the depth of his analysis of America" (emphasis added). There had, then, been a sudden and indeed revolutionary shift in intellectual styles in 1938, as Marshall and Drescher conveyed by using the term "fashionable." Before then all was darkness—"the pre-Pierson years," as in prehistoric.[6]

Marshall and Drescher's study reinforced this sense of time immemorial by neglecting the question of when such ignoring of Tocqueville might have originated. Rather than having a beginning, it just always was. What they wished to examine was the commencement and development of the subsequent Tocqueville fashion, rather than that which had preceded it, so their neglect of origins was understandable. But their essay, whatever its manifold virtues, did establish a distinctive picture of a sudden rise in fashion preceded by an indistinct period of utter neglect.

These images of Tocqueville's work as fashion or stock price, besides their suggestion of triviality, also underscored the themes of chance and fluctuation. Stocks, like fashion, are fickle. They are also cyclical. Fashion and fortune revolve, but seldom in sync with each other. Tocqueville, then, by extension from the metaphor, could be seen as having emerged out of nowhere, like toreador pants or Microsoft. What needed explanation, therefore, was how and why the fashion arose when it did, seemingly out of the void.

Eight years after Marshall and Drescher's article, the time-immemorial "pre-Pierson years" were furnished with a fairly specific beginning. By providing this point of origin, Robert Nisbet's influential essay about "Many Tocquevilles" gave a more definite shape to the alleged period of Tocqueville's neglect. In his discussion of the various uses to which Tocqueville's writings had been put, Nisbet provided both more precision and less data than Marshall and Drescher had done. After Nisbet wrote, the alleged abandonment of Tocqueville became more firmly established as a definite historical fact that did not need to be revisited. But in the hands of later scholars, the duration of this supposed time period tended to expand, even as its status as a distinct epoch crystallized.

Both the originating date of the period of forgetfulness and the time of Tocqueville's sudden reemergence kept shifting throughout the course of Nisbet's essay. At first, he contended that the descent into irrelevance began "by the 1870s," after which time *Democracy in America* was "only occasionally studied and footnoted." Nisbet also bracketed the era by providing an end point: "about 1940," he thought. So, the era of Tocqueville's neglect spanned approximately seventy years, or three generations. But later in the essay, Nisbet expanded that era at the front end and contracted it at the rear: it became "from the late 1860s until the late 1930s"; and still later, he postulated a contraction, with the *Democracy*'s undergoing a "decline, in both intellectual and popular regard, by 1880," but being "restored . . . to . . . extraordinary importance since about 1940."[7] Thus, the sinking of Tocqueville was diversely said to have occurred by the 1870s, the late 1860s, and 1880, with the rise happening in the late 1930s or about 1940. Nisbet's decision not to impose a false precision on murky and uncertain data was, on the whole, commendable. Unlike its celestial counterpart, there could be no precisely calculated moment when Tocqueville's eclipse took place; instead, it developed over a few years and ceased at an approximate time. But Nisbet's article did provide crucial scaffolding to support this construct of a completely forgotten, then suddenly resurrected, Tocqueville. It furnished the supposed period of neglect with a point of origin, something that had not been on Marshall and Drescher's agenda.

After the mid-1970s, then, the almost mythical drama of a lost oracle or prophet who returned from the nether regions with lore and guidance for a new age was well established. Central to the myth was the element of oblivion. While the exact dates of forgetfulness remained somewhat vague, the length of the time span actually increased in the accounts of later scholars. For example, one careful historian, Wilfred M. McClay, wrote that "the postwar period saw an extraordinary rebirth of interest in Tocqueville," which in his account was chiefly due to the 1945 Bradley edition of the *Democracy*. "Hard as it is to imagine today," McClay wrote, "Tocqueville had been a negligible influence upon American thinkers in the years between the Civil War and World War II." McClay thus stretched the period of oblivion by a decade, from seventy to eighty years. His source was Nisbet's impressionistic, undocumented essay.[8]

James T. Kloppenberg also stretched the period to eighty years, but with his additional years coming at the front end, rather than, as in McClay's version, at the back: it lasted "from the outbreak of the Civil War until the outbreak of World War II." Kloppenberg took issue with both Nisbet and McClay—significantly, however, not about the length of the period of Tocqueville's supposed eclipse, but only about its cause. As against Nisbet and McClay's thesis, which held that Tocqueville faced too much competition in the marketplace of celebratory works about American institutions after the 1870s (or perhaps it was the 1860s), Kloppenberg argued that the sinking of Tocqueville's reputation happened because the multiple strains and antagonisms of American life had rendered his commentary of dubious value: "It was instead the prevalence of conflict that submerged the *Democracy*. Conflict caused Americans to doubt the wisdom of Tocqueville's analysis, because they interpreted *Democracy in America* as stressing an underlying national consensus on basic values." In this version, again, the forgetfulness is associated with drowning and submergence in waters of oblivion.[9]

Certainly many American scholars did interpret the *Democracy* as a text depicting and to some degree even celebrating a consensual democratic society, despite the copious evidence within that book that can be marshaled against such a conclusion. The adequacy of this interpretation, on which both McClay and Kloppenberg were in agreement, is not the issue here. What is significant, rather, is the way this entire discourse about Tocqueville's alleged disappearance begged the question. Kloppenberg took issue with McClay over the causes of a phenomenon whose existence was assumed rather than established. Tocqueville's absence from American intellectual life for eighty years was simply taken for granted, while these two distinguished intellectual historians engaged in a courteous disagreement as to its causes. The controversy would then be conducted on the worn-out old terrain of the relative balance between "conflict and consensus" in the Gilded Age, Progressive Era, Twenties, and Great Depression. This, then, was a particularly clear example of a circumstance that historians often face: finding causes for a phenomenon that might not have existed, at least in the form in which it has been projected.

An illuminating lecture that the Cornell historian Michael Kammen delivered at the Library of Congress in 1997, although it is a work of lasting importance for the sharpness and sensitivity of its critical insights, nevertheless also serves to illustrate the sheer obduracy of this received opinion concerning Tocqueville's alleged neglect. Speaking of James Bryce's *The American Commonwealth*, which had been published in 1888 (and citing Nisbet as his source), Kammen declared, "Bryce's emphasis on the enduring stability of political institutions in the United States seemed more comforting to that conservative era [the late nineteenth century, 'starting in the later 1870s'] than Tocqueville's litany of open-ended speculations about the potential for tyranny by the majority, never mind his praise for broadly based participation in local government and civic affairs as the very root and branch of American democracy." And with regard to the subsequent generation of the Progressive Era, he contended: "Political scientists and historians of the so-called Progressive era preferred to emphasize change through conflict. The calmly consensual society depicted by Tocqueville in 1835, one that did not even have two major political parties worthy of the name, seemed hopelessly irrelevant."[10] Thus were two completely antithetical explanations incongruously yoked together in the space of three sentences. According to Kammen's account, during the Gilded Age in the late nineteenth century, which was a conservative era, Tocqueville's rather unsettling commendation for broad-based citizen participation in public affairs and his warnings about the potential for a democratic despotism provided less comfort to Americans than Bryce's portrayal of stable political institutions. During the Progressive Era of the early twentieth century, however, the reigning emphasis on change through conflict made Tocqueville seem irrelevant because he had emphasized a society of calm consensus. Kammen thereby managed to conjoin the arguments of both McClay and Kloppenberg: Tocqueville was neglected because of consensus *and* conflict. It seems poor Tocqueville just could not get it right: in a conservative era he was ignored because he emphasized activity and participation; in the ensuing progressive age, he was neglected because he stressed consensus rather than conflict. When two such contradictory statements are brought to bear on a subject, the dogmatic nature of that subject—in this case the idea of Tocqueville's neglect—is plainly visible.

The genealogy of this notion of oblivion must be kept in mind. Drescher and Marshall had certainly been correct in maintaining that, based on the number of publications at least, interest in Tocqueville accelerated after 1940 and especially after 1960. What they went on to assert, however, was something altogether different, namely that prior to that time only an occasional European political scientist or sociologist had evinced any interest in Tocqueville. Thus, they laid a foundation on which a distinct and binary opposition would be constructed. It was not enough to demonstrate a quickening interest in Tocqueville in the postwar years; it was also necessary that the pre-Pierson years be depicted as *absolutely* lacking in scholarly interest, an almost complete blank, rather than portrayed as deficient in a proportional sense. However, they left it at that; they made no other empirical claims about that earlier era, which was not in the purview of their specific research. It was left to Nisbet to take the next step. He provided a point of origin—a moment of dusk that ushered in the night of forgetfulness of which Pierson was the dawn and Bradley the sunrise. In doing so, Nisbet endowed the period with a distinctness that it had lacked in the time-immemorial trope of Drescher and Marshall. Once that periodization had occurred, the notion of Tocqueville's erasure or oblivion, what McClay called his "negligible" status, became, rather than a subject of scholarly inquiry in its own right, a solid historical datum for which it was the task of historians to provide explanations. That is, they had to historicize the presence of Tocqueville after 1945, given what was understood to be his complete absence for so many preceding decades.[11]

And so, gradually, and not as the result of the work of any one scholar, what should have been a fruitful subject of comparison, a study of relative, fluid, shifting interest and influence, of pros and cons and in-betweens, congealed and at last crystallized into a stark opposition, an explosion of interest in Tocqueville that came almost out of nowhere. On the "right," or privileged, side of this chronological binary opposition were the editions, translations, and books and articles of the postwar era, and on the "left" side was . . . oblivion.

Cultural critics at the end of the twentieth century were famously enjoined to "always historicize!" because by doing so they might, however temporarily, locate a perspective from which the seemingly enduring elements of culture could be revealed as the utterly contingent products of play and power that they are.[12] This imperative was by no means a task taken to heart solely by the political or cultural left. It is tautologically the function of any historian to furnish a history to events—since by themselves events can never be history. They must be constructed into a history by means of ordering and interpretation. But the drive to endow events with the status of history—an unproblematic cultural labor, it would seem, to anyone with an open mind—does contain certain pitfalls. These are not the dangers of subverting precious traditions or casting down the revered pillars of what Friedrich Nietzsche referred to as "monumental history"—heroic achievements sculpted in stone—but rather are psychological perils, errors of perception and apperception. When a historian scans the landscape of current or prior structures of thought and notices a higher level of interest in a particular subject, he or she is driven to seek the reasons for that surge in the shifting moods and currents of the time. But in foregrounding and focusing on any given object of study, the background out of which it emerges as if in relief can come to be thought of only in terms of its contrast, negation, or radical difference from that object. That is what happened to the efforts to contextualize Tocqueville's thought in postwar America. The evident postwar rise in interest in Tocqueville induced Nisbet, Marshall, Drescher, McClay, and others to portray the prewar period as a blank backdrop providing a stark contrast to the rich tapestry of postwar scholarship.

In truth, there have seldom been more convenient candidates for the historicizing impulse than scholarly and popular interest in Tocqueville's works after 1945. Tocqueville was the nineteenth century's premier philosopher of democratic culture and mores and their relation to despotism and revolution, and these were major preoccupations of postwar America's public intellectuals. Sixties Tocqueville was historicism made easy. In fact, it was too easy, and efforts to establish Tocqueville as postwar America's "icon"[13] were accomplished only at the expense of significant erasures and distortion. Part of the distortion was to portray the Civil War–to–World War II period as devoid of interest in Tocqueville.

But this image is simply incorrect. Tocqueville was in fact a continuing presence in American intellectual life of this whole period. Although his prominence did diminish from the heights of the 1840s and 1850s, he was never absent from publications and classrooms; more importantly, he continued to be a presence in and through the acts and writings of men and women, some of whom had known him personally, whose careers in education, scholarship, or journalism were notable features of that long era.

Our concern in this book is with Tocqueville's treatment at the hands of American intellectuals, but it also merits mention that one can observe an analogous misrepresentation or blowing out of proportion with regard to the fashioning of Tocqueville's reputation in France. Conclusions that should be understood as measured and qualified become exaggerated as they crystallize into a dogmatic account. In its sheer blunt directness, Eric Keslassy's version of Tocqueville's reputation furnished an excellent synopsis of received opinion about Tocqueville's French fortunes. Keslassy wrote in 2003, "After his death, which occurred in 1859, the writings of Tocqueville rapidly lost their audience to finally fall into oblivion at the beginning of the 1870s."[14] The essay in which this remarkable legend appeared lacked footnotes, but it is obvious that the source of such a conclusion is Françoise Mélonio's magisterial study, *Tocqueville and the French*. By Mélonio's account, however, *De la démocratie en Amérique* was reprinted continuously during both the "decline" after 1859 and the "oblivion" after 1870, with the last edition coming out nearly eighty years after the book's original appearance. This last edition was followed by a thirty-four-year hiatus (from 1913 to 1947)—that is, a gap of about one generation. The *Ancien Régime,* however, filled in part of the gap caused by the lack of *De la démocratie* reprints during that generation. Print runs after the first edition included those of 1866, 1876, and 1886, followed by a small print run of five hundred copies in 1900, which was reprinted seven times, the last as late as 1934.[15]

Given this copious body of evidence, an obvious question presents itself, namely, Is this the record of a writer who had been consigned to oblivion? Or is it rather a record of extraordinary continuity punctuated by the typical rises and falls sparked by generational change? What major historian or political theorist of the nineteenth century would not have been proud, relieved, and delighted to know that his major works would be more or less continuously appearing in new reprints for seventy-five years after his death?

Just as the ruling trope for Tocqueville's comparative displacement came to be that of oblivion, so also the renewal of interest in his work was often exaggeratedly expressed as a triumphant "return." Mélonio's discussion of the period following oblivion came under the heading of "Tocqueville's Return." The phrase had a special resonance for European intellectuals because it connoted a double movement in time and space. First, Tocqueville came back from the underworld of forgetfulness after a long absence, and, second, he made the journey home from America, to France and to Europe. This latter meaning was especially salient and poignant after the implosion of the despotic communist regimes of Central and Eastern Europe. Indeed, several writers took to referring to late-twentieth-century interest in Tocqueville as a "second return" and linked the homecoming with the departure or ejection of communism from the house of Europe. Oxford's Jack Hayward, for example, in a review of Mélonio entitled "Tocqueville's Return Again from America," pointed out that "Tocqueville . . . has a message for the late twentieth century. It was not by chance that when France, always seeking to communicate with the universe, had to decide what it might offer the newly liberated countries of Central and Eastern Europe, it sent a Furet-led cavalcade of *Tocquevilliens* to instruct them in the art of democratization." According to Martin Malia, an American scholar of Soviet history and politics at the University of California, Berkeley, the leading role that had been played in social and political philosophy by Tocqueville in the years around the

1848 revolution of was taken over in the late nineteenth and early twentieth centuries by Karl Marx and Max Weber, but the fall of communist tyranny drew new attention to Tocqueville. Although his chronology of "return" was vague, Malia did connect the late-twentieth-century keenness for Tocqueville to the death of communism: "as the spectre of communism gave way to 'market democracy,'" he wrote, "Tocqueville's magisterial sociology of modern politics was carried forward on a second wave of enthusiasm." Malia, one of the most distinguished Soviet scholars of the twentieth century, had never written about Tocqueville until his own field of study faced its demise; then he joined other scholars in hailing a second return of Tocqueville. Kloppenberg also perceived a "wave" that "crested twice," corresponding to a shift in interest from the first to the second volume of the *Democracy*, with the second crest occurring at the century's end. Keslassy joined the chorus of writers who professed to discern a second return—"le nouveau retour de Tocqueville"—also at the close of the century.[16]

These scholars all emphasized not Tocqueville's *continuing* presence and relevance, but rather his postwar influence as a phenomenon that occurred in an intermittent, wavelike manner. The ubiquity of this trope in the scholarly literature revealed both a hunger for academic novelty and a need by scholars to represent their own work as being on the cutting edge. Sixty to seventy years after the beginning of what everyone agreed was a rise in interest in Tocqueville's work, it nevertheless remained the scholarly fashion to position one's own work on the leading edge of newly discovered waves, returns, reduxes, or price increases, all implicitly accompanied by their respective ebbs, absences, or slumps.

And all agreed that the most extreme of the periods of absence was the post–Civil War era in the United States. To mount a contrary argument is unheard of. I do, however, mean to argue that the notion of oblivion is not just exaggerated, it is completely mistaken. That does not mean that Tocqueville was the cynosure, icon, or focus of intellectual attention, both laudatory and critical, in the late nineteenth and early twentieth centuries that he would become from World War II to the beginning of the twenty-first. Of course Tocqueville's reputation was subject to a degree of fluctuation. To undermine one dubious binary opposition in order to construct another is not my purpose or method. I have tried not to establish a position on this issue as extreme as the argument I seek to modify.

But the evidence for Tocqueville's nonoblivion is overwhelming. In the face of such evidence Robert Nisbet's assertion that the *Democracy* was only infrequently studied after the Civil War is utterly astounding. It is true that

The Old Regime appeared in only one American translation after 1856, that of *Harper's* editor John Bonner. But no fewer than seventeen editions or reprintings of *Democracy in America* appeared in the half-century after the end of the Civil War. There were three new editions between 1898 and 1904 alone, at the supposed nadir of Tocqueville's importance. The first was prepared by the most important educator in America at that time, Johns Hopkins University's founding president, Daniel Coit Gilman, and the 1904 edition contained an introduction by John T. Bigelow, former New York *Post* editor and U.S. ambassador to Paris during the Civil War. It was reprinted three times, the last in 1912.[17]

In the late 1880s, well into this era of abandonment and oblivion, one Hopkins Ph.D., Woodrow Wilson, wrote of Tocqueville as being unsurpassed in the philosophical study of democracy. In an article astutely assessing the work of James Bryce, who had taken pains to position his *American Commonwealth* as an advance over Tocqueville's *Democracy*, Wilson wrote, "Mr. Bryce does not feel called upon to compete with de Tocqueville in the field in which de Tocqueville is possibly beyond rivalry." Portraying Tocqueville in the most respectful, almost reverential manner, Wilson took issue with Bryce, whose quarrel with Tocqueville Wilson thought was misguided, and whose method he termed dangerously ahistorical.

Indeed, Bryce himself had directed a graduate seminar on Tocqueville at Johns Hopkins in November of 1883—and he showed up looking for trouble; that is, he urged his students to dig up examples of mistakes that Tocqueville had made in the *Democracy*. Among the attendees at that seminar were John Dewey, J. Franklin Jameson, Albert Shaw, and Wilson. Working "from pencil notes that I took while Mr. Bryce was talking," Shaw later wrote that "a good instance of Mr. Bryce's method [can] be found in the way he utilized that very occasion when he was reviewing and criticizing De Tocqueville, (for he was engaged at that time upon his own work,) and kept steadily in mind the opportunity to draw from each one of us his own impressions as to points made by the Frenchman in the thirties." These "impressions" duly appeared in a separate monograph that Bryce published four years later, enumerating Tocqueville's errors. The most critical point that Tocqueville had missed in his drive for general points about the democratic social state in America, Bryce believed, was that the Americans were, in all important respects, merely imitation Englishmen. Tocqueville's allegedly insufficient knowledge of English history and society, and of the extent to which England was the source of American institutions, led to this, his greatest error. "The American people," Bryce wrote, "is the English people, modified in some directions" by its colonial history and democratic government, "but in essentials the same."[18] Such was the advance in the philosophical under-standing of American democracy provided by Bryce over poor, outdated Tocqueville.

It was surely no accident that Bryce confronted Tocqueville in the semi-nar rooms of the Johns Hopkins University in Baltimore. The founding of Johns Hopkins in 1876 was the most important single event in the history of American higher education in the entire postbellum era, with the possible exception of the establishment of postsecondary educational institutions for African American students at Hampton, Howard, Atlanta, Fisk, and Tuskegee. And Hopkins would be to Tocqueville in the Gilded Age what Harvard had been in the age of Jackson and Yale would be in the time of George Wilson Pierson and James T. Schleifer. It is not, then, by numbers of publications that Tocqueville's presence in American intellectual life during this era can be measured; it is also by the people who studied and taught his works, and by their social location.

In the famous Hopkins Seminary (seminars), graduate students like Woodrow Wilson, J. F. Jameson, John R. Commons, John Dewey, Avery Cra-ven, and Frederick Jackson Turner often came to grips with Tocqueville, his evidence, and his key concepts. The single most efficacious force behind the development of the Hopkins history department—as well as a founder of the American Historical Association and a pivotal figure in the organization of the discipline of history in America—was Herbert Baxter Adams. Adams, who, as the great historian James Ford Rhodes recalled, "had more to do with the founding and conduct of that Association than any other one man," was a Tocqueville scholar, the biographer of Jared Sparks, and the author of a still-valuable monograph on the relationship between Sparks and Tocque-ville, published in 1893. Hopkins' president, Gilman, brought out a major new edition of *Democracy in America* in 1898, together with a scintillating introduction that was published separately in *Century* magazine. During the 1860s, as a young man of tremendous energy and gifts, Gilman had become friends with the equally indefatigable Francis Lieber, Tocqueville's friend and translator; when he served as librarian of Yale University, Gilman made sure that Lieber had a steady provision of books, which the Prussian constantly asked for. Lieber, that passionate and inveterate creator of neologisms, play-fully called the librarian "the kindly keeper of my bibliotecarian integrity."[19] Gilman was a bridge between the intellectual generation of Lieber and Tocqueville and that of the Progressive Era. Two of his major contributions as a scholar were editions of the two men's works.

Lieber exercised an influence on the curriculum and intellectual life of both Yale and Columbia that was roughly analogous to that of Gilman at Hopkins—leaving out of the analogy Gilman's monumental importance in the history of university administration. In both cases, the influence of Tocqueville was obvious and strong. Indeed, Lieber established the discipline of political science in America.

The illustrious polymath Theodore Dwight Woolsey, after stepping down from the presidency of Yale University, perpetuated Lieber's legacy by bringing out a revised edition of Lieber's most important book, *Civil Liberty and Self-Government*, in 1874, just after Lieber's death. Woolsey, in fact, as he noted in his preface, had taught the *Civil Liberty* at Yale almost as soon as it came out in 1853. His correspondence with Lieber's widow, Matilda, reveals how proud Woolsey was of this new edition and of his association with Lieber. Professing himself "gratified by your kind words in regard to my editorial preface [which] make me feel not ashamed of what I have done," Woolsey gladly took on a second Lieber assignment: a revision of the Prussian's other major book, the *Manual of Political Ethics*, without compensation. In his preface to the *Civil Liberty*, Woolsey flatly identified Lieber as the founder of political science in America. Woolsey wrote that Lieber "influenced political thought more than any of his contemporaries in the United States." In preparing the edition of the *Political Ethics* a few months after the *Civil Liberty*, his veneration for Lieber as elevated as ever, he wrote to Mrs. Lieber, "I took more liberties with the style . . . than in revising the *Civil Liberty*. My guide was the enquiry 'would Dr. Lieber consent to this if he were alive'?"[20]

Lieber's political thought veers far from Tocqueville's analyses in key respects, but in others they show deep affinities and undoubted influence. Pierson called Lieber the person "who, more than any other publicist in the United States, would parallel Tocqueville's political philosophy in his own writings."[21] Lieber especially relied on Tocqueville's investigation of political and administrative centralization. This influence is clearest in the *Civil Liberty* itself. Lieber somewhat comically referred to the influence's flowing in the other direction, however; he actually allowed to appear in print his ludicrous opinion that Tocqueville's *The Old Regime* was a sort of gloss on Lieber's book—"a continued historical commentary on all that is said in the present work on Gallican political tendencies," he called it. Thus, he echoed the conclusion that Samuel Tyler had reached in his 1858 *Princeton Review* article comparing Lieber and Tocqueville.[22]

Like his revered uncle before him, Timothy Dwight, "the pope of Connecticut," Woolsey would also serve as president of Yale. His tenure lasted a remarkable twenty-five years (1846–1871), during which time he took numerous steps to upgrade and modernize the curriculum. In this endeavor a key ally had been the youthful Gilman. Gilman shook the drowsy and slovenly library awake; when he was made assistant librarian the library was open only five hours per weekday and contained about twenty thousand volumes. Of even greater significance, as Hugh Hawkins showed, Gilman took over and breathed life into the moribund Sheffield Scientific School, which became a leader in specialized scientific education, emphasizing "attention to European counterparts, dethroning of the classics, laboratory teaching, study beyond the bachelor's degree, and emphasis on faculty scholarship."[23] After his resignation as president in 1871, Woolsey not only undertook his homage to Lieber in the new editions of *Civil Liberty* and *Political Ethics* but also produced his own textbook, *Political Science* (2 vols., 1886), which was long a basic work in the still-young discipline. Like Lieber, Woolsey focused on the concept of centralization as the most important contribution made to political science by Tocqueville (whom Woolsey deemed "honored alike at home and with us").[24]

During his long scholarly career, and especially before the Franco-Prussian War in 1870, Lieber had been closely affiliated with two other world-famous scholars—one from Heidelberg and one from Paris—whose collegueship, shared scholarly concerns, and wide circle of influences caused them, and with justice, to think of themselves as "a scientific clover-leaf" of international scope and renown. The Paris connection was Édouard Laboulaye, a lecturer in the Collège de France and later the director of that august institution, whose field of expertise was American constitutional history and constitutionalism. He was a great friend and lover of America. (The Laboulaye family remains one of the principal exponents of Franco-American amity through diplomacy and cultural exchange.) Laboulaye was the leading figure behind the project to present the United States with the Statue of Liberty as a gift from the people of France. He was also a good friend and intense admirer of Tocqueville and the author of an insightful reminiscence of the older statesman. René Rémond wrote that the name of Laboulaye "dominated the history of intellectual relations between France and the United States between 1850 and 1860 as did that of Lafayette before 1830 and that of Tocqueville during the July Monarchy." A staunch defender of the North among the intellectuals of Paris during the American Civil War, he won the undying gratitude of the American ambassador, John T. Bigelow, for his efforts. He was indeed, as Drescher wrote, "the leading exponent of American ideals and institutions" in France after Tocqueville. Laboulaye's *Histoire des États Unis* was drawn from the first course of lectures on American history ever delivered in France. And, in a marvelous extra offering of his many gifts, Laboulaye was probably best known in America from the 1860s to the 1920s as a best-selling author of fairy tales, most of which were translated and published in American editions.[25]

The third facet of the clover-leaf, the Swiss-born Johann Bluntschli, had less to do directly with Tocqueville but was, with Lieber, the leading international jurist of the late nineteenth century. At Heidelberg, he trained Hopkins faculty members Herbert Baxter Adams and Richard T. Ely. When Bluntschli died in 1881, the German citizens of Baltimore took up a subscription to transfer his library of twenty-five hundred books and three thousand pamphlets from Heidelberg to Johns Hopkins, where they were displayed in a special depository by early 1883. The minutes of the Hopkins Seminary show virtually all the meetings after January 1884 as taking place in the Bluntschli Library. The Bluntschli donation led to the university's receiving significant portions of the libraries of the other two men, as well.[26]

Bluntschli "exerted a more profound personal influence upon Adams than did any of his other teachers," wrote one student of Adams's career in Germany. The two became very close. Adams never forgot the comfort he received when Bluntschli sat beside him during his nerve-wracking doctoral examination. As part of his training in German studies, Adams also read intensively in the works of Lieber and Laboulaye. Adams joined the Hopkins faculty after Gilman had unsuccessfully tried to lure Herman von Holst (who went on to inaugurate the history department at the University of Chicago) and Henry Adams, who wrote to Gilman on November 8, 1877, that he declined "to become again a Professor on any terms." But H. B. Adams did more than, as one adviser to Gilman wrote in 1868, "at least suppl[y] our needs." His tremendous capacity for work was reminiscent of the young Lieber. Edward A. Freeman once said Adams "was the most energetic man he knew in two hemispheres."[27]

The department at Hopkins grouped history, politics, and economics. The conjunction of these fields was symbolized by the motto on the wall of the Hopkins seminar room: "History is Past Politics," a pearl from the once revered E. A. Freeman, an English historian not appreciated by American audiences, as Adams himself admitted, nor they by him. In an 1894 paper read to college and prep school teachers, Adams traced the politics-history conjuncture in America to Lieber. Not only Hopkins, but Cornell, Harvard, Michigan, and Wisconsin all grouped history with politics.[29]

The Scientific Clover Leaf. Special Collections, Milton S. Eisenhower Library, Johns Hopkins University, Baltimore, Maryland.
"Three great international jurists have been commemorated in Baltimore—Bluntschli of Heidelberg, Lieber of New York, and Laboulaye of Paris. In view of their intimate relations and close concord, somebody called them an 'international clover leaf.' This might pass as a metaphor, but when photographs of the three faces were pasted upon a huge trifolium the metaphor vanished and the reality was more amusing than artistic."—Daniel Coit Gilman, 1902[28]

Thus, with Gilman, Adams, Lieber, and, to a lesser extent, Laboulaye as sponsors, the legacy of Tocqueville remained vibrant at Johns Hopkins up to and beyond the beginning of the twentieth century. And under Gilman and his successor Ira Remsen, Hopkins itself would exert an influence on American intellectual life far out of proportion to its size and age. Yale University may have awarded the first American Ph.D. in 1863, but Hopkins was established to dedicate itself to graduate education almost exclusively. Indeed Hopkins was the single greatest spur to the development of American graduate education. Harvard's move toward launching a graduate school, for example, arose to a large degree from the competition that Hopkins posed. In 1880, Gilman proudly noted to Basil Gildersleeve, Hopkins's renowned professor of Greek, "J. H. U. is often quoted *to* Pres. Eliot, & by him; & he has now announced that the chief topic of discussion in the Faculty next year is to be 'Graduate instruction.'" Gilman, a great administrator, was independently recommended to be the president of the new institution by four of America's most distinguished university presidents, Charles W. Eliot, Noah

Porter, Andrew Dickson White, and James B. Angell. "Unquestionably," concluded Frederick Rudolph in his standard history of American universities, "the Johns Hopkins University at Baltimore *was* different, speaking a language, breathing a spirit that had long been anticipated but never before achieved in the United States." The state universities, emerging into greatness with the support of the endowments provided by the Morrill Act of 1862, would become the academic homes of many of the young men and women who fanned out of Baltimore with their new Ph.D.'s, but the influence of Hopkins was felt everywhere by 1900, in all fields of research and all types of institutions. "Johns Hopkins elevated man's reason to a position it had not before attained in the United States," Rudolph wrote. "It released the energies of scholarship, combined them with the national impulse to human betterment and material progress. The task it set for itself was immense and unending, and in time the spirit of Johns Hopkins would penetrate everywhere."[30]

And so, as the academic disciplines that constitute the body of knowledge and methodology that came to be known as the social sciences were taking shape, Tocqueville was far from absent. In the field of history, one Tocqueville enthusiast, Henry Adams, produced two of the great classics of the field, while another (unrelated) Adams, Herbert Baxter Adams of Hopkins, oversaw the Hopkins seminars and founded the American Historical Association. Woodrow Wilson said of Adams in this regard, "The thesis work done under him may fairly be said to have set the pace for university work in history throughout the United States. That is the whole thing in a nutshell."[31] The "father of political science" was Tocqueville's friend, informant, translator, and commentator, Francis Lieber. Harvard's Francis Bowen, the reviser of the Henry Reeve translation of the *Democracy*, a version that would remain standard for a century, was a prominent economist and author of a major textbook in that developing field. As I explained in chapter 3, Bowen's economics volume is alive with Tocqueville's spirit and insight.[32]

A fourth discipline-defining Tocqueville enthusiast was Charles Horton Cooley, who performed at the University of Michigan a feat comparable to those of Adams at Hopkins or Lieber at Columbia: he was one of the founders of sociology in America. Cooley's foundational 1909 work *Social Organization* made extensive use of Tocquevillean concepts, which were liberally acknowledged. Cooley examined the place of sentiment and idea in the social body as a whole; like Tocqueville he was concerned about the effects of democracy on consciousness itself. Part III of *Social Organization*, called "The Democratic Mind," was the first effort to extend Tocqueville's insights from Parts I and II of the second volume of *Democracy in America*. Such an effort to understand the reciprocity of society and consciousness made him, as Dorothy Ross noted, "more influential [than E. A. Ross, sociology's other American pioneer] on the psychological course of American sociology."[33]

Therefore, the social sciences in America—economics, sociology, history, political science—were founded or developed by scholars deeply familiar with and influenced by Tocqueville. Two of them were Tocqueville translators, and three wrote specific commentaries on Tocqueville's works.

In addition to being a critical figure among discipline shapers like Lieber, Adams, Bowen, and Cooley, institution builders like Gilman, key university presidents like Gilman and Woolsey, and public figures like Wilson and Bigelow, Tocqueville was a writer the knowledge of whose work was actively cultivated at prestigious and culturally strategic institutions like Hopkins, Columbia, Yale, and Harvard. Tocqueville was also the explicit subject of a steady, if thin, stream of articles, many of great value and insight, in the "pre-Pierson years" after 1870 and on up through the 1930s. Moreover, these studies came from the pens of some of the most important public intellectuals of the Gilded Age, Progressive Era, Twenties, and Great Depression, including E. L. Godkin, Woodrow Wilson, John Graham Brooks, Matthew Josephson, and Albert Salomon.

In 1976 Robert Nisbet could only recall an utter absence of Tocqueville during all his years of formal education. He wrote, "I can attest that in the 1930s, during seven years of a better-than-average education, undergraduate and graduate, at Berkeley, I did not once hear the name Tocqueville in class or seminar." But if Nisbet had been educated on the East Coast he would have had a different experience. Tocqueville's works were a regular feature of the curriculum at Yale between 1870 and 1920, where the required course of instruction for seniors included the *Democracy* as well as Lieber's *Civil Liberty*. Professor Arthur M. Wheeler taught the *Democracy* along with François Guizot's *History of European Civilization*, the latter book a deeply formative text for Tocqueville's own developing historical mind. William Graham Sumner assigned Tocqueville to his students for a short time; he also taught the works of Lieber and Woolsey in his courses. In the 1920s and 1930s, Yale became the epicenter of Tocqueville scholarship under the leadership first of Paul Lambert White, then John M. S. Allison, and finally George Wilson Pierson. Yale acquired the bulk of its great Tocqueville manuscripts collection in the early 1920s. During the 1930s and almost certainly before, students in Harvard's undergraduate American government course were faced with large amounts of mandatory reading from the *Democracy*. The evidence, although circumstantial, is also strong that Tocqueville was in the curriculum at City College, Fordham, and The New School in the 1930s, and likely at Syracuse and Cornell in the 1940s. In short, while perhaps not a central figure, Tocqueville was no more absent from American classrooms than he was from the journals in those "pre-Pierson years."[34]

Thus, the importance of Tocqueville in American intellectual life after the Civil War cannot be reckoned by toting up articles. Regardless of whether key shapers of American higher education, journalists, and scholars endorsed, critiqued, or merely referred to Tocqueville, the thesis that he was drowned in waters of oblivion in this era cannot be sustained. Accounts of Tocqueville's demise were greatly exaggerated, is how Mark Twain, who probably *was* oblivious of Tocqueville, would have expressed it.

Civil War

During the 1860s, I have argued, American interest in Tocqueville continued to be abundantly evident in new publications, articles, and reviews in the American journals. It is simply not the case that, in James T. Kloppenberg's words, Tocqueville suffered a "disappearance" that commenced at "the out-break of the Civil War." On the contrary, at the outbreak of the Civil War the *Christian Examiner* declared that "as a historian and a political philoso-pher [Tocqueville's] pre-eminence is undeniable," and Charles Eliot Norton observed in the *Atlantic Monthly* that Tocqueville's "reputation and the weight of his authority are continually increasing."[35] Meanwhile, in the spring of 1862, a superb two-volume edition of Tocqueville's unpublished let-ters and essays, along with an excellent biography by Gustave de Beaumont himself, arrived in American bookshops; and in the autumn of that year, Bowen completed his labors on the new, revised translation and edition of *Democracy in America* that would remain the standard edition until World War II.

But the interest in Tocqueville during the 1860s was perforce of a different character than that which had gone before. The main reason for the change was not Tocqueville's death, for new works by him continued to appear quite steadily until 1868. It was different because of the war. Works by Tocqueville came out during each year of the war and in the early phases of Reconstruc-tion. American writers recognized in these new writings the same Tocque-ville they had known before, but they approached him differently. There is not a single comment from the 1860s on Tocqueville that stresses a novel or unexpected quality in the new works that were being published. What was different, of course, was America itself—and yet somehow Tocqueville retained his relevance to the nation. In a strange way, it was not that the Civil War caused Americans to look at Tocqueville differently so much as it brought about a new America that the same old unchanged Frenchman, Tocqueville, helped them to understand.

Of course, such transitions are not clean, univocal, or uncontested. The 1860s were, however, a decade in which some of the most enduring conventions of Tocqueville discourse were pieced together and began to solidify. These conventions would retain their currency for over a century.

The general-interest periodical article on Tocqueville conforms to a distinctive "ideal-typical" arrangement that originated in the Civil War years. This is who Tocqueville was, the article says, an aristocrat who traveled to the United States as a young man in order to understand a new kind of social formation—democracy—that, in a myriad specific shapes, will constitute the generic form of the future social and political condition of all the nations of the West—or the Christian nations, as they were often called. This aristocratic foreigner wrote the best commentary on our institutions and customs. His character was sober, shy, and earnest. A public servant and politician, he was a member of the Chamber of Deputies and a foreign minister. His book on democracy in America made his reputation both at home and abroad. He made many remarkable predictions, many of which were borne out, but he also committed a number of errors, which arose out of his aristocratic worldview. America has undergone momentous changes since he wrote that noble philosophical study of democracy—yet, so much of what he said is still pertinent. Thinking people can appreciate the impartiality with which he analyzed his subjects—both democracy and America. He was a sincere, because unflattering, friend of American democracy, however intense his fears about its progress in France and Europe.

American readers could be edified by this basic article, as a kind of theme with variations, in 1861 or 1898 or 1959.[36] The immediate occasion for the development of this particular artifact of American intellectual culture was the conjunction of the Civil War with the publication of Tocqueville's works in two editions, one in English, one in French.

The first publication event after Tocqueville's death was the appearance of Beaumont's biography-cum-reminiscence in 1862. It is still a valuable work: an indispensable portrait by the best lifelong friend Tocqueville ever had and a reliable source of accurate information about its subject. Nearly four decades after it was written, Gilman wrote that he believed Beaumont's study would never be surpassed. The biography appeared as part of a two-volume set of previously unpublished material: some of Tocqueville's essays plus a selection of the correspondence. With the alacrity that often accompanied the appearance of Tocqueville's work, this set too was translated almost immediately.

The title page of *Memoir, Letters, and Remains* provided a hint of the treasures that lay within this English-language edition. It announced that Ticknor and Fields was publishing the work "with large additions" to the French original. These additions, in that era before international copyright, were of great significance to American scholars. The additional material furnished American readers with a collection of Tocqueville's previously unpublished works that was considerably richer than that which was available in the French edition. Desiring to present a fuller picture of Tocqueville to American readers than the one that could be gleaned from Beaumont's French edition, the anonymous editor explained, she undertook to obtain from the great English economist Nassau Senior the journals wherein he had recorded, at length and close to verbatim, the many extended conversations he had held with Tocqueville.

Further indication of the editor's industry, tact, and literary judgment emerges from her preface to the *Memoir, Letters, and Remains*. For the American edition, she contacted not only Senior but also Tocqueville's other closest English friend, John Stuart Mill, about her translation project, obviously explaining a plan to expand the original and present a fuller portrait of Tocqueville than Beaumont had allowed to appear in his original edition. From Senior, astonishingly, she extracted both his journals and all the originals of the correspondence between him and Tocqueville "from which M. de Beaumont selected those which are published in the second volume." This gesture by Senior indicates that he was dissatisfied with the content, the number, or the editing of the selections that Beaumont had included in the French volumes; here, for English speaking readers, Senior was granted an opportunity to present a fuller picture. But it was not just the letters that he allowed to be made public; it was also his journals with their record of Tocqueville's conversations. The selections from those conversations were fully up to the task that the editor had set for them—that of producing a richer and more accurate portrait of Tocqueville through both his voice and his pen than the cautious Beaumont had allowed to appear in his edition. In Tocqueville's letters, "the depth and seriousness of his mind, combined with an almost feminine grace and delicacy," are on open display. "He attached an almost exaggerated importance to style; he so shrank from exhibiting his ideas, unless expressed in the very best language, corrected and re-considered again and again, that to change their form is a greater responsibility with regard to him than to almost any other author." But with the addition of the Senior conversations, she was able "to exhibit M. de Tocqueville in two characters, in each of which he was eminent—that of a converser and that of a practical politician."[37]

From Mill, on the other hand, the editor received permission to publish Tocqueville's essay on "France before the Revolution," which Mill had published in the *London and Westminster Review* in 1836.

As a result of her enterprise and editorial skill, this edition contained fifty-eight pages of letters and conversations not found in the Beaumont edition and provided still another valuable document besides those and the 1836 essay: the letter to the *London Times* that Tocqueville had written in December 1851 describing the coup d'état of Louis Napoleon. Taken in its entirety, then, this was the most valuable edition of Tocqueville, except for the *Democracy* and *The Old Regime*, that the nineteenth century produced in any language. It was an indispensable source for English readers, and it was far superior to its French counterpart. Indeed, there would be nothing like it for over a century, until the translations of Drescher and George Lawrence. None of Tocqueville's nineteenth-century translators—not Lieber, Reeve, Bowen, Sparks, Bonner, or Alexander Teixiera de Mattos—served Tocqueville nearly so well as the anonymous translator of the *Memoir, Letters, and Remains*.

The *Memoir* provoked a series of extended critical articles. The first notice drew attention to the excellence of the English over the French version. "It is a fortunate thing for the readers of these Letters that they were translated in England," began the commentary in the *New York Times*. In Paris, Beaumont had been "under a thousand restraints of personal relations and delicacy of feeling, which have prevented him from publishing what were, no doubt the choicest of the letters," and government censorship further curtailed what he could print of his friend's political opinions. But "the English Editor has had no such restraint. His additions are the most racy part of these deeply interesting volumes."[38]

The confluence of the appearance of the Beaumont and Bowen editions and the onset of the Civil War led to a sharpening of the features of Tocqueville's image. He began to acquire his stereotypical traits of sagacity, impartiality, and goodwill toward the democratic experiment, traits he had developed in spite of the European and aristocratic milieu out of which he had arisen.

The Tocqueville literature of the early 1860s was heavily biographical.

One reason for the biographical slant lay in the nature of the publications that came out after 1862. What was really novel in them were Tocqueville's correspondence and Beaumont's splendid "Memoir." Beaumont provided American readers with a great deal of information that had simply not been available, and so the focus on Tocqueville's fascinating life and exemplary character, as they were unvaryingly presented, was to some extent simply a function of the demands of periodical publishing. But the biographical slant signaled a complex, contradictory shift in status, as well: Tocqueville's prestige reached greater heights than ever before, but at the same time writers felt compelled to explain to readers just *why* this was so, to issue what might be called cultural reminders to Civil War audiences. The assumption was that readers knew who Tocqueville was, and why he was important, but required a certain memory prompting if he was to retain his stature for a radically different America than the one he had visited thirty years before.

The Tocqueville of the early 1860s literature was, first of all, a European. This obvious trait received special attention; Tocqueville was indeed the most "completely cosmopolitan" of all statesmen and men of letters, according to the *Christian Examiner*, which emphasized his familial, spiritual, and intellectual ties with England, Italy, and Germany. "No foreigner has entered so thoroughly into the spirit of our institutions," another author wrote in the same journal six months later, while a third author expressed gratitude "to find, at last, a man, born in Europe and educated in the conservative atmosphere of its higher circles, who could bring a candid and honest mind to the study of our democracy."[39]

Second, Tocqueville was a Christian. One enthusiastic clergyman, Ray Palmer, even tried to portray Tocqueville as a Protestant at heart. For, although "De Tocqueville was educated in the Romish Church, and not under the full influence and in the atmosphere of spiritual Christianity," Palmer wrote in the *New Englander*, he "died a Christian in a far higher sense than this"—that is, than having received the last rites on his deathbed, as Beaumont reported. Beaumont, of course, had failed to furnish any facts confirming this judgment of Palmer's, but it was no matter: "We attribute this [dearth of information about the state of Tocqueville's soul] to the want of a competent reporter, and to his own imperfect understanding" as a born Catholic.[40] But this was an exceptional opinion; most writers were happy to leave Tocqueville to Rome.

A third aspect of the 1860s Tocqueville concerned his method as a scholar—and, by extension, the unprejudiced quality of his views. Charles-Augustin Saint-Beuve once said that Tocqueville "began to think prior to having learned anything."[41] Tocqueville's alleged preference for abstract reasoning was well captured by Saint-Beuve's bon mot and by the gibe in the ninth-edition *Encyclopaedia Britannica* article about the "excess of the deductive spirit" in his works. Yet such was not the general view among American writers during the Civil War. Some of them minimized this supposed fault, others tried to evade it, and one even portrayed Tocqueville's method as essentially empiricist—"Baconian"—rather than deductive at all. "He has no theory set up beforehand which he is anxious to support," Palmer argued. "In true Baconian fashion, his object is to observe facts carefully, and then to ascend to their proper significance and law." Another critic, C. C. Smith, set out to write about both volumes of the Beaumont correspondence plus both *Democracies*, but he completely ignored the second, more abstract volume and limited his comments to the 1835 book. Why this restriction? "In reading his book," Smith argued, "what first strikes an American reader is the extraordinary minuteness of his information, even more than the general accuracy of his statements."[42]

This angle on Tocqueville—that he was not in fact excessively deductive, that his work on America derived its power from closely observed detail, that the empirical amassing of facts had greater significance than the generalizations of Volume II—signaled an important shift in American perceptions. This quintessential Frenchman was, to begin with, subtly anglicized in these portraits. French philosophy will always be perceived in the mold of its modern founder, René Descartes, just as a British mode of philosophizing will forever be associated with Descartes's philosophical antipode, Francis Bacon. Many interpretations of Tocqueville's methodology have appeared over the course of more than a century and a half, but never before or since has Tocqueville been called a Baconian. Yet this was only an extreme statement of a more general anglicizing, empiricist trend in portraying Tocqueville. Writers drew attention to Tocqueville's English friends, marriage to an Englishwoman, and admiration of English liberal traditions. "By marriage, his affections, interest, and friendships became largely English; much of his most intimate correspondence is across the Channel; and in his despondency as to the fate of France, he turns . . . to the stability of English law and the staunchness of English nationality," wrote J. H. Allen.[43]

By stressing the factual over the philosophical, the empirical over the metaphysical, in Tocqueville, writers such as Smith, Palmer, and G. M. Towle were striking a blow for the Union. For there was not a single publication about Tocqueville during the 1860s that did not draw attention to the desperate struggle for democratic nationhood that was raging beyond the comfortable living rooms and paneled libraries where the journals were perused. The *North American Review* gave the clearest statement of the link. "Ancient political foundations are apparently undergoing great and continual changes, symptoms of momentous commotions already appear," Towle wrote, "and the question whether democracy can or cannot survive the excesses of its own elements, is put to the test with all the severity which a conflict between twenty millions and nine millions can produce. The rapid sale of these volumes [of Tocqueville's works] encourages the hope that the wise and moderate precepts therein contained may be speedily disseminated through our community."[44]

The tilt toward supposedly English over French traits in describing Tocqueville also had its roots in the agonies of the war's early phases. The appearance in 1862 of Tocqueville's correspondence and his *London Times* article on Bonaparte's coup d'état enormously strengthened his appeal as a steadfast enemy of despotism at a time when Napoleon's government was distinctly unfriendly to the Union cause. Thus, three elements were conjoined in the Tocqueville portrait: his hatred of Napoleon III's despotism, the emperor's hostility to the Union, and Tocqueville's conversion into a more "English," or empirically sound, and less "French," or Cartesian, writer. As the *New York Times* wrote, Tocqueville's "candor and accuracy in regard to this country rendered him highly credible" in regard to his own. "We learn from this philosophic observer, whose most intimate relations were with England, that the popular dislike of England is still intense in France." Tocqueville's analysis of the French political scene threw light, the *Times* believed, on the fact that "the Emperor is regarding the French Princes with deep distrust, and that their reception into our army, and their gallant conduct here, has rendered him cold to our National cause." Charles Eliot Norton also represented the Beaumont edition as a remonstration against the regime of Napoleon III. "M. de Beaumont's notice of the life of Tocqueville, and Tocqueville's own later correspondence, appear to a thoughtful reader as accusations against Imperial despotism, as protests against the wrongs from which freedom is now suffering in France," Norton declared.[45]

This interpretation of Tocqueville as an ethnographer, a meticulous and accurate observer of American democracy who valued facts over theory, would have a lasting influence. As the facts of Tocqueville's biography became known, so also did this way of construing its meaning for Americans. Tocqueville, the describer of American society, began his ascendancy over Tocqueville, the political philosopher. A century later, bitter attacks on

Tocqueville by the historian Edward Pessen and others would be based on this Civil War–era interpretation.

When Marie de Tocqueville died in 1865, she bequeathed all of her husband's papers to Beaumont, thus opening a rift between the Tocqueville and Beaumont families that persisted for a century. The Tocquevilles felt that Alexis's papers should have remained within the family. In 1891, a settlement was reached by which the Tocquevilles purchased the archive from Beaumont's heirs.[46] But Mme. de Tocqueville's decision was not merely a snub of a family who could have treated her with more warmth; it was also a means by which she could be assured that her husband's legacy would be passed on to future generations in a reliable, scholarly form that met the best editorial standards of her day.

And so it was that after the incredible Tocqueville bounty of 1862 with the American publication of the two Beaumont and two Bowen volumes, Tocqueville's works received still further attention throughout the 1860s owing to a major publishing venture in France, namely a full-scale, multivolume edition of Tocqueville's complete works, undertaken jointly by Mme. de Tocqueville and Beaumont. This version, still used by scholars, usually referred to as "the Beaumont edition" and cited as O. C. (B), appeared in nine volumes between 1865 and 1868. Only the last three volumes contained previously unpublished material, however. Volume VIII (1865), of great if belatedly recognized scholarly importance, comprised the notes for Tocqueville's projected second volume about the French Revolution. Volume VII (1866) consisted of unpublished correspondence, and Volume IX (1868) contained economic and political essays. The prior six volumes comprised the *Democracy*, *The Old Regime*, and the 1860 Beaumont "Memoir" and correspondence that had appeared in the two-volume edition of 1862. Thus, it was in 1865, as the Civil War ended, that a stream of new material began to appear. None of these last three volumes containing new material would appear in English translation during the nineteenth century.

The fact that these last three volumes of the Beaumont edition did not acquire a translator is not in itself an indication of a decline in Tocqueville's prestige. The Bowen-Reeve translation of the *Democracy* and the translation of the letters and remains had both been published just three or four years earlier, while the Bonner rendition of *The Old Regime* was ten years old. The final tomes in the *Oeuvres complètes* consisted of miscellaneous short notes and speeches; mostly they were journal entries and notes for an unfinished book. In the mid-nineteenth century, scholarly conventions and expectations were not such that every volume in an exhaustive complete works must be translated; indeed, early in the twenty-first century, much of Tocqueville's correspondence was still not available in English.

Because the last volumes were not of the highest importance for understanding Tocqueville, only the two pillars of highbrow reviewing in the United States, the *North American Review* and the *Nation*, published articles on Tocqueville in the late 1860s.

In the *North American Review*, Edward Brooks, furious with Tocqueville for perpetrating alleged misconceptions about American federalism, all but accused him of having persuaded England and France to accord the Confederacy the status of a belligerent power during the Civil War's early phase. The British action, which came in a proclamation of neutrality on May 13, 1861, was in strict accordance with international law, for President Lincoln had ordered a naval blockade of Southern ports—an act of war. But Northern opinion was outraged at the promptness as well as the timing of the proclamation, and most observers considered it to be a prelude to outright diplomatic recognition of the Confederacy. To Brooks, five years later, the British action was still an open wound. He did not attribute the British action to calculations of national interest, however, but to an idea—and that idea, he believed, had been derived directly from Tocqueville. "He was, in fact, the oracle in all that related to the institutions of the United States," Brooks fumed. "On the strength of his opinion, our Union was looked upon, without the least question, as a mere partnership of States, which any one of the partners might dissolve at will." Brooks depicted Europe as a continent "filled with emissaries from the South enforcing the same notion, and quoting M. de Tocqueville in its support."[47] Brooks's attack on Tocqueville foreshadowed those of a century later. In pointing to Tocqueville's deficiencies as an empirical observer, Brooks ironically extended the tradition that had begun earlier in the 1860s. Although his article marked a rare and passionate dissent from the respectful assessments that had appeared during the war, it nevertheless shared with them the assumption that Tocqueville was an observer first and foremost, a philosopher second.

Michael Heilprin, on the other hand, viewed Tocqueville in a more comprehensive way: as a philosophic observer, and in a pair of articles at the end of the Civil War he managed to publish the most insightful commentary of the entire decade. The life of this prodigiously gifted Hungarian Jew seemed to symbolize the history of the nineteenth century. Heilprin was a thoroughly Magyarized or assimilated Jew who, in 1842, had moved with his wife, child, and parents to Hungary, a more liberal land than the obscure and benighted Polish province in which he had been born in 1821. He soon became a leading liberal voice, writing poetry and criticism that expressed the desire for independence and human rights for Jews and Hungarians living under Austrian domination. After the 1848 revolution, he became a member of the Kossuth government, but upon the suppression of that revolution and the relentless Habsburg pursuit of people who had held responsible positions in the Hungarian government that the revolution had established, Heilprin and his family fled to Paris. Eventually, in 1856, they emigrated to Philadelphia. Heilprin arrived with a letter of introduction from Kossuth in his pocket. From Philadelphia, the family moved to Brooklyn, where Heilprin had close relations with other 1848–1849 refugees, including the sister of Kossuth.

Master of fifteen languages, a staunch liberal, and by every account a man of persistent kindness, humor, and generosity of character, Heilprin eventually became a regular contributor to the *Nation,* writing scores of articles in the two decades after the Civil War. He had an astonishing memory. A contemporary author and close friend, Unitarian clergyman John Chadwick, recalled:

> Mr. Heilprin's knowledge of history was nothing less than an epitome of its universal course. His stomach for facts was something wonderful. His command of dates was by tens of thousands. . . . He would run his eye along the pages of a dictionary of dates and make corrections by the half-dozen or the dozen upon every page. The time and place of the six hundred battles and engagements of our Civil War were all at his tongue's end. . . . His confidence in his memory was very great, and he wrote the most elaborate historical reviews without a particle of special preparation.[48]

In two of his articles for the *Nation,* Heilprin gave concrete form to two themes that would become staples of Tocqueville commentary. These themes had been asserted by previous writers, but Heilprin articulated them more fully; he made them come alive with clear, specific references. The first was that Tocqueville was the writer on American society and international affairs who had a special affinity for the discerning general reader. Heilprin commended the complete works "to the reading, or rather thinking, public in this country." In a land where the reading public was vast (over 90 percent of native-born whites were literate in 1860), the thoughtful, discriminating reader, at the end of the Civil War especially, could benefit from a contemplation of Tocqueville's life and writings.[49] Tocqueville "more than any other man, helped [Americans] to understand the philosophy of their own political institutions and social phenomena." Second, Tocqueville exhibited an unsurpassed "candor, impartiality, and philosophical independence which he applied to the performance of his task."[50]

Later, Heilprin expanded on this notion of Tocqueville's impartiality, enumerating a list of seeming paradoxes in Tocqueville's personal, familial, and historical milieu that, taken together, left him in the position of a man at the conjunction of many boundaries. Tocqueville had written to Reeve in 1837 about "the chance of birth" that had molded his life and its effect on his entire *weltanschauung.* "I came into the world at the end of a long Revolution, which, after having destroyed the old state, had created nothing durable," he wrote. "Aristocracy was already dead . . . and democracy did not yet exist. . . . I was so thoroughly in equilibrium between the past and the future that I felt naturally and instinctively attracted toward neither the one nor the other." Although this account could hardly be more self-serving, many scholars have taken it more or less at face value, because, I believe, it actually does capture a truth about the historical moment of transition that Tocqueville understood more clearly than any of his contemporaries. But Heilprin, without benefit of the Reeve letter, which had not yet been published, elaborated on Tocqueville's supposed lack of bias and attributed it to this array of contradictory elements. The concluding volume of the complete works, he wrote, "presents to us De Tocqueville entire, as he was in the period of his maturity and vigor." "De Tocqueville entire" had been an aristocrat preparing the path that led to political equality; "the friend of democracy in the New World who trembles at its advent—under different auspices—in the Old; the . . . republican by conviction who sincerely defends the constitutional throne of Louis Philippe"; the advocate for the poor who hates socialism; the Catholic who favors church-state separation.[51]

In the winter of 1863, twenty-five-year-old Henry Adams, secretary to his father Charles Francis Adams, American ambassador to the Court of Saint James, wrote to his brother Charles, "I have learned to think de Tocqueville my model, and I study his life and works as the Gospel of my private religion." Adams was engrossed in the study of both Tocqueville and John Stuart Mill, two thinkers who, as Alan Kahan showed, exemplified a special form of "aristocratic liberalism." Yet it is difficult to detect overt signs in the form of concepts, themes, or methods of Tocqueville that appeared in the later work of the great American pessimist. Tocqueville's influence on Adams was based on a temperamental similarity that was not quite a congruence but that helped Adams to move, as J. C. Levenson wrote in his ageless study of Adams, "from a limited vision of his own family which, though it included great men and deeds within its purview, might have become a real confinement of the mind."[52]

In an indispensable yet seldom cited essay of 1965, Richard Ruland addressed the evident contrast between Adams's early and late relation to Tocqueville: Tocqueville as "Gospel" for the young Adams, yet absent from the work of the mature writer save in an occasional evocative gesture. "Influence there certainly was," Ruland concluded, "but it operated at a level beneath idea borrowing or stylistic echo." Tocqueville's influence flowed like a subterranean stream for over forty years, according to Ruland's account, and emerged to the surface when Adams wrote *The Education of Henry Adams* in 1905. The essential affinity between the two books consisted of the fact that "the *Education* can be read as a sequel to Tocqueville's study of equality's effect on Western man. . . . The Frenchman's forced sympathy for what is uncongenial gives way, under increasing pressure, to the irony of Adams' account of what has clearly gone wrong."[53] That which Tocqueville had portrayed with hope, Adams perceived to be a failure.

A synopsis such as this is inadequate to bring out the historical and psychological subtleties of Ruland's study. It is a kind of tour de force of empathy with deceased predecessors. Ruland, however, did place a lot of pressure on his limited direct evidence. He wrote of "the natural affinity which made Tocqueville a spiritual ancestor of Adams,"[54] a claim, however credible, that had an uncomfortable proximity to Ross Hoffman's sense of "morphological resemblances" between Tocqueville and Edmund Burke.

One month after Adams wrote his brother about spending his free time studying Tocqueville and Mill—that is, in February 1863—Adams made the acquaintance of Mill in London. Historian Max Baym has shown that Mill communicated to Adams an "enthusiasm for Tocqueville. . . . For Adams, Mill's works constituted a school of French thinking." Adams's entrée into both English and French intellectual culture was made smooth by his friendship with the Yorkshire writer Richard Monckton Milnes. It was Milnes who introduced Adams to Mill as well as to A. C. Swinburne. Adams also "had personal dealings" with Tocqueville's translator, Reeve. Milnes was close to a galaxy of French society, including Tocqueville, about whom he wrote a warm article in the *Quarterly Review* in 1861. Adams met Milnes just at this time, upon arriving in London. In addition to Mill, Milnes himself greatly "stimulated Henry Adams's interest in [Tocqueville's] writings," Baym wrote.[55] Baym's study, based on underscorings and marginal notes of the books in Adams's personal library, is the strongest documentary link between the two writers. It strengthens Ruland's case that Adams's *Education* can be read as part of a dialog spanning an ocean and two generations between Tocqueville and Adams.

Americanism

Daniel Coit Gilman was not, at the close of the nineteenth century, the most honored man in Baltimore. That distinction belonged by universal consent to the leading Roman Catholic prelate in the United States and the shepherd of its most historic diocese, James Cardinal Gibbons. "Taking your life as a whole," Theodore Roosevelt once told Gibbons, "I think you now occupy the position of being the most respected and venerated and useful citizen of our country."[56] Born in Baltimore to Irish immigrant parents, Gibbons undertook a reverse migration to Ireland as a young boy due to his father's ill health. The father died of tuberculosis when Gibbons was thirteen, and his mother took him and his six siblings with her back to Baltimore via New Orleans. Young James Gibbons was, therefore, an Irish immigrant who was more American than Irish.

In his youth, Gibbons was made aware of a calling to the priesthood when he attended a religious mission in New Orleans that was directed by one of the most remarkable figures in American religious history, Father Isaac Hecker. Father Hecker, "the Yankee Paul," developed during a thirty-year apostolate a fusion of American democracy and Catholic Christianity that in later years and in a distorted, inaccurate version, would be embraced by some French Catholics, and excoriated by many more, under the banner of "Américanisme." Central to the ideas of the Americanists, especially in France but also in America, was the portrayal of American Catholics that Tocqueville had drawn in *Democracy in America*. At the very end of the century, the "errors" of Americanism would be roundly censured by Pope Leo XIII in an encyclical letter, *Testem Benevolentiae*, which was addressed to Cardinal Gibbons.[57]

Shortly after Hecker died, in 1888, John Henry Newman wrote that he felt a "sort of unity in our lives—that we had both begun a work of the same kind, he in America and I in England." It is deeply ironic that an ideology with such a distinctly national name—Americanism—came to be, however erroneously, associated with the name of Father Hecker, for he was truly, as Walter J. Ong, S.J., called him, "a man between two worlds."[58] Born in 1819 in New York to a nonreligious German immigrant baker and his wife, Hecker as a young man became an ardent member of the radical "Locofoco" party of Jacksonian Democrats in New York City. During the depression following the Panic of 1837, he and his brother distributed their bread for free to the distressed unemployed laborers of the city. In his early twenties, Hecker heard Orestes Brownson speak on "The Democracy of Christ," and the encounter set him on the long path to Roman Catholicism, the priesthood, and, in 1858, the foundation of a new religious order dedicated to missionary work in America: the Paulists.

But before he reached those destinations, Hecker had first to absorb the works of Immanuel Kant, take inspiration from the New England transcendentalists, and eventually sojourn with the builders of a utopian future at George Ripley's experiment in communal living, Brook Farm, in West Roxbury, Massachusetts. A valued and popular member of the celebrated commune, Hecker put his artisanal skills to productive use as the baker for the cooperative. His roommate there was Charles A. Dana, and of course he was acquainted with Nathaniel Hawthorne, Ralph Waldo Emerson, Margaret Fuller, and other seekers after social perfection. When, in 1843, after he left the community, Hecker placed himself under instruction in preparation for entering the Catholic Church, he tried earnestly to get his great friend Henry David Thoreau to join him. "The gate out of the present era of folly is close," he told Thoreau, "the gate lies at your feet"—it opens out on to the road that leads to Rome.[59]

This man between two worlds studied for the priesthood in Belgium and served as a parish priest in England before he returned to the United States in 1851. Although he had been ordained as a Redemptorist, Hecker was expelled from that order and encouraged by Pope Pius IX to found his own congregation. His response was to found the Missionary Society of St. Paul, an order dedicated to laboring in the thorny fields of the American mission, where nativism and anti-Catholicism flourished. In choosing Paul as the order's patron, Hecker was giving expression to a perhaps still-obscure sense of loving affinity with the Apostle to the Gentiles. In Ong's words, "St. Paul was caught not only, as we all are, between the worlds of body and soul and, further, between the world of the temporal order and the spiritual order, but between two still further worlds, the Hebrew and the Christian. For Paul was both Jew and Christian, a Jewish Christian, and one who kept this two-sided aspect of his character spectacularly evident to all the world."[60] Thus also, by analogy, was the mission of Isaac Hecker. He wished to bring the church to America, but almost equally, to bring the message of America to the church. "He was the main source of the apologetical bridge between Catholicism and American nationalism," wrote Edward Langlois; as Hecker put it, he could be "all the better Catholic because I am an American; and all the better American because I am a Catholic."[61]

"There can be no doubt of the fact that an interior dialogue with Europe formed, matured, and finally opened up to all the world the characteristic American attitudes of Father Hecker," Ong wrote. Hecker described himself as "an International Catholic." This is the ironic aspect of so-called Americanism: it was universalist in inspiration and aspiration, like the church in which it developed, but sadly, a counterfeit version of it was conveyed to Europe. Cardinal Gibbons was being perfectly candid when he told Leo XIII, "this doctrine that I willingly call extravagant and absurd, this Americanism, as it has been called, has nothing in common with the views, aspirations, doctrine, and conduct of the Americans."[62]

Americanism was a broad term encompassing a range of diverse ideas and denoting numerous ethnic and theological interests within the church, but at base, Americanists believed that American democratic and national traditions were harmonious with active participation in the Catholic Church. In the twenty-first century, such a proposition seems so obvious that it does not need to be articulated, but in the age of Pius IX and of anti-Catholic movements in the United States, this position needed to be clearly spelled out. Cardinal Gibbons and other leading Americanists were "more or less consciously moving along lines marked out by Father Hecker and the Paulists," and Hecker's own contribution was to have "translated American symbols into Catholic language (and vice versa)."[63] Americanism, then, was but one mode—one of the most important ones—by which immigrants sought to escape their outsider status without relinquishing the beliefs and practices that had defined their cultural identity in former times. Yet at the same time it was seen by many as a means by which the church could be called to a fuller understanding of its own "deposit of faith," because Americanism viewed democracy not as a development that was antithetical to the hierarchical church polity, but rather as the expression in itself of the Gospel's message of the full dignity of the individual in a temporal order directed toward the common good of the multitude. Many years after the Americanism controversy had subsided, another French philosopher (and careful reader of Tocqueville) who had been forever changed by his years in America, Jacques Maritain, was the most profound, eloquent, and philosophically rigorous proponent of this democratic leaven in the church's heritage of faith. And Father Hecker, who had been stung by the declaration of the doctrine of papal infallibility at the First Vatican Council in 1869—a council he had looked forward to hopefully but left early in disappointment—would be on the minds of many of the delegates to the Second Vatican Council over ninety years later. As Sydney Ahlstrom observed, "No nineteenth-century Roman Catholic in America so clearly foreshadowed the *aggiornamento* which Pope John XXIII would begin to call for when he became pope—on the centenary of the Paulists' founding."[64]

The essential core of Americanism may be easily recognized by the careful reader of *Democracy in America*, for it bears a striking family resemblance to Tocqueville's commentary on Catholicism in America, a discourse that, following a rhetorical strategy Tocqueville often employed, is embedded in a larger discussion about the extent to which religion serves to maintain a democratic republic. His account of and predictions for Catholicism in America occur in the most crucial chapter of the 1835 volume, chapter 9 of Part II. Jean-Claude Lamberti called this chapter "the true conclusion" to Volume I[65] because the long chapter on "the three races" that succeeds it is really an excursus on American racial mores. That democracy got underway in America is a historical problem; that it be maintained is a sociological and philosophical one. It is the persistence, not the inception, of democracy that Tocqueville was most concerned to elucidate; indeed, he insisted that to explain this continuity is "the principal purpose of this book" (*DIA* 319). The causes of such persistence fall into three categories: first, circumstances, which he called "accidental or providential causes" (*DIA* 319); second, laws; and third, mores. It is the last of these that is by far the most important category. "Laws do more to maintain a democratic republic in the United States than physical causes do, and mores do more than laws" (*DIA* 352).

And, of the elements that combine to constitute mores, religion is pivotal. It exerts both direct and indirect influences on American political culture: direct because America was settled by Europeans whose religious beliefs and ecclesiastical polity, Tocqueville wrote, "I can only describe as democratic and republican"; indirect because, by placing a check or brake on desires, Christian morality helps to instruct citizens in maintaining a liberty that remains ordered and not purely self-interested.

It is in this portion of the *Democracy*, showing how religion (for all practical purposes, Christianity, but by no means exclusively Christianity in principle) supports democratic institutions, that Tocqueville brought in the subject of American Catholicism. Tocqueville typically advanced his arguments by presenting some sort of paradox, real or imagined, and then showing how the paradox could be resolved by a proper understanding of democratic or American institutions, history, or mores. That was the strategy he used to introduce the issue of Catholicism in Protestant America, a land where, because its ur-Christianity, Puritanism, had been democratic, "from the beginning, politics and religion were in harmony" (*DIA* 332). Because of the Irish immigration and Catholic conversions in the general population, he observed, there were about one million Roman Catholics in the United States by the 1830s. "These Catholics demonstrate a great fidelity in their religious practices and are full of ardor and zeal for their beliefs. Nevertheless"—here he introduced the paradox—"they constitute the *most* republican and democratic class in the United States" (*DIA* 332; emphasis added). This was the core of the ideology advanced by Father Hecker in the 1860s and embraced by the Americanists up through the 1890s: Catholics would be both devout and democratic; Catholicism does not necessitate loyalty to a distant, absolute monarchy, contrary to the slanders purveyed by the rising nativist tide of the 1880s and 1890s.[66]

Both Tocqueville and Hecker considered that widespread conversions to Catholicism would figure prominently in the American future. Hecker's reasons for this conclusion were theological; he believed that the Holy Spirit was especially hovering over America and that the nation had a special role to play in the divine plan for salvation. Tocqueville's predictions, on the other hand, were sociological and anthropological: Catholic beliefs were more amenable to doctrines of equality than were those of Protestantism, while American Catholics, being in the main from lower classes, knew that only a democratic government would afford them a chance to participate in public affairs. "It is a mistake . . . to regard the Catholic religion as a natural enemy of democracy," Tocqueville concluded. "Of the various Christian doctrines, Catholicism seems to me, on the contrary, among those most favorable to equality of conditions" (*DIA* 332). Only by recalling that the Principles of 1789, and of French republican tradition ever since then, had embodied bitter hostility to the church, and that the church had responded with anathemas to republican doctrines, can the originality of Tocqueville's statement be appreciated. Indeed, he was among the first in a century-long line of French intellectuals, culminating in Maritain, who argued for the full compatibility of democracy and Catholic Christianity.

Therefore, it should occasion no surprise that Tocqueville was closely identified with the so-called Americanists in France in the 1890s, after Leo XIII had called for a policy of *Ralliement* with the Third Republic— essentially, a cease-fire followed by mutual tolerance between church and state in France. As one prominent republican politician, Eugène Spüller, wrote in 1894, Tocqueville had "the honor of in some degree having founded the *rallies* party." Father Hecker and his Paulist mission were also notable features of Americanism for French supporters of the *rallié*.[67]

The key to the successful merging of Catholicism and democracy in the United States was the absence of the church from the realm of govern-ment—the separation of church and state. As Leo XIII called for in the Ral-liement, the two should be able to coexist. When clergy, as Tocqueville put it, depart from the sanctuary and take up a position in a social hierarchy that promotes the existing order, there can be no real détente between Catholi-cism and the republic. However, when, as is the case in the United States, the clergy as such are excluded from the government, "no faith does more than the Catholic faith to encourage adepts to take the idea of equality of conditions and carry it over into the world of politics" (*DIA* 333). Moreover, the American clergy had enthusiastically embraced the beliefs and institu-tions of democratic equality: "The Catholic priests of America have divided the intellectual world into two parts: in one they have left revealed dogmas, to which they submit without discussion; in the other they have placed polit-ical truth, and this they believe God has left for man to investigate freely" (*DIA* 334). The historical, political, and surely the theological validity of this contention may certainly be called into question. To some degree, in fact, that is what Leo XIII did in *Testem Benevolentiae*. As Françoise Mélonio observed, however, few Frenchmen were persuaded by the argument. "For most readers [in 1840s France], Catholic institutions had a natural affinity with monarchy and none at all with democracy."[68]

But the conclusion that, in Tocqueville's tidy phrase, "American Catho-lics are at once the most docile believers and the most independent citizens" (*DIA* 334) was precisely the basis for the optimism of Father Hecker and the Americanist laity, priests, and bishops of the 1880s and 1890s such as Gib-bons and Archbishop John Ireland of St. Paul. Tocqueville, then, had a role to play in the ecclesiastical controversy. In France, that role was distinct and widely acknowledged. In the United States, it was more suppressed and indistinct. This was largely because the American version of the controversy involved many issues besides the relationship of the church to American democratic institutions. But the thought of Hecker and Gibbons in particu-lar, by echoing so harmoniously with Tocqueville's observations, inevitably brought Tocqueville into the arena of discussion.

As a central aspect of their mission in the United States, Hecker and the Paulists founded the *Catholic World*, "a monthly magazine of general litera-ture and science," in 1865; Hecker himself edited it until his death in 1888. It was the most important Catholic periodical in America in the post–Civil

War era. In November 1880, an article appeared in *Catholic World* about the life, work, and significance of Tocqueville. On a surface reading, this essay simply furnishes a clear, straightforward, biographical sketch and synopsis of Tocqueville's major ideas from a Catholic perspective. Yet it contains comparisons and allusions that reveal it to be, at a deeper level, a document of Americanism. It furnishes the documentary link—so abundant in France but lacking in the United States—between Americanism and Tocqueville.

The article is replete with references—obscure today even to most educated Catholics, resonant with them then—that go beyond mere explanations or apologias but appear to be carefully placed stones in an arching argument that connects Tocqueville's French with the Paulists' American Catholicism. At the outset, the author, Wilfred C. Robinson, emphasized the connection between Tocqueville's "life as a citizen and as a Christian."[69] The purpose of the article would be to elaborate on and elucidate that association. Tocqueville, Robinson wrote, viewed the historical development of France during his lifetime "as so many steps made along the path to democracy which he considered all people would have to tread" (157). Thus was Christianity linked to democracy in the Paulists' publication via the honored symbol of Alexis de Tocqueville.

Tocqueville's allegedly upright character was sentimentally extolled, and of course he was represented as having died in the church's embrace: "seeing his end approaching," Robinson assured his readers, "he carefully fulfilled his religious duties" (160). This remark was probably intended as a dig at Beaumont, who, in his "Memoir" of Tocqueville's life, at that time the only biography, had minimized the specifically sacramental elements of Tocqueville's death. Beaumont had written bluntly, "His death was that of a Christian, as had been his life. Conversion has been wrongly spoken of. He had no need of conversion, because he had never been in the slightest degree irreligious." In 1861, this was hardly devotional discourse, and it reflected the outlook of the unbeliever Beaumont more than that of Tocqueville. A century after this was written, in fact, an angry John Lukacs was provided with documentary evidence by the sisters from the order who had nursed Tocqueville through that final illness, the sisters of Notre-Dame de Bon Secours de Troyes, that supported the conclusion that Tocqueville died "in peace with himself and his church," and he berated Beaumont for being an "unscrupulous editor" of Tocqueville's correspondence. Although scholarly opinion tends to hold, with André Jardin, that Tocqueville's doubts served to keep him aloof from the church's embrace, Lukacs continues to believe otherwise; in fact, he considers his research on Tocqueville's last days to be his most important contribution to the scholarship in the field. In 1880, certainly, Robinson's gentle rejoinder to Beaumont was not without warrant.[70]

Robinson made many more allusions that brought out the Catholicity, as well as the democratic nature, of Tocqueville's thought. Robinson, for example, is the only commentator to point out the fact that Tocqueville considered Louis Bourdaloue (1632–1704) "the greatest of all French spiritual writers" (160). For today's readers, this is an abstruse reference. No mention of Bourdaloue appears in the modern secondary literature on the subject— namely in the work of Jardin, Doris Goldstein, Lukacs, or James T. Schleifer, all of whom focused on Tocqueville's religious thought.[71] Tocqueville admired Bourdaloue deeply, however.[72] Bourdaloue was a Jesuit, a contemporary of Bishop Bossuet, a saintly confessor, and a devotional writer of genius who was renowned as the greatest preacher of his age. It was said of him that "the Jesuits answered Pascal's attacks on their moral teaching by making Bourdaloue preach."[73] This reference can be construed as another piece in the Paulist argument connecting a symbol of democracy with not only Catholic spirituality but Jesuit spirituality and intellectual rigor.

In referring to Tocqueville's public career, Robinson emphasized the Frenchman's service to the causes of slave emancipation, colonial administration, and prison reform. "Bad political news affected him as much as some personal sorrow," Robinson wrote (162). Praising Tocqueville's vaunted prescience, he singled out the idea that future generations would be, as Tocqueville put it, "more and more inclined to divide into two parties, one deserting Christianity altogether, the other entering into the bosom of the Roman church" (162).

At the conclusion of this remarkable essay, Robinson drew a comparison between Tocqueville and "another noble Frenchman who left his literary labors incomplete . . . Ozanam" (166). Frédéric Ozanam (1813–1853) was a contemporary of Tocqueville and one of the great laymen and apologists of French Catholic history. Indeed, it is surprising that there is no record of acquaintance between the two, for Ozanam, who had a genius for friendship, was close to many people in Tocqueville's circle of acquaintance, such as Jean-Jacques Ampère, the liberal Catholic Charles de Montalembert, and the Dominican Jean Baptiste Lacordaire (who would be elected to the chair in the Académie Française left vacant by Tocqueville's death).

The significance of Ozanam for this article about Tocqueville rests on two of Ozanam's great achievements. First, Ozanam founded the Society of St. Vincent de Paul, the linchpin of Catholic service to the poor and, without too much of a stretch of the imagination, a counterpart to the Paulists. Second, and of greater importance, Ozanam was a leader in the movement that became known as Christian Democracy. Originating in France as a kind of "reaction against reaction," this movement for democracy and social justice ultimately, with the urging of Cardinal Gibbons among many others, was embraced by Pope Leo XIII in both his great social encyclical *Rerum novarum* (1891) and, later, in *Graves de communi* (1901), in which he adopted and approved the term explicitly.

Robinson thus concluded his exposition of Tocqueville's life and work for a Catholic audience with a peroration from Ozanam: "Do you think," Ozanam wrote to Lacordaire, "that God has made it the duty of some to die for the cause of civilization and of the church, and left to others the task of living, their hands idle, dozing on a bed of roses? Workers in science, Christian men of letters, let us show that we are not cowardly enough to believe in a division such as it would be wrong to charge God with making and a shame for us to accept. Let us hasten to prove that we, too have our battlefields, wheron, if need be, we know how to die." To fully drive home the point, Robinson positioned Tocqueville in the company of Ozanam on the roster of those who were both great Catholics and supporters of a Christian democracy, that is, Americanists manqué: "Alexis de Tocqueville, like Ozanam, was not among those who dozed. Both were numbered among those who died laborers to the last" (166). By thus associating Tocqueville with Ozanam, Robinson brought Tocqueville directly into the Americanist controversy, the single most important episode in American Catholic intellectual history between the Civil War and World War II.

The story of the eventual censure of Americanism by Leo XIII is a wonderwork of narratology: it is a story that creates the conditions for its own interpretation. That is, a bald, factual telling of the tale furnishes the reader with the metaphorical structure by which to understand it. Simply put, the censure was sparked by a bad translation from English into French. In condensed form, the story is this: shortly after Father Hecker died in 1888, his close companion and brother Paulist Walter Elliott published a warm and rather uncritical biography. Elliott's *Life of Father Hecker* was translated into French by the Countess de Revilliary in 1897. This French edition contained a preface by Abbé Félix Klein in which Hecker's ideas were commended and his life extolled. Between them, however, the translation and the preface managed to present a simplified and distorted exposition of Hecker's ideas.

Elliott's *Vie de Père Hecker* subsequently served as the object of a slanderous, alarmist polemic entitled *Études sur l'Américanisme: le Père Hecker, est-il un saint?* by a Vincentian priest of reactionary views, Charles Maignen. His answer to the question posed in his own title was "a shrill negative," as he proceeded to tear down Hecker and "Heckerism" as a species of individualist cant and a potential denial of papal authority.[74] Maignen was associated with extreme elements of French Catholicism who were monarchist in their political sentiments—in 1897!—and who opposed Leo XIII's call to French Catholics for a cessation of hostilities with the bitterly anticlerical Third Republic. An anguished Cardinal Gibbons wrote to the Vatican "to protest with all the energy in my soul and conscience against this incriminating tendency brought against us, against these perverse insinuations of which we are the object and these revolting calumnies against an episcopate and a clergy entirely devoted to the salvation of souls and filled with veneration for the Holy See and in particular for the sacred person of Leo XIII."[75]

It is notable that Leo XIII, knowing that the *Vie de Père Hecker* was a weak translation, felt bound to censure ideas that the book *might have contained*. "You are aware, beloved Son," the pope began, "that the book entitled, 'The Life of Isaac Thomas Hecker,' chiefly through the action of those who have undertaken to publish and interpret it in a foreign language, has excited no small controversy."[76] His larger task, of course, was to clarify the relationship between the American church and the Vatican, especially, as the historian John Tracy Ellis emphasized, "at a time when the German Church had only recently emerged from Bismarck's *Kulturkampf*, when the anticlerical government of Italy was making it increasingly difficult for the Church to carry on its mission in that country, and when France was in the throes of one of its worst crises between Church and State."[77] In any case, *Testem Benevolentiae* was careful not to ascribe the rebuked ideas to Hecker himself. Indeed, the entire letter was, in grammatical terms, an enormously extended exercise in the subjunctive mood: *if* those are the ideas that some Catholics hold, then they cannot be upheld by Catholic clergy and laity. "We cannot approve the opinions which some comprise under the head of Americanism. . . . If [the term Americanism] is to be used not only to signify, but even to commend the above doctrines, there can be no doubt but that our Venerable Brethren the bishops of America would be the first to repudiate and condemn it. . . . For it raises the suspicion that there are some among you who conceive of and desire a church in America different from that which is in the rest of the world."[78]

The consensus of scholarly opinion is that *Testem Benevolentiae* retarded the course of theological debate in the American church for almost half a century. As the Jesuit historian Gerald P. Fogarty put it with perhaps some exaggeration, "The condemnation of Americanism cast the American

Church into a dogmatic slumber from which it would not awaken until the 1940s." Although the state of theological reflection is not the concern of the present study, it is worth remembering that in this controversy, so crucial to late-nineteenth and early-twentieth-century American intellectual history, but completely absent from systematic studies of that subject, Tocqueville played a significant role. But it was a role that would elude the investigator who draws conclusions based on the frequency with which Tocqueville shows up in footnotes. Finally, it is also worth noting that Tocqueville had plenty of company in being ill served by his translators.[79]

Not only Catholic, however, but also Protestant and Jewish immigrant voices were heard on the subject of Tocqueville in the half-century after the Civil War. Seeing Tocqueville as a judicious supporter, as well as an analyst, of democratic society and a symbol of its peculiarly American form, immigrant intellectuals such as Michael Heilprin and E. L. Godkin admired him and even wished to establish a philosophical proximity to him as a fellow European who understood what was distinctive about American democracy. However, one immigrant intellectual censured Tocqueville with an astonishing bitterness born out of a grievance that he had nursed for fifty years. In a rancorous article that appeared in *Forum* magazine in 1898, Tocqueville was compared to "a self-righteous and self-constituted Timon." Shakespeare's Timon of Athens is a character of such breathtaking misanthropy that, when he discovers a fortune in gold on his property, he decides to do something even more antisocial than spending it all on himself: he distributes it where he knows it will do the most harm. This was the character brought to the mind of Karl Blind by the mention of Tocqueville. In spite of the calumnious distortions his article contained, Blind felt he had a very good reason for his caustic resentment of Tocqueville. A half-century earlier, Blind had been arrested on orders of the Foreign Ministry of France when Tocqueville served as foreign minister in the Barrot government of June to October 1849.

Blind was a German Forty-Eighter and a radical democrat. In his relentless assault on Tocqueville's character and judgment, Blind recounted the story of how in 1849, "as a member of an embassy of the democratic governments of Baden and Rhenish Bavaria" to Paris, he had been arrested and thrown into the prison of La Force.[80]

In addition to Timon as symbol of misanthropy, then, Blind's metaphor points to Timon who was formerly of, but was exiled from, Athens, the symbol of democracy. Tocqueville, therefore, was an exile from and despiser of democracy. Tocqueville as Timon was a generalized emblem of alienation.

However, Blind's self-description as a legitimate diplomat was a bit of a stretch. From the French perspective, he was an envoy of an illegal revolutionary provisional government sent to Paris to agitate for still further revolutionary change. Of course the Foreign Ministry had him clapped in irons.

The occasion of Blind's article was the publication in English of yet another problematic translation of Tocqueville's works, this time of the *Souvenirs*, or "Recollections," that had been published in France in 1893, forty years after Tocqueville had completed the work, which he had intended as a private exercise rather than a public accounting. The translation that appeared in 1896 by Alexander Teixeira de Mattos is notable for its collection of, in Sherman Kent's words, "appalling and inexplicable errors and gaucheries," and one can only be grateful for the George Lawrence translation, which did not appear until 1970.[81]

Blind attempted to match Tocqueville in caustic scorn, but that was a mighty task that he simply was not equal to, as Tocqueville's own portraits in the *Recollections* are famous for their harsh, mocking, mordant quality. Tocqueville did not set out to be fair in the *Recollections*; he tried to set down his reactions to people and events surrounding the Revolution of 1848. For judicious, measured opinions, one looks elsewhere in Tocqueville's work. As soon as the original *Souvenirs* was published, Lord Acton noted this sardonic quality in the memoir, so unexpected by the reader who was familiar with the rest of Tocqueville's published work. "Swift could hardly have excelled him in his bitter and comprehensive irony," Acton wrote. He was struck by "such strange vituperation in one so dignified and so impersonal."[82]

A particular target of Tocqueville's scorn had been the socialist Louis Blanc, author of the plan for workshops for the idle labor force that had been adopted and then abandoned by the 1848 Provisional Government in Paris, leading to the awful June Days with their massacre of unemployed workers. Tocqueville described the tumultuous events of May 15, 1848, when radicals invaded the Chamber, with a particularly cruel portrait of Blanc. "Just then some of the common people took Louis Blanc up in their arms and carried him in triumph through the hall. They held him over their heads by his little legs; I saw him vainly trying to escape, twisting and turning in every direction, but never succeeding in slipping through their hands, and talking the whole time in a choking, strident voice. He reminded me of a snake having its tail pinched."

Blanc had been a special friend of Blind's, and Blind found this portrait in particular to be intolerable. (Both J. P. Mayer and A. J. P. Taylor also singled it out as one of the most unfair descriptions in the volume.) But Blind merely sputtered in rage. The article contains perhaps a dozen exclamation marks. "What a bitterness of unjust judgment! What a reactionary turn of mind!" he wrote (744).[83]

The unreasoning fury of Blind reached a nadir of vituperation when, echoing long-outdated notions of phrenology, he even assailed Tocqueville's physical appearance: "A look at De Tocqueville's portrait, which is given in the front of the book, will perhaps satisfy the student of physiognomy that there is a strong indication of this shrewish habit in the formation of the mouth and its surrounding parts" (752–53).

The *Nation* also printed a two-article notice on the *Souvenirs* as soon as the book was published in France. In their tone of esteem approaching hero-worship, these articles formed a mirror-image to the furious attack by Blind. The author, Auguste Laugel, writing from Paris, sentimentally depicted Tocqueville as a sort of Diogenes, "lost among men, like some superior spirit," a mysterious figure who walked as "a sort of stranger among his contemporaries." Tocqueville's *Souvenirs* was "at times . . . truly prophetic," Laugel added—prescience being already a required trope where Tocqueville was concerned.[84]

Laugel's articles were elegiac in tone, regretting the loss of Tocqueville's presence among a younger generation of French intellectuals. "How distant already seems the figure of Alexis de Tocqueville!" he exclaimed. "Tocqueville is already become an 'ancient.' " The thesis of Tocqueville's being forgotten shows up here for the first time. But the assertion, again, belongs in a particular context. Laugel had been a friend of Tocqueville and of Laboulaye and, along with Laboulaye, a leading defender of the Union cause in Paris during the Civil War. He was the brother-in-law of Maria Weston Chapman, in whose abolitionist newspaper, the *Liberty Bell*, Tocqueville had published his antislavery "testament" in 1855. Godkin appointed Laugel the Paris correspondent of the *Nation* when he founded the magazine in 1865, and the following year, Laugel published, in French, English, and Spanish, a popular travel account entitled *The United States during the Civil War*. Among the anecdotes he there recounted was the edifying story of encountering a Kansas farmer reading the *Democracy* on a Mississippi steamboat. Laugel thought of his friendship with Tocqueville as a great "privilege" of his life and was as eager to exalt as Blind was to disparage the author of the *Souvenirs*.[85]

Notes

1. Tocqueville to Hubert de Tocqueville, February 23, 1857, OC, XIV:329; Herr, *Tocqueville and the Old Regime*, 36; see also, Edward T. Gargan, "The Formation of Tocqueville's Historical Thought," *Review of Politics* 24, no. 1 (January 1962): 48–61.

2. William James, *Principles of Psychology* (Chicago: Encyclopedia Britannica, 1952), 502.

3. See, for example, Gary W. Gallagher and Alan T. Nolan, eds. *The Myth of the Lost Cause and Civil War History* (Bloomington: Indiana University Press, 2000), Charles Reagan Wilson, *Baptized in Blood: The Religion of the Lost Cause, 1865–1920* (Athens: University of Georgia Press, 1980), and, especially, David W. Blight, *Race and Reunion: The Civil War in American Memory* (Cambridge, Mass.: Belknap Press, 2001).

4. Max Beloff, "Tocqueville and the Americans," *The Fortnightly* 170 (September 1951): 573. "Tocqueville's stock fell as that of twentieth-century thinkers like Clifford Geertz, Antonio Gramsci, and E. P. Thompson rose." Ronald G. Walters, "Reforming Tocqueville," *The Tocqueville Review/La Revue Tocqueville* 9 (1988): 283; a half-century after Beloff, the *Wilson Quarterly* tiresomely chimed in: "While Karl Marx has fallen sharply on the intellectual stock exchange in recent years, Alexis de Tocqueville has dramatically risen." "Tocqueville in the 21st Century," *Wilson Quarterly* 24, no. 2 (Spring 2000): 97.

5. *TBSR*, following p. 200.

6. Marshall and Drescher, "American Historians and Tocqueville's *Democracy*," 513, 514.

7. Robert Nisbet, "Many Tocquevilles," *American Scholar* 46, no. 1 (Winter 1976): 59, 60, 61.

8. Wilfred M. McClay, *The Masterless: Self and Society in Modern America* (Chapel Hill: University of North Carolina Press, 1994), 235.

9. James T. Kloppenberg, "Life Everlasting: Tocqueville in America," *La Revue Tocqueville/The Tocqueville Review* 17, no. 2 (1996): 22.

10. Michael Kammen, *Alexis de Tocqueville and Democracy in America* (Washington, D.C.: Library of Congress, 1998), 11.

11. The influence of Nisbet's article is as widespread and unchallenged as it is specious. In addition to McClay, Kloppenberg, and Kammen, André Jardin cited it in the last chapter of his biography (Jardin, *Tocqueville*, 534n3), while Joseph Epstein referred glowingly to it in his introduction to the Bantam Classic edition of the Reeve translation and drew special attention to Nisbet's never having heard Tocqueville's name during his Berkeley education ([New York: Bantam, 2000], xxxi).

12. Fredrick Jameson, *The Political Unconscious: Narrative as a Socially Symbolic Act* (Ithaca, N.Y.: Cornell University Press, 1981), 9.

13. See, for example, Isaac Kramnick, introduction to *Democracy in America*, trans. Gerald Bevan (London: Penguin Classics, 2003), ix–xii.

14. Eric Keslassy, "Le nouveau retour de Tocqueville," *The Tocqueville Review/La Revue Tocqueville* 24, no. 1 (2003): 189.

15. Françoise Mélonio, *Tocqueville and the French*, trans. Beth G. Raps (Charlottesville: University Press of Virginia, 1998), 149, 162–69.

16. Martin Malia, "Did Tocqueville Foresee Totalitarianism?" *Journal of Democracy* 11, no. 1 (January 2000): 179; Mélonio, *Tocqueville and the French*, 189–208; Jack Hayward,

"Tocqueville's Return Again from America," *West European Politics* 18, no. 2 (April 1995): 447; Kloppenberg, "Life Everlasting," 23, 28; Keslassy, "Le nouveau retour."

17. Bradley, *Democracy in America*, app. 4, II:482–85; Alexis de Tocqueville, *Democracy in America*, ed. Daniel Coit Gilman, 2 vols. (New York: Century, 1898); Alexis de Tocqueville, *Democracy in America*, ed. John T. Bigelow, 2 vols. (New York: Appleton, 1904).

18. Woodrow Wilson, "Bryce's American Commonwealth," *Political Science Quarterly* 4, no. 1 (March 1889): 154; Abraham S. Eisenstadt, "Bryce's America and Tocqueville's" in *Reconsidering Tocqueville's Democracy in America*, ed. Abraham S. Eisenstadt (New Brunswick, N.J.: Rutgers University Press, 1988), 229–30; Edmund Ions, *James Bryce and American Democracy, 1870–1922* (London: Macmillan, 1968), 118–20; Albert Shaw, "De Tocqueville," *New York Times—Saturday Review of Books and Art*, December 10, 1898, 844; James Bryce, *The Predictions of Hamilton and De Tocqueville*, Johns Hopkins University Studies in Historical and Political Science, Fifth Series, Vol. IX (Baltimore, Md.: Johns Hopkins University Press, 1887), 26.

19. *Herbert B. Adams: Tributes of Friends* (Baltimore, Md.: Johns Hopkins University Press, 1902), 59; Francis Lieber to Daniel Coit Gilman, May 28, 1865, Lieber papers (JHU).

20. Theodore Dwight Woolsey to Matilda Lieber, May 5, 1874, Lieber papers (H); Woolsey, "Introduction to the Third Edition" in *On Civil Liberty and Self-Government*, by Francis Lieber, 3rd ed., 2 vols. (Philadelphia: Lippincott, 1877), I:6; Anna Haddow, *Political Science in American Colleges and Universities, 1636–1900* (New York: D. Appleton-Century, 1939), 114.

21. *TBA*, 375–76.

22. Francis Lieber, *On Civil Liberty and Self-Government*, 1st ed. (Philadelphia: Lippincott, Grambo and Co., 1853), I:275; Lieber, *Civil Liberty*, 3rd ed., I:254 n.

23. Abraham Flexner, *Daniel Coit Gilman: Creator of the American Type of University* (New York: Harcourt, Brace, 1946), 10–11, 13–15; Hugh Hawkins, "Charles W. Eliot, Daniel C. Gilman and the Nurture of American Scholarship," *New England Quarterly* 39, no. 3 (September 1966): 293, 294–96.

24. Theodore Dwight Woolsey, *Political Science*, 2 vols. (New York: Scribner's, 1886), II:367–71.

25. [Daniel Coit Gilman], *Bluntschli Lieber and Laboulaye* (Baltimore: Privately printed for a few friends, 1884), Special Collections Department, Milton S. Eisenhower Library, Johns Hopkins University, Baltimore, Maryland; Wilton S. Dillon and Neal G. Kotler, eds., *The Statue of Liberty Revisited: Making a Universal Symbol* (Washington, D.C.: Smithsonian Institution Press, 1994); Édouard Laboulaye, "Alexis de Tocqueville," in *L'État et ses limites*, 3rd ed. (Paris: Charpentier, 1865), 138–201; Walter D. Gray, *Interpreting American Democracy in France: The Career of Édouard Laboulaye, 1811–1883* (Newark, N.J.: University of Delaware Press, 1994), 27; Rémond quoted in Gray, *Interpreting American Democracy*, 27; Seymour Drescher, review of *Interpreting American Democracy in France: The Career of Édouard Laboulaye, 1811–1883*, by Walter D. Gray, *American Histor-*

ical Review 100, no. 5 (December 1995): 1589; on the fairy tales, see Édouard Laboulaye, *Laboulaye's Fairy Book: Fairy Tales of All Nations*, trans. Mary L. Booth (New York: Harper and Brothers, 1867); Édouard Laboulaye, *Contes bleus*, ed. George Ellas Wisewell (New York: Allyn and Bacon, 1924).

26. [Gilman], *Bluntschli Lieber and Laboulaye*, 5–7; [Herbert B. Adams], *Bluntschli's Life-Work* (Baltimore, Md.: Privately printed, 1884); Marvin E. Gettleman, ed., *The Johns Hopkins University Seminary of History and Politics: The Records of an American Educational Institution, 1877–1912*, 5 vols. (New York: Garland, 1987), Seminary Records in Facsimile, after January 4, 1884.

27. Raymond J. Cunningham, "The German Historical World of Herbert Baxter Adams: 1874–1876," *Journal of American History* 68, no. 2 (September 1981): 270, 273–74; Hugh Hawkins, *Pioneer: A History of the Johns Hopkins University, 1874–1889* (Ithaca, N.Y.: Cornell University Press, 1960), 169, 172; W. Stull Holt, ed. *Historical Scholarship in the United States, 1876–1901: As Revealed in the Correspondence of Herbert B. Adams* (Baltimore, Md.: Johns Hopkins University Press, 1938), 1–17, 29–34.

28. Daniel Coit Gilman, "Pleasant Incidents of an Academic Life," *Scribner's* 31, no. 5 (May 1902): 618.

29. Herbert B. Adams, "Freeman the Scholar and Professor," *Yale Review* 4, no. 3 (November 1895): 241, 245; Adams, "Is History Past Politics?" 19, 20, Herbert Baxter Adams papers, Special Collections Department, Milton S. Eisenhower Library, Johns Hopkins University, Baltimore, Maryland.

30. Laurence Veysey, *The Emergence of the American University* (Chicago: University of Chicago Press, 1965), 96; Frederick Rudolph, *The American College and University: A History* (New York: Alfred A. Knopf, 1962), 270–71, 274–75.

31. *Herbert B. Adams, Tributes of Friends*, 46. This is not to argue that Adams was himself a great historian, as John Higham made clear in a thorough study, "Herbert Baxter Adams and the Study of Local History," *American Historical Review* 89, no. 5 (December 1984): 1225–39.

32. Francis Bowen, *Principles of Political Economy Applied to the Condition, the Resources, and the Institutions of the American People* (Boston: Little Brown, 1859); Francis Bowen, *American Political Economy* (New York: Scribner's, 1870).

33. Charles Horton Cooley, *Social Organization: A Study of the Larger Mind* (New York: Scribner's, 1909), 105–205; Dorothy Ross, *The Origins of American Social Science* (Cambridge: Cambridge University Press, 1991), 240; see also 240–53; Robert Cooley Angell, introduction to *Cooley and Sociological Analysis*, ed. Albert J. Reiss Jr. (Ann Arbor: University of Michigan Press, 1968), 1–12.

34. Nisbet, "Many Tocquevilles," 60; George Wilson Pierson, *Yale College: An Educational History, 1871–1921* (New Haven, Conn.: Yale University Press, 1952), 70–71; Pierson, "Tocqueville's Visions of Democracy," *Yale University Library Gazette* 51, no. 1 (July 1976): 8–11; *Selections from Democracy in America* by Alexis de Tocqueville. Printed for the use in the course "Government I" at Harvard University, 1932 (Cambridge, Mass.: Harvard University Press, 1932); this volume comprises chapter 3, "Social Condition of

the Anglo-Americans," chapter 4, "The Sovereignty of the People," chapter 8, "Government of the Democracy in America," chapter 15, "Unlimited Power of the Majority," and chapter 16, "The Causes Which Mitigate the Tyranny of the Majority," all from Volume I. Phillips Bradley taught at City College and the New School during the 1930s. Albert Salomon was his colleague at the latter institution. Ross J. S. Hoffman taught at Fordham in the late 1930s. Bradley also moved to Syracuse and Cornell in the 1940s.

35. Kloppenberg, "Life Everlasting," 22; C. C. Smith, "Alexis de Tocqueville," *Christian Examiner* 78, no. 3 (November 1862): 402; Norton, "Alexis de Tocqueville," 551.

36. See, for example, Smith, "Alexis de Tocqueville"; Gilman, "Alexis de Tocqueville and His Book on America—Sixty Years After," *Century Magazine* 56, no. 5 (September 1898): 703–15. J. A. Lukacs, "Reading, Writing, and History: De Tocqueville's Message for America," *American Heritage* 10, no. 4 (June 1959): 99–102.

37. Anon., preface to *Memoir, Letters, and Remains*, by Alexis de Tocqueville, 2 vols. (Boston: Ticknor and Fields, 1862), vi, vii.

38. *New York Times*, July 4, 1862, 2.

39. J. H. Allen, "History and Biography," *Christian Examiner* 72, no. 2 (March, 1862): 297; Smith, "Alexis de Tocqueville," 381; Rev. Ray Palmer, D.D., "Alexis de Tocqueville," *New Englander* 21, no. 4 (October 1862): 669.

40. Palmer, "Alexis de Tocqueville," 683, 692, 694.

41. Quoted in François Furet, "The Intellectual Origins of Tocqueville's Thought," *Tocqueville Review* 7 (1985–1986): 118.

42. Smith, "Alexis de Tocqueville," 390–91.

43. Allen, "History and Biography," 297.

44. G. M. Towle, "Alexis de Tocqueville," *North American Review* 95, no. 1 (July 1862): 139.

45. *New York Times*, July 6, 1862, 4; Norton, "Alexis de Tocqueville," 551.

46. [George Wilson Pierson], "GWP—Instructions for the Further Use of These Tocqueville MSS," Yale Tocqueville Manuscripts, Ms. Vault Tocqueville, Beinecke Rare Book and Manuscript Library, Yale University.

47. Edward Brooks, "The Error of De Tocqueville," *North American Review* 102, no. 2 (April 1866): 330–31; James M. McPherson, *Battle Cry of Freedom: The Civil War Era* (New York: Oxford University Press, 1988), 382–91.

48. John Chadwick in the *Unitarian Review*, September 1888, quoted in Gustav Pollak, *Michael Heilprin and His Sons* (New York: Dodd, Mead, 1912), 9–10; on Heilprin, see also Emil Lengyel, *Americans from Hungary* (Philadelphia: Lippincott, 1948), 65–68; Robert Perlman, *Bridging Three Worlds: Hungarian-Jewish Americans, 1848–1914* (Amherst: University of Massachusetts Press, 1991), 98–101.

49. For the development of a serious reading public in the United States after 1860, see Louise L. Stevenson, *The Victorian Homefront: American Thought and Culture, 1860–1880* (New York: Twayne, 1991), esp. 30–47.

50. Michael Heilprin, "De Tocqueville in the United States," *Nation* 1, no. 8 (August 24, 1865), 247.

51. Tocqueville to Henry Reeve, March 22, 1837, *Letters,* 115–17; Michael Heilprin, "De Tocqueville as a Legislator," *Nation* 2 (March 1, 1866), 278.

52. Elizabeth Stevenson, *Henry Adams: A Biography* (New York: Macmillan, 1956), 57–58; Richard Ruland, "Tocqueville's *De la Démocratie en Amérique* and *The Education of Henry Adams,*" *Comparative Literature Studies* 2, no. 3 (1965): 195–207; J. C. Levenson, *The Mind and Art of Henry Adams* (Boston: Houghton Mifflin, 1957), 20.

53. Ruland, "*De la Démocratie* and *The Education,*" 195, 196.

54. Ruland, "*De la Démocratie* and *The Education,*" 196.

55. Max I. Baym, *The French Education of Henry Adams* (New York: Columbia University Press, 1951), 22, 24, 29.

56. John Tracy Ellis, *The Life of James Cardinal Gibbons,* 2 vols. (Milwaukee, Wis.: Bruce Publishing, 1952), II:500.

57. David J. O'Brien, *Isaac Hecker: An American Catholic* (New York: Paulist Press, 1992); James T. Fisher, *Catholics in America* (New York: Oxford University Press, 2001), 84–90; Sydney Ahlstrom, *A Religious History of the American People* (New Haven, Conn.: Yale University Press, 1972), 825–41; Martin E. Marty, *Pilgrims in Their Own Land: 500 Years of Religion in America* (Boston: Little, Brown, 1984), 276–84; Patrick Allitt, *Catholic Converts: British and American Intellectuals Turn to Rome* (Ithaca, N.Y.: Cornell University Press, 1997), 112–16; Mélonio, *Tocqueville and the French,* 177–79; William Portier, "Isaac Hecker and *Testem Benevolentiae:* A Study in Theological Pluralism," in *Hecker Studies: Essays in the Thought of Isaac Hecker,* ed. John Farina (New York: Paulist Press, 1983), 11–48; Edward J. Langlois, C. S. P., "Isaac Hecker's Political Thought," in Farina, *Hecker Studies,* 49–86. Leo XIII's letter, *Testem Benevolentiae,* January 29, 1899, was intended for all American bishops but sent to Cardinal Gibbons as senior prelate; it is published in John Tracy Ellis, ed., *Documents of American Catholic History,* 3 vols. (Wilmington, Del.: Michael Glazier, 1987), II:537–47; Cardinal Gibbons's reply of March 17, 1899, withheld from publication for forty-five years, appeared in *Catholic Historical Review* 30 (October 1944): 346–48.

58. Walter J. Ong, S.J., "Man between Two Worlds," *Catholic World* 186 (May 1958): 86–87.

59. O'Brien, *Isaac Hecker,* 90–91, 93 (quote), 103.

60. Ong, "Man between Two Worlds," 86–87.

61. Langlois, "Isaac Hecker's Political Thought," 49.

62. Gibbons to Leo XIII, 347.

63. Ahlstrom, *Religious History,* 380; Langlois, "Isaac Hecker's Political Thought," 53.

64. From Jacques Maritain's dozens of books and articles on the subject, a useful anthology was gathered by Joseph W. Evans and Leo R. Ward, *The Social and Political Philosophy of Jacques Maritain* (New York: Doubleday, 1965); see also Bernard Doering, *Jacques Maritain and the French Catholic Intellectuals* (Notre Dame, Ind.: University of Notre Dame Press, 1983), 168–205; Matthew J. Mancini, "Maritain's Democratic Vision: 'You Have No Bourgeois,'" in *Understanding Maritain: Philosopher and Friend,* ed. Deal W. Hudson and Matthew J. Mancini (Macon, Ga.: Mercer University Press, 1988), 133–52; Ahlstrom, *Religious History,* 544.

65. Lamberti, *Tocqueville and the Two Democracies*, 50.

66. John Higham, *Strangers in the Land: Patterns of American Nativism, 1860–1925* (New York: Atheneum, 1971), 5–7, 35–105.

67. Mélonio, *Tocqueville and the French*, 178 (Spüller quote), 179.

68. Mélonio, *Tocqueville and the French*, 79.

69. W. Robinson, "Alexis de Tocqueville," *Catholic World* 32 (1880): 157. Subsequent references appear parenthetically in the text.

70. John Lukacs, "The Last Days of Alexis de Tocqueville," *Catholic Historical Review* 50:2 (July 1964), 158, 159; Jardin, *Tocqueville*, 528; Lukacs interview.

71. Jardin, *Tocqueville*, esp. 528–32, 61–64, 364–67; Doris S. Goldstein, *Trial of Faith: Religion and Politics in Tocqueville's Thought* (New York: Elsevier, 1975); Lukacs, "The Last Days of Alexis de Tocqueville"; James T. Schleifer, "Tocqueville and Religion: Some New Perspectives," *Tocqueville Review* 4, no. 2 (Fall–Winter 1982): 303–21.

72. "What admirable language! What consummate art! It is impossible to study him sufficiently," Tocqueville wrote to Francisque de Corcelle, December 31, 1853 (*Memoir, Letters, and Remains*, II:244; also found in OC XV, pt. 2, 89). In another letter to Corcelle that Beaumont did not publish in the 1861 *Memoir, Letters, and Remains* (and that therefore Robinson could not have known about), Tocqueville wrote again of Bourdeloue's mastery of literary form and his ability to bring his hearers straight along on a path toward the spiritual truths he held out for them. OC XV, pt. 2, 130–31. Robinson's contention that Tocqueville admired Bourdaloue as the greatest French spiritual writer seems warranted—provided we place Blaise Pascal in the category of philosopher rather than spiritual writer.

73. T. J. Thomas, "Louis Bourdaloue," *Catholic Encyclopedia* (New York: R. Appelton, 1907) II:717–19.

74. Ellis, *Life of Cardinal Gibbons*, II:58–62; Portier, "Isaac Hecker and *Testem Benevolentiae*," 19–23; Ahlstrom, *Religious History*, 825.

75. Ellis, *Life of Cardinal Gibbons*, II:60.

76. Leo XIII, *Testem Benevolentiae*, 538.

77. Ellis, *Life of Cardinal Gibbons*, II:2.

78. Leo XIII, *Testem Benevolentiae*, 546.

79. Gerald P. Fogarty, S.J., "American Catholics, 1865–1908," *Encyclopedia of American Catholic History*, ed. Michael Glazier and Thomas J. Shelley (Collegeville, Minn.: Liturgical Press, 1997), 78.

80. Karl Blind, "Alexis de Tocqueville's 'Recollections' and Self-Revelations," *Forum* 24 (1897–1898): 759. Subsequent references appear parenthetically in the text.

81. Sherman Kent, review of Tocqueville, *Recollections*, *Annals of the American Academy of Political and Social Science* 270 (July 1950): 195.

82. Lord Acton, "Tocqueville's Souvenirs," *Nineteenth Century* 33 (January–June, 1893), 885.

83. *R*, 150–51; Mayer, "Introduction" to *R*, xix; A. J. P. Taylor, *From Napoleon to Lenin* (New York: Harper Torchbooks, 1966), 58.

84. [A. Laugel], review of *Souvenirs*, by Alexis de Tocqueville, *Nation* 270 (April 13, 1893): 270 and (April 27, 1893): 311.

85. Laugel, "Review," 270; Allan Nevins, foreword to *The United States during the Civil War*, by Auguste Laugel (1866; repr. Bloomington: Indiana University Press, 1961), ix–xxxi. Nevins was successful in his "effort to rescue [Laugel] from almost complete oblivion" (vii) in his foreword, which remains an indispensable source. See also Georges J. Joyaux, "Auguste Laugel Visits the Army of the Potomac," *Virginia Magazine of History and Biography* 69, no. 4 (October 1961): 469–88.

CHAPTER FIVE

❄

Enduring Sage

Early in the twenty-first century, the central component of the common understanding of what Tocqueville's standing at the start of the twentieth century had been, was that his interpretation of America, while it had been insightful, had been pertinent to a bygone era. A corollary to this idea of a dated Tocqueville was the relevance, or at least the superior timeliness, of a new book that had been published a half-century after *Democracy in America* and had superseded it: James Bryce's *The American Commonwealth*.

In fact, however, the belief that most commentators thought of Bryce's two volumes as having eclipsed Tocqueville's was both vastly overstated and short-lived. By the time of World War I, it had disappeared.

How can we account for this erroneous yet persistent belief that Tocqueville had been superseded at the turn of the century? The great medieval historian Marc Bloch was renowned for his brilliant use of a technique he called the "regressive method." The basic idea was to work backward in time from the incomplete and sketchy evidence of more recent days. A version of that method can be deployed to reveal the genealogy of the supersessionist dogma that Bryce had come to overshadow Tocqueville around the turn of the twentieth century. As is the case for a correct understanding of other errors concerning Tocqueville's reputation, so also the genealogy of this one should begin with Robert Nisbet's oft-cited 1976 essay, "Many Tocquevilles." There Nisbet claimed, "By the 1870s [*Democracy in America*] had become a text only occasionally studied and footnoted. In England, Dicey lamented that he could not interest students in a work that had been virtually the staple of his and his contemporaries' education."[1] Nisbet's assertion carried the unmistakable implication that Dicey had cried out his lament about students not reading Tocqueville during the 1870s. However, the article in which Dicey commented that Tocqueville was not much read by students appeared in 1893, not in the 1870s, and it is certainly questionable, given Dicey's own commitments and loyalties by the 1890s, whether it was a lament at all.

Nisbet was referring to Albert Venn Dicey, the nineteenth century's leading authority on English constitutional development. As holder of the Vinerian Chair of English Law at Oxford, lecturer at the London School of Economics during its formative years, and author of *The Law of the Constitution* (1885), Dicey wielded enormous intellectual authority.

As a matter of fact Dicey *had* written about Tocqueville during the 1870s, but at that time he betrayed no sign of disillusion and no shortage of admiration for his subject. In an essay written in 1872, which had been occasioned by the publication of Nassau Senior's notebooks and correspondence with Tocqueville, Dicey was outspoken about Tocqueville's greatness. Indeed he called Tocqueville "the greatest historical writer whom this century has produced." Dicey did add a caveat to this encomium by specifying that Tocqueville had been "not exactly a great historian." He was, rather, "a great critic of history," because "he did not propose to himself to narrate the transactions of the past"—which evidently was Dicey's criterion for being a great historian—"but to explain them." He depicted Tocqueville in his familiar role as an oracle who "possessed a kind of prophetical foresight" in his speech to the Chamber of Deputies anticipating the February 1848 revolution. And he concluded that "the source of De Tocqueville's foresight is the same as the origin of his greatness as a theorist. In both cases, his strength lies in an unrivalled capacity for critical analysis."[2]

These fulsome expressions of esteem were considerably modified twenty-one years later when Dicey reviewed the first French edition of Tocqueville's *Souvenirs* for a British journal. Here Dicey introduced the comparison between Tocqueville and Bryce that was intended to highlight the Frenchman's supposed deficiencies. Dicey's 1893 opinions appear to have been quickly forgotten, however, or as seems more likely, not much noticed to begin with. In the mid-1960s, in a rambling introduction to the hardcover edition of the George Lawrence translation of the *Democracy*, J. P. Mayer called this second Dicey article "a little-known essay on Tocqueville which deserves to be reprinted," and this remark almost certainly provided Nisbet with the idea of looking Dicey up. It is not only the obscurity of this essay that leads to this conclusion but also the facts that Mayer called the essay

Dicey's attempt "to evaluate Tocqueville's permanent place in the history of political thought" and that it is Nisbet's only mention of Dicey.[3]

Thus, although Dicey wrote about Tocqueville twice, in 1872 and 1893, the first time praising Tocqueville extravagantly and the second treating him more disparagingly, Nisbet referred only to the latter article, and at the same time clearly implied that it was a product of the 1870s.

The central contention of the 1893 article was that the once-vibrant observations of Tocqueville had become passé. Two interrelated developments had brought on this relative decline. First, Dicey contended, the men who, in England, had so ardently championed Tocqueville during his lifetime had themselves suffered a falling off in their reputation. And second, Bryce's *The American Commonwealth* furnished such a painstakingly thorough, accurate, and timely account of American political culture and institutions that readers in the era of the internal combustion engine who were interested in learning about such matters no longer had to turn to Tocqueville's excessively abstract observations dating from Andrew Jackson's first term of office.

Dicey imagined a black disklike shadow inexorably moving across the light once shed by Tocqueville and his English colleagues:

> Will Alexis de Tocqueville take his place among the writers whose works are true classics[?] Will he stand in the records of French literature near, or by the side of, Montesquieu?
>
> Some thirty or thirty-five years ago even to ask this question would have savoured of intellectual blasphemy. Tocqueville's rank among French thinkers and men of letters had before 1860 obtained general recognition. Mill, Grote, Senior, Greg, all the men, in short, who then guided the educated opinion of England, had proclaimed Tocqueville's eminence. He was canonized in his lifetime. Unfortunately, the fame of the thinkers to whom Tocqueville was an oracle is itself for the moment under a kind of cloud. The reputation of some of them is dead. . . . The fame of Tocqueville himself suffers under an eclipse like that which dims the reputation of his friends.[4]

At the end of his article Dicey professed to be noncommittal on the question of Tocqueville's ultimate importance. After all, he wrote with arresting political metaphors, the reputation of many great writers had suffered after their deaths: "The dictatorship of Johnson did not long survive his life"; Montesquieu's "intellectual supremacy . . . had passed away by the end of the 18th century. . . . In such matters nothing is decisive but the judgment of time" (782, 783).

But, as Dicey certainly knew, time itself renders no judgments. It is the statements of men and women offered over time—often self-interested, careless, hasty, misleading, or misguided statements—that come to seem cloaked in the impersonal judgment of time itself. Thus, it would have been advisable for Mayer and Nisbet to have first acquainted themselves with Dicey's own very considerable bias in the 1890s in regard to Tocqueville, and especially to *Democracy in America*, before relaying his opinions as though they were the impartial observations of a disinterested scholar. In fact, Dicey had a clear parti pris regarding Bryce's *American Commonwealth*, which had been published just five years before. "*La Démocratie en Amérique*, as a picture of modern America, would in any case be out of date," Dicey wrote, but "Bryce's *American Commonwealth* is now the only book worth consulting as a source of information about American institutions" (783). In addition, Dicey denigrated Tocqueville's scholarship ("Erudition was never his strong point") and characterized the Frenchman's knowledge of American institutions as "superficial." In short, "As a repertory of information about the United States *La Démocratie en Amérique* cannot stand comparison for a moment with Bryce's *American Commonwealth*" (773).

That such statements would, even years later, be taken at face value is testimony to the fragility and transience of historical memory and to the momentum achieved by "standard" approaches to problems in intellectual history. But Dicey's devaluation of Tocqueville's standing must be understood in a specific context. Bryce, as we have seen, had made every effort to position himself as a writer who had displaced Tocqueville as the leading foreign commentator on the United States. He had been working to that effect at least since 1883, and he wrote every line of his *American Commonwealth* while casting a backward glance at the ghost of Tocqueville hovering over his shoulder. It was, without a doubt, a major portion of his self-imposed task to argue that he had written "the only book worth consulting" on his subject.

What did Dicey have to do with this? To begin with, we might note that *The American Commonwealth* is dedicated to Albert Venn Dicey. Dicey and Bryce had been intimate friends ever since their student years at Oxford together. In 1870, the two comrades jointly undertook the journey to the United States that would eventually result in Bryce's *American Commonwealth*. Their six-week American sojourn was a defining experience in both their lives. Thirty-seven years later, Dicey wrote his friend: "It is curious to think how much in one way or another our journey in 1870 affected both our lives, and I should say on the whole affected them happily. One may pretty well assume that neither *The American Commonwealth* and probably neither the *Law of the Constitution* nor certainly *Law and Opinion* would have been produced but for this journey."[5] In other words, A. V. Dicey was James Bryce's Beaumont. Yet, in another instance of the consistent lapses in critical discernment that haunt Tocqueville's reception at almost every turn, Mayer, Nisbet, and others imbibed Dicey's claim about Tocqueville's alleged "eclipse" straight up, as it were: they understood it to be a neutral remark made by an impartial contemporary observer.

To summarize Dicey's part in the Tocqueville story: Bryce had endeavored to displace Tocqueville as the preeminent foreign commentator on American institutions. He had conducted a graduate seminar at Hopkins at which the students' assignment was to seek examples of Tocqueville's errors, and he published a separate monograph on the issue. His own *American Commonwealth* was the highly praised result of an exhaustive effort to describe American institutions. Dicey had been Bryce's traveling companion in America. Dicey had praised Tocqueville effusively in the 1870s, but after *The American Commonwealth* appeared he made an about-face, declared that Tocqueville was passé, and disingenuously maintained that he could not get his students—these were Oxford University scholars studying constitutional law under his tutelage—to read Tocqueville's book. In 1966, Mayer took up this preposterous claim and reported it straight, without irony or context, as evidence of Tocqueville's supposed eclipse. In the mid-1970s, Nisbet, probably after noticing Mayer's report, reiterated Dicey's opinion, but this time with the strong implication that it dated from the 1870s. This was part of the chain of events that led to the notion that Tocqueville was considered passé and deemed merely of historical interest to intellectuals, beginning in the 1870s.

The Progressive Era provided but one version of a Dicey-like interpretation of Tocqueville, and it was a gentle, moderate version at that. It came in a book by a prominent Progressive intellectual, John Graham Brooks. In many ways, Brooks represented the typical Progressive leader. He was a Unitarian clergyman and social Gospel advocate, possessed of an elite education, sensitive to developments in the arena of social welfare in Europe, confident in the power of publicity and scholarly investigation to assuage social illnesses, nationalistic in the sense that he favored a strong central state and believed in the special qualities and role of the American people, and finally, liberal insofar as he rejected socialism as a remedy for America's myriad of social and economic problems. A firm and committed enemy of the trusts, Brooks was the president of the National Consumers' League from 1899 to

1915. Brooks truly did fall rapidly into obscurity after his death in 1938 at the age of ninety-one, but in the glory days of Progressive improvement he was one of America's best known and most respected reform figures. Jane Addams wrote of the "incentive and reassurance his position on social affairs" had provided her, while Felix Frankfurter, in 1940, issued the remarkable, if utterly mistaken, judgment: "I do not know of any sociological writings, say between 1890 and 1920, that will have more enduring value for scholars fifty years hence than the writings of John Graham Brooks."[6]

Brooks had spent the years between 1882 and 1885 in Europe, attending the great German universities of Berlin, Jena, and Freiburg and investigating labor organizations in France, Belgium, Germany, and England. These experiences infused the pages of his first book, *Compulsory Insurance in Germany*, published in 1895 for the U.S. Department of Labor. Ten years later he wrote the unsettling *The Social Unrest*. The year after that, he took up the presidency of the American Social Science Association (ASSA), whose previous leaders had included Francis Lieber. The ASSA was already a fading organization because the breadth of its disciplinary reach ran counter to the trend of increasing disciplinary separation and growing professionalization of academic social scientists. Yet it was a perfect fit for Brooks, whose own background and training came out of that older, broad-based concern with social problems. His major work, *As Others See Us*, published in 1908, was a series of meditations on the lives and work of the foremost European commentators on the United States, ranging from Tocqueville to Hugo von Münsterberg. Written as a series of articles for *The Chautauquan*, the book testified to his faith in immigrants and evinced an awareness of that transatlantic reciprocity which, since the groundbreaking work of James T. Kloppenberg in the mid-1980s, scholars have come to recognize as a crucial element in social reform in the decades before World War I.[7]

Of all the Europeans he surveyed, Brooks reserved his strongest praise for the British traveler to whom he dedicated his book: James Bryce. Brooks dubbed him "our greatest critic."[8] In Brooks's opinion, Bryce's great book breathed a generosity of spirit, openness to cultural diversity, and unflagging willingness to look for the cultural and social structures that lay behind the peculiarities of American attitudes and behavior. Brooks attributed this fundamental liberality to the incredible variety of Bryce's own experiences. "If he is discussing American manners or morals," Brooks believed, "his judgment means something because he has watched manners and morals in many countries. . . . It is this large mastery of contemporary political and social experience which makes Mr. Bryce, not only superior to de Tocqueville, but clearly our greatest critic" (236).

Brooks occupied a prominent place in the crowded ranks of Bryce's American friends. During the summer when Brooks was writing *As Others See Us,* the two outdoor enthusiasts went trout fishing and mountain climbing together at Brooks's summer retreat in New Hampshire.[9] Perhaps as a result of this friendship with one of the most eminent British public figures of his time, Brooks's treatment of Bryce in *As Others See Us* bordered on flattery. His book was written just when Bryce, who was certainly used to being lionized, arrived in the United States to take up his duties as the British ambassador to Washington. Whether because of Bryce's status as a newly arrived guest, the book's dedication, or Brooks's concern as a Progressive with the problems that Bryce directly addressed, Brooks wrote like a diplomatic envoy himself when he delicately brought up what he said was "the one critical weakness" in Bryce, namely his unrelenting optimism (242). Because that note of bright hopefulness in *The American Commonwealth* verges on the risible to readers a century later, it is reassuring to note even the minimal critical insight that Brooks was able to muster concerning it. Brooks contended that Bryce's popularity in the United States "has much to do with" the fact that "the net judgment of this profound study should be (I cannot help using the word) so *doggedly* hopeful." "The serenity of the author's optimism falls in with that most persistent trait of the American character, hopefulness" (241).

This feeble effort at criticism lost its bite, however, when Brooks tried to explain the reasons behind Bryce's dogged hopefulness. "The main ground of Mr. Bryce's optimism about us is our inveterate, underlying hopefulness," he tried to argue (242). That is to say, the grounding of Bryce's optimism about the American people was the optimism of the American people. A second source of hope was America's democratic educational system "as it acts upon public opinion." Thus, all of the "shadows" that Bryce observed in the American polity seemed to dissipate—"they neither discourage nor seriously alarm him"—when viewed through such a hopeful lens, and the reader was left with the sense of the "cheer" exuded by Bryce's volumes (252).

Few commentators would accuse Tocqueville of dogged hopefulness. Brooks came close, however, in the generally optimistic approach he took throughout his study to the question of America's then current social problems. And although Brooks awarded the laurel for greatest foreign critic to

Bryce, he also displayed a deep admiration for Tocqueville. That is to say, unlike Dicey he did not feel he had to deprecate Tocqueville as part of a strategy for elevating Bryce.

As Others See Us supports the idea that Tocqueville was both well known and highly respected during the Progressive Era. No indication of exoticism or oblivion emerges from Brooks's pages, just straightforward exposition and analysis, combined with the same thoroughgoing presentism that he brought to the discussion of his other subjects. In the case of Tocqueville, however, the presentist temptation was even stronger than for the others, for *Democracy in America* was, for him, virtually a point of departure for a full understanding of the most pressing issues of early twentieth-century social reform. "It adds to the impressiveness of de Tocqueville's faith in our destinies that with all his continuous study of the United States until the time of his death, his confidence increased rather than diminished" (169), Brooks argued, again counter to a large body of evidence. This "converted aristocrat" (158) had displayed "a prophetic insight" (150) into the nature of our social problems, and because it had been so prophetic, his analysis was also enduringly relevant. Like more recent journalists and commentators who focus upon the unanswerable question of what Tocqueville would say, do, favor, or deplore if he were alive today, Brooks remade Tocqueville into a Progressive reformer—indeed into kind of forerunner of Herbert Croly, whose *The Promise of American Life* was published the same year as *As Others See Us*. "The level from which de Tocqueville speaks is that of the National Whole and the Common Welfare. He has not in mind temporary interests; much less mere private interests" (162), he wrote in approximately the middle of his chapter, the remainder of which he devoted to examples of the importance of applying such a perspective to contemporary social problems ranging from conservation to race relations to the trusts. Brooks subtitled his book "a study of progress in the United States," and in the figure of Tocqueville, he presented his strongest claim for the durability of Progressive social and political ideals. By transforming Tocqueville into a Progressive—translating Tocqueville's prose, as it were, into the present tense—Brooks also placed him in proximity to the camp of the American optimists: "As we follow his pages, we see our troubles as through mists, but the mists are radiant and the light of a great hope shoots through them" (155).

At the time, the reality was very different. While writers only infrequently referred to Tocqueville's empirical observations, they continued to praise his analytical acumen. In his comprehensive, authoritative, and widely influential *History of Political Theories* (1920), for example, Columbia University's

William A. Dunning explained how and why Tocqueville "established a new canon in political science." The "observations" of Tocqueville to which Dunning specifically referred were not ethnographic but structural, not remarks about what he witnessed or heard about American society but inferences concerning "the workings of democratic governments under a written constitution."[10]

Dunning was probably the most influential political scientist in America in 1920. His own connections to the Tocqueville legacy, while indirect, were nevertheless significant. If Francis Lieber was the "father of political science in America," his successor in his endowed chair at Columbia University, John W. Burgess, was its consolidator and first important institution builder. Although their philosophies diverged somewhat, with Lieber's Kantian emphasis on law or universal formulas contrasting with Burgess's Hegelian stress on the formation of the American nation, Burgess was a worthy holder of Lieber's chair at Columbia.[11] As an administrator he also left a deep mark on his field. Burgess founded the School of Political Science at Columbia in 1880 and built it by 1900 into the leading center of political research and teaching in the United States.

Burgess was a fervent adherent of Teutonism in historical scholarship and of Germany's state development in politics. While a student in Berlin, he had been thrilled to witness the Prussian army march past in review just after its awesome victory in the Franco-Prussian War. "It was," he recalled, "more to us [students] to see the power of the new Germany make its triumphal entrance into the new imperial capital than to have heard a few lectures which we would have only partially understood. It gave us a more correct conception of the new Germany than we could ever have obtained from the reading of books or the hearing of lectures and addresses." Burgess shared numerous political preoccupations, ideas, and prejudices with his predecessor Lieber, but without the latter's breadth of achievement or bluff bonhomie. Another important influence on Burgess was Johann Bluntschli, member of the celebrated "Scientific Clover Leaf" with whom Burgess studied in Germany, and whose own ideas owe such a debt to those of Lieber.[12]

The most brilliant graduate student of Burgess's early Columbia years was Dunning. Upon Burgess's recommendation, Dunning was appointed the first holder of the Francis Lieber Professorship of History and Political Philosophy at Columbia, making him, as it were, third in a line of succession. Dunning came to be known most widely for his role in promoting a now thoroughly discredited narrative of the Reconstruction period, both through his own book on the subject, *Reconstruction, Political and Economic, 1865–1877*

(1907), which he prepared for the prestigious American Nation series, and through of the work of his several talented Southern-bred graduate students, such as Mildred C. Thompson and J. G. de Roulhac Hamilton, who formed a veritable "Dunning School" with their state studies depicting a helpless white South in the grip of political regimes dominated by incompetent, corrupt, racially inferior freedmen. Dunning's scholarly reputation has been molded by this perception, which is somewhat justified, but also misleading insofar as it is based more on work by his students than by himself and focuses too narrowly on one aspect of a wide-ranging scholarly career. Regrettably, his book on Reconstruction is one of the laziest volumes in an otherwise distinguished series. An astute study by Philip R. Muller has shown just how little real research, or even careful writing, Dunning devoted to that volume. Muller concluded that Dunning "never saw it as a serious scholarly chore requiring a significant investment of time or energy."[13]

On the other hand, Dunning lavished enormous energy and years of research and writing on a project that he did consider to be of serious scholarly importance, a three-volume *History of Political Theories* published between 1904 and 1920. It is a work, Muller wrote in 1974, "of enduring value to students of the subject."[14] After the second volume was published in 1905, fifteen years went into the making of the third, most important one, *From Rousseau to Spencer*, and this culminating work exudes a balance, grace, and unaffected accessibility that mark it as a crowning achievement. In this, the standard history-of-ideas text of its age, Dunning portrayed Tocqueville as an "amazingly acute and judicious" political theorist. Indeed, the Frenchman's "acute observation and brilliant literary expression established a new canon in political science." Dunning did not hesitate to hold Tocqueville up to direct comparison with the most exalted of the ancient and Renaissance political thinkers from Aristotle to Niccolò Machiavelli. It was Tocqueville, he said, who articulated such major categories of modern political thought as the judicial function and administrative decentralization, "issues first brought into prominence among European thinkers by the descriptions and eulogies framed by Tocqueville. From his time to the present day they have been continuously in the focus of historical, constitutional, and juristic discussion."[15]

The summer after Dunning's history appeared, a young, charismatic Army veteran with an "unusually vivid personality" named Paul Lambert White made an astonishing discovery in Normandy: the manuscripts of Alexis de Tocqueville. White was a Hoosier who migrated east at the age of twenty in order to enroll in Bowdoin College. From the time of his graduation from

Bowdoin in 1914 until his shockingly premature death from appendicitis only eight years later at the age of thirty-two, White's life was dominated by the Great War and its aftermath. He became one of the great American Francophiles of the early twentieth century. Out of his contagious enthusiasm, there gradually emerged a treasury of scholarship whose dimensions could scarcely have been imagined when the war stumbled to its bitter close.

White moved south from Maine to Pennsylvania as war broke out in Europe. He received a master's degree in history from the University of Pennsylvania in 1916, then studied law for a while back in Indiana. The seeming lack of direction that his studies might indicate came to a sudden end with the American entry into the war. White was commissioned lieutenant and shipped off to France where he served as an aide-de-camp to Gen. Harry C. Hale of the Eighty-fourth Division. After the Armistice, White remained briefly in France for a period of study in Paris at the Sorbonne and, by 1920, was an instructor in history at Yale, as well as the husband of Helen van Keuren; they were married in June of that year. It was during the following summer that White returned to France and met Tocqueville's heir.

George Wilson Pierson rather fancifully reconstructed the events that followed in a 1976 public lecture.

> And so presently there was the young Yale instructor sitting down on the terrace outside the old turreted chateau in Normandy, near Cherbourg, with Comte Crétien de Tocqueville, the great-nephew of Alexis, and talking about White's enthusiasm and Franco-American relations, and what he hoped to be able to do, and weren't there papers and wouldn't he be allowed to use them? . . . Minutes went by and the Comte was polite but totally uninterested. At the end of the hour, out from under the great triple arch of the stables, a groom led a horse for the Comte's morning constitutional and Paul White took a look at the horse and said, "What a magnificent animal!" "Hein? You are interested in horses? Would you like to come ride with me?" So they went riding together and, after the second hour, White had access to the Tocqueville papers, access into the tower *chartrier* where Tocqueville had worked.[16]

In the fall of 1922, the *Yale Review* published a jumble of juicy quotations that White had assembled from Tocqueville's previously unexamined notebooks in order to open a window on American mores during the age of Jackson. The article produces an unsettling effect, for its lightness of tone clashes jarringly with the darkly censorious content of Tocqueville's observations.

The *Democracy*, White wrote, "has been a source of pride and instruction among us for nearly a century."[17] But until White wrote, no one had seen and reported on the private correspondence, as well as the diary and note-book entries, out of which that work had emerged. White's debunking pur-pose in the *Yale Review* piece was to point out the contrasts between the "pride and instruction" that the *Democracy* had so long provided and the disparaging, even harsh, responses to Americans that Tocqueville had con-fided to his private journals. White's own authorial approach, however, placed him in an antagonistic relationship to the object he tried to accom-plish. That is to say, he tried to present a gently bemused authorial persona of himself, the writer of the article, while building up a portrayal of a Tocque-ville who was repulsed by American manners. And unquestionably, White's portrait of Tocqueville is of a much less sympathetic character than the typi-cal image that Tocqueville had come to possess since the mid-nineteenth century. Tocqueville's popularity, after all, had been due in no small part to his purported curiosity and openness to American manners and mores, in obvious contrast to such foreign visitors as Charles Dickens and Mrs. Anthony Trollope, who, Americans complained, had been unable to see beyond the bad food, coarse manners, poor roads, and crude accommoda-tions they had to endure in their own heroic forays onto American soil. White, by contrast, argued that "Tocqueville saw with much the same eyes as Mrs. Trollope" (129). But, because Tocqueville's published reflections conveyed such an impression of "integrity and generosity" and "keenness as an observer" (129), the disparaging observations that fill his notebooks and letters must come as a surprise. Tocqueville "has so long been thought of as a solemn commentator on our institutions," White contended, "that it is difficult to cast him in another role—that of an amused recorder of the lighter side of American life" (116). According to White, Tocqueville viewed Americans as lacking in humor, devoid of imagination, and glaringly deficient in plain good manners (except in Boston), in addition to being greedy, "socially pretentious" (125), and excessively religious. In short, White argued that Tocqueville's response to America was one that rein-forced, rather than contradicted, the harping criticisms of the Trollopes and Dickenses.

This odd and internally contradictory article provides a useful signpost indicating the direction that White would probably have gone in with the wealth of material that he had gathered. It was a different direction from the one taken by his successor, Pierson. But White died one month before his article appeared in print.

Pierson had been working on the Tocqueville manuscripts for many years under the direction of John Allison at Yale. Indeed, *Tocqueville and Beaumont in America* began as his dissertation. It had at least a local notoriety, because the dissertation itself, which made up the book's first eight chapters, was awarded the prestigious John Addison Porter University Prize in 1933. When the book was published Pierson was an assistant professor of history at Yale. He was promoted to associate the following year at the age of thirty-five.[18]

In the decade and a half between the appearance of White's article and the publication of Pierson's *Tocqueville and Beaumont in America*, formal academic articles on Tocqueville began to appear in the fairly new outlet of the scholarly journals. One of the first, appearing in the same year as White's, was a comparative study by William Henry George of Tocqueville's adaptation of Montesquieu, the first such article on this important topic. Now long surpassed by the definitive study on the subject by Melvin Richter in 1970,[19] the essay is nevertheless of some historical interest, largely because George engaged with contemporary forms of radical political theory, that of syndicalism in particular. The essay, however, was almost pure exposition; the only references were to *La Démocratie en Amérique* and *l'Esprit des Lois* directly, except for the first two footnotes. George constructed a far-ranging contrast of a "'corporative' (in contrast with a pulverized) society," corporative in this case signifying a society made up of intermediary bodies. "De Tocqueville," George pointed out, was "the first publicist in France to make an adaptation of Montesquieu's doctrine." He offered a fine exposition of Tocqueville's concept of democratic despotism and closed with a call for a form of "administrative syndicalism" to "render the syndicalists' protest without substantial foundation in fact." "They [the syndicalists] represent a protest against centralized, unitary and authoritative political control," George somewhat naively concluded. "So does De Tocqueville."[20]

Tocqueville made his appearance in discussions of literary theory, as well. In 1926, Katherine Harrison was the first to draw attention to the ways in which the poetry of Walt Whitman conformed to Tocqueville's prediction in Volume II of the *Democracy* that Americans would produce a literature that focused not on society but "on man alone." Had Tocqueville read *Leaves of Grass*, Harrison wrote, he "would have felt that the real American poetry was beginning. Whitman fulfills miraculously the Frenchman's prophecy; he is the representative democratic poet." Sixty years later, Cushing Strout pointed to Harrison's article as "the first to cite Whitman as proof of Tocqueville's prescience." Undoubtedly, he carefully called it "the first," because Strout's old teacher, Lionel Trilling, had also noted the phenomenon in 1945, when, in a review of the Bradley edition of *Democracy in America*, he described Tocqueville's speculations on democratic poetry as "a precise account of Whitman before *Leaves of Grass* had been conceived."[21] Here as elsewhere, Strout distinguished himself among Tocqueville commentators between 1970 and 2000 by being almost alone in looking back at the Tocqueville literature of the early twentieth century. Even Richter, unquestionably among the giants of twentieth-century Tocqueville scholarship, paid no attention in his Montesquieu essay to the aforementioned study by George.

In 1928, the *Romanic Review* at Columbia University published correspondence between Tocqueville and such American informants and friends as Jared Sparks, John C. Spencer, and Charles Sumner. The letters had been discovered at Harvard University and the Historical Society of Pennsylvania, and while not of fundamental importance to the state of Tocqueville scholarship as it stood at the time they did reveal that Yale's collection gathered by White contained some gaps. In an opening footnote that could not have escaped Pierson's attention, the scholar who found the letters, Richmond Laurin Hawkins, wrote, "The existing biographies of Tocqueville are antiquated and incomplete. . . . Tocqueville's published correspondence with Frenchmen and Englishmen is fairly abundant; his correspondence with Americans is virtually inedited."[22]

The 1938 appearance of Pierson's volume, then, rather than being seen at the time as rescuing Tocqueville from oblivion and thereby demarcating a rigid boundary between two distinct epochs in the history of Tocqueville's reception, was instead saluted as a superlative achievement within an established, ongoing field of study. The reviews of *Tocqueville and Beaumont in America* are almost uniform in this regard. Of fifteen reviews that appeared immediately after its publication in the major journals, newspapers, and magazines, ten made specific reference to Tocqueville's *Democracy* as famous, familiar, well-known, a classic, universally recognized as "one of the world's great books," or other such expressions indicating widespread knowledge of the author and his "famous journey." The *Atlantic Monthly* reviewer summed up much of the contemporary sentiment when he said that the *Democracy* was superior to Bryce's tome and was a book that "has been world-famous for a hundred years," while the editor of *New York History* wrote, echoing the most common response, "Every well-informed political scientist of today knows the work well. Few persons, however, know the genesis of that critical study, and this work supplies the explanation."[23]

Four reviewers situated Pierson's book in the larger context of centennial events; that is, they specifically discussed not merely the fact that *Tocqueville and Beaumont in America* issued from the Oxford University Press one hundred years after the *Democracy* appeared in an American edition, but that its publication was but one episode in an ongoing series of events that marked the appearance of Tocqueville's masterpiece. Indeed, the mid-1930s, prior to the publication of *Tocqueville and Beaumont in America,* had seen the publication of many centennial Tocqueville articles: one by Pierson himself, as well as others by Albert Salomon, David S. Muzzey, William Lingelbach, Harold W. Stoke, Phillips Bradley, and Matthew Josephson, all in major scholarly journals.[24] The most imposing of such centennial commemorations, however, occurred on June 27, 1935, when Tocqueville's great-great-nephew, Comte Jean de Tocqueville, accompanied by André Le Febvre de Laboulaye, who was the French ambassador to the United States and Édouard de Laboulaye's grandson, presented a bust of Tocqueville to President Franklin Roosevelt in a ceremony at the White House.[25]

Several *Tocqueville and Beaumont* reviewers drew specific attention to the legacy of White, to whose memory Pierson had dedicated the book with a generous inscription. Robert Spiller and Crane Brinton both mentioned the young veteran's manuscript discoveries and his early death. Gilbert Chinard alluded to this and other commemorative proceedings in his *Yale Review* notice: "Recent centenary commemorations have again attracted attention to Tocqueville's great book, 'Democracy in America.' Among the several studies published in connection with them, none stands so high in scholarly merit as this contribution by Mr. Pierson." Other intellectuals who sounded the centennial theme—such as Bradley, Lingelbach, and Salomon—had themselves published valuable studies of Tocqueville in the preceding two or three years. That is, they were contributors to the very centennial events to which they drew attention.[26]

One scholar who included all of these threads of discourse into his review—the *Democracy*'s enduring fame, the centennial observations, and White's pioneering labors—and whose review might therefore be said to typify responses to Pierson just before World War II—was Lingelbach, the dean of the University of Pennsylvania's College of Arts and Sciences (and, after the war, the innovative archivist and librarian of the American Philosophical Society). The frequently told tale of Tocqueville and Beaumont's expedition, Lingelbach wrote, "is here retold with a freshness and finality." He judged that the true value of Pierson's book lay in its uncovering of Tocqueville's source materials rather than in an exposition of Tocqueville's political philosophy. Those were the sources "in the possession of the Tocqueville family to which Paul Lambert White some years ago was first given access." Lingelbach indeed had probably known White, for the latter had received an advanced degree in history at the University of Pennsylvania while Lingelbach was on the history faculty.[27]

While his response to Pierson's book was generally favorable, Lingelbach's review revealed a vague sense of dissatisfaction. The book was repetitious and just too long. In his concluding paragraph, Lingelbach wrote of his own partiality in the matter of Tocqueville's usefulness. "In these days of new ideologies and plebiscitarian dictatorships," he urged, "*Tocqueville and Beaumont in America* should stimulate a renewal of interest in the great foreign commentators on American democracy, for the legacy of Tocqueville's teachings in the education of Americans has by no means been exhausted."[28]

Lingelbach's emphasis on dictatorship and centennial grew out of his own previous scholarly work, for he had only recently produced an important essay on Tocqueville that he explicitly situated in that commemorative, centennial mode. A year and a half before *Tocqueville and Beaumont in America* appeared, Lingelbach wrote that the great merit of Tocqueville lay in his "prophetic" character, especially "in the light of the appearance of the postwar totalitarian states in Europe, not to mention the drift in that direction in other states." (It was Lingelbach who, however unintentionally, was being prophetic here: that sentence is a prototype of some of the Tocqueville commentary that was written well after World War II, not in 1937.) As a young professor, Lingelbach had been stranded in Russia when World War I broke out, and he had written one of the early American accounts of the Russian Revolution. Anticipating the theme of his Pierson review, Lingelbach emphasized the "philosophical analysis" that Tocqueville brought to bear on his subject, a contribution that he considered to be of greater long-term significance than "the historical picture" that Tocqueville had presented in 1835. Because of that analysis, Lingelbach wrote, the *Democracy* "will always assure to its author a foremost place among our historians and political theorists."[29]

Other Pierson reviewers who were already becoming prominent names in the Tocqueville scholarship were Phillips Bradley and Albert Salomon. Like Lingelbach, both of them had written centennial essays in the previous couple of years. Bradley, of course, was soon to make his reputation as the most influential *Democracy* editor since Francis Bowen. Bradley built a fascinating career around the edges of political philosophy and history, not in those fields. Indeed, a striking feature of Bradley's career is the fact that he was not by professional affiliation either a historian or a political theorist. His first article on Tocqueville described Tocqueville's book, in what would become stupefyingly clichéd terms, as "the most delightful, and in many ways the most penetrating, study of American life."[30]

Bradley, born in 1894, received his bachelor's degree from Harvard in 1916 and served in the Navy in World War I. During the 1920s, he taught at Wellesley and Amherst, but spent a great deal of those years in London. Awarded a Carnegie Fellowship to the University of London in 1928, he studied economics and labor relations. He earned a Ph.D. from the London School of Economics in 1936. Evidence indicates that Bradley was a restless, perhaps somewhat abrasive, character. Rather than settling into a stable career at one top institution, he bounced from one first-rate university to another after receiving his Ph.D. In the two decades after he left London, Bradley taught at Vassar College, Queens College, the New School, Cornell University, the University of Illinois, and Syracuse University. In none of these positions did he work in the field of political philosophy or history. Rather, his area was public administration with a specialty in labor and industrial relations. When he moved to Cornell in 1945, it was to take up the position of director of extension programs and professor of industrial and labor relations at Cornell's School of Industrial Relations. The next year, he moved to the University of Illinois, where he directed that university's School of Industrial and Labor Relations. Forced out of this post in 1950, he obtained a position at Syracuse University's Maxwell School of Citizenship and Public Affairs, then as now one of the nation's leading institutions of public administration.[31] Bradley, in short, was not making his career and reputation as a scholar of Tocqueville, meticulous and useful as his Knopf edition of the Democracy was, but as a student of modern industry. Surprising though it may seem to students and teachers of the Democracy, Bradley's obituaries were almost completely silent concerning his edition of Tocqueville's masterwork.

Evidently Bradley liked Pierson's book quite well, for he reviewed it twice. The pair of reviews, like all of Bradley's prose, convey little information about his own ideas and tend to substitute platitudes for analysis. Taken together, they also echo the themes of other scholars, Lingelbach in particular. Classifying Pierson's work as "a fitting centennial tribute to the first American edition of Tocqueville's Democracy in America," Bradley emphasized the degree to which Pierson had eschewed analysis of Tocqueville's political thought in favor of travel narrative and description of American manners and customs. "The main outlines of Tocqueville's visit to America are well known," Bradley wrote. "What Professor Pierson has done is to weave the day-to-day activities" of Tocqueville and Beaumont into a detailed account.

Bradley's centennial article on the *Democracy* appeared in the same month as Lingelbach's. Bradley was a painstaking scholar and assiduous researcher, but he was more of a compiler of data than an analyst of the material he collected. Fifty years after Bradley's *Democracy* edition appeared, the political theorist Alan Ryan rightly said of his appendices and bibliography that "any serious scholar of Tocqueville will still find these serious and interesting"—but Ryan chose to exclude them from his own reprint edition of the 1945 *Democracy*.[32] Given such reticence, Bradley's modest 1937 article is of some interest, because in it he said more about political theory than in all the one hundred pages of his *Democracy* appendix. After marking the centennial of the *Democracy*'s appearance, Bradley moved directly to the issue of the book's lasting importance, which lay, Bradley wrote, in the author's having attended "not only to the study of American institutions but also to the principles and practices of democracy everywhere." Tocqueville "had translated a single episode into universal terms."[33]

One of Bradley's colleagues during his three years at the New School, years during which he completed much of the work for his edition of *Democracy in America*, was the great sociologist Albert Salomon. Salomon typified a group of Central European immigrant intellectuals, often Jewish refugees, fascinated by Tocqueville's defense of liberty and repelled by the emergence of totalitarian states with their monstrous myths of race and history, who were about to assume prominent roles in the field of Tocqueville studies. Salomon, like Bradley, had been deeply engaged in studying the problems of the working class and industrial relations. Born in Germany just a few months after Bismarck's departure from the great arena of statesmanship, Salomon studied "the science of society" at Heidelberg, the academic home of such predecessors as Johann Bluntschli, H. B. Adams, and John W. Burgess. He received his Ph.D. in 1921 at the age of thirty. Salomon would go on to experience some of Germany's and Europe's bitterest tragedies, while barely escaping from others. A member of a significant, if not politically powerful, group of intellectuals in the German Social Democratic Party, Salomon served as editor of the party's social scientific journal *Die Gesellschaft* between 1928 and 1931. Salomon's socialist convictions were deeply important to his formation, but, as he said in later years, he would "come to experience his 'Jewish existence as destiny.'"[34]

As a socialist intellectual and a Jew, Salomon became perforce an exile as well. Salomon met Hannah Arendt in Paris in 1933; she pleaded with him to leave Europe for the United States. His departure two years later must in small part have come from Arendt's example.[35] Finally fleeing his native Germany, then, he arrived in New York in 1935 and took up a post at the New School, that haven for Central European scholars and, by virtue of that status, one of the great sources of the enrichment of American intellectual life in the twentieth century. Salomon's last endeavor before leaving Europe was to edit, with commentary and introduction, a volume of selections from Tocqueville's works. The house of Rascher in Zurich published the tome, and it was to the best of my knowledge the first appearance of Tocqueville in the German language in the twentieth century.[36]

Salomon's arrival in America coincided exactly with his first scholarly publication in English, which was an authoritative, pioneering essay on Tocqueville on the occasion of the centennial of the publication of *Democracy in America*. Published in the journal *Social Research* in November 1935, Salomon's article remains, in the twenty-first century, a point of departure for anyone wishing to consider Tocqueville as more than an ethnographer. Reflecting his life experience and his dark times, Salomon presented a deep and nuanced view of his subject. "[Tocqueville's] optimism concerning democracy is to be explained only as a pedagogic and didactic attempt," Salomon contended. "The actual content of all his work is deeply pessimistic as to the future of political and social development."[37]

Salomon always wished, in the words of Thucydides that he quoted in 1962, "not to become shrewder next time, but wise forever."[38] Salomon mingled his Marxist and his Tocquevillean outlook, coming during the 1950s to view Tocqueville as a kind of "conservative Marxist": conservative because his critique of modernity came from a unique perspective on the advantages of the past and from an aristocratic perspective; Marxist because, first, of his radical critique of the bourgeoisie and, second, because he viewed social classes rather than individuals as being the key historical actors. Yet, Salomon's Tocqueville was also—this essay having been written in 1959—an existentialist, because, like Friedrich Nietzsche, Jean-Paul Sartre, and Albert Camus, he understood the inward universe of passions and freedom to constitute the milieu of human thought and action.[39]

The prestige and deference accorded to Bradley's edition of the *Democracy* was not contemporaneous with its 1945 publication but was a later development. Indeed, for all its later renown, the Bradley edition was met at the time of its appearance with a courteous but surprisingly muted welcome. Toward Tocqueville himself and his celebrated book praise was universal and unwavering, but the package in which the Frenchman's classic study was wrapped was more variably received. Reviews in the scholarly journals ranged from tepid to hostile; moreover there was a clear correlation between the care taken by the reviewer and the degree of harshness in his response.

Some reviewers settled for descriptive accounts of the volumes' contents combined with vague formulas about the timeliness of their appearance. "Both the editor and the publisher seem to have been moved by something of Tocqueville's sense of obligation and lofty purpose in making available this distinguished edition," Southern historian Charles S. Sydnor wrote. Whatever the precise intent of that sentence, it falls in with the most common theme of the reviews, namely Tocqueville's immediate, transparent relevance to problems and opportunities faced by a world utterly transformed by the most massive and deadly war in human history. Indeed, if the discussion of Tocqueville became so insistently focused on his current relevance in the second half of the twentieth century, that particular emphasis arose from the fact that the *Democracy*, appearing as it did almost simultaneously with the end of the war in Europe, was held by every commentator on record to be important precisely and primarily because of its purported messages to the world of 1945. "It is hard to believe that the first section of *Democracy in America* appeared 110 years ago," wrote Paul Kiniery in the *Catholic Historical Review*, "much of it might have been written within the past year, so applicable is it."[40]

But most Tocqueville experts were far from enchanted with Bradley's efforts. Anticipating themes of later reviews directed at other new translations—and continuing the pattern inaugurated by the caustic Bowen in 1862—these reviewers raised the perfectly sensible question of why the Henry Reeve translation had been resurrected in the first place. Some of them also criticized the wooden, undertheorized essay by Bradley by means of which the outdated text was supposed to be provided with a context meaningful to contemporary readers.

William Anderson was among the first to observe that Bradley's text, despite its tinkering with the Reeve-Bowen version, "still falls far short of excellence," and he furnished as many examples of those shortcomings as the word limit of his book-review format would allow. Typical of the negative reviews that greeted the Bradley version was Anderson's insistence on "the great merit of de Tocqueville's masterpiece," alongside the conclusion that, notwithstanding such merit, "there is still need of a completely new American translation."[41] Unfortunately, when George Lawrence did provide that translation two decades later, his massive labors were met with a similar skepticism.

Anderson devoted most of his review to a critique of the *Democracy*'s translation and a few lukewarm words of commendation for the introduction; Donald J. Pierce in the *American Sociological Review*, by contrast, blasted the introduction while more gently criticizing the translation itself.[42] But it was left to Thomas I. Cook in the *American Historical Review* to gather up these two strands of criticism in one tight fist and strike it hard on the seminar table. Cook noted an important but overlooked fact (again, in contradistinction to those who point to the *Democracy*'s having been out of print as evidence of Tocqueville's neglect), namely that "secondhand copies of previous editions and translations are still readily available at modest prices," and therefore "a new two-volume edition, selling at six dollars, has to justify itself by cogent virtues." This, Cook believed, the Bradley volumes signally failed to do. Any new edition "should either be a new, and a better, translation, or it should be preceded by an introduction which adds to scholarly knowledge or gives new philosophical or historical information. Unfortunately, the present work meets neither of these criteria." Cook's dismay was intense enough to cause him to stray onto the path of prediction, something historians are well advised to avoid. So flawed was the Reeve-Bowen text, even as revised by Bradley, Cook thought, that "I venture to suggest that the widespread distribution and reading of this work, through a popular edition, is unlikely unless and until a really effective modern translation is made." He was, to put it mildly, proven wrong on this point. But Cook went beyond expressions of dismay at the translation's flaws; he was equally harsh concerning the shortcomings of Bradley's "unilluminating and uninspired" introduction, which he thought made no contribution to the scholarship; nor was it "a masterly philosophical disquisition" such as Tocqueville deserved and needed; nor even a popular, accessible introductory essay.

Cook put forward a second forecast that proved to be more valid than his first: "It is perhaps to be feared that the appearance and existence of this edition will prevent rather than encourage" a wholly new translation, he wrote. About this point he was exactly right: just six years after Bradley's volumes appeared, the definitive French edition of *De la démocratie* was completed under the auspices of the national commission set up to oversee the publication of Tocqueville's complete works. But fifteen years would elapse before English readers would be able to enjoy a translation made from that French original. Surely the sway of the flawed Bradley edition was one reason they had to wait so long.[43]

Indeed, the marketing behavior of academic publishers was almost as reliable a gauge of Tocqueville's stature as were the opinions of professional experts. In the second half of the twentieth century, the publishers' relationship to Tocqueville stretched across the tiny spectrum from the savvy to the cynical. In its treatment of Pierson's *Tocqueville and Beaumont in America*, the Johns Hopkins University Press fell squarely into the latter category. When it picked up the text of Pierson's book after it had entered the public domain in 1996, the Press expunged Beaumont from the volume almost entirely, and when it did grant him a marginal role, did so in ways that actually underscored the cynicism of his exclusion.

In 1968, Seymour Drescher published a thoughtful and convincing essay advocating that scholars should study Beaumont and Tocqueville *jointly*. While conducting his own research in Harvard's Widener Library in 1964, Drescher had had occasion to examine Jared Sparks's first-edition copy of Beaumont and Tocqueville's *Du Système pénitentiare*, published in Paris in 1833. There Drescher found, pasted inside the back cover, an advertisement for a forthcoming joint work by the same two authors to be entitled *Institutions et moeurs Américains*. The story of how this joint project came to be disaggregated (with Tocqueville going on to write the *Democracy* and Beaumont his novel *Marie*) is now well known, but the enduring partnership of these two lifelong comrades is a firmly established fact. "It would be pointless," Drescher contended, "to attempt to disentangle the fabric of Tocqueville and Beaumont's social thought in order to allot credit for each insight which found its way into print over the name of one or the other. . . . [M]any of their ideas were discussed at length before either, or both, attempted to put them down on paper. During their journeys to America and England dialogue almost always preceded travelogue. This process was so clearly the rule that it is often impossible to discover who originated a given idea." The intimacy of Tocqueville's and Beaumont's ideas mirrored that of their friendship, as such contemporaries as Jean-Jacques Ampère and Heinrich Heine noted. "These two inseparables whom we always see joined together, in their travels, in their publications, in the Chamber of Deputies, perfect each other superbly," Heine wrote. And as James T. Schleifer pointed out in his study of the *Democracy*, the great Yale Tocqueville manuscripts collection was "based on the premise that the lives of Tocqueville and Beaumont are inseparable."[44]

Pierson himself made a strong argument for the same position. During his long years of research, he said in a lecture at Yale, he had reached the conclusion that "Beaumont had played a very large role in this trip and that he and Tocqueville had exchanged thoughts and ideas and discoveries and often it wasn't possible to tell who had first had an idea."[45] No doubt Pierson had carefully chosen his title to reflect this very theme. But Pierson's obvious preference was irrelevant to the Hopkins Press as it tried to capitalize on Tocqueville's name without confusing potential buyers with the unfamiliar name of Tocqueville's companion. The book's 1996 title, then, was *Tocqueville in America*.

This blunt title was unnecessarily confusing for another reason. In 1959, the same year that Doubleday Anchor published John Lukacs's version of Tocqueville's history of the French Revolution and correspondence with Arthur de Gobineau, that ambitious publisher brought out an abridged version of Pierson's classic, with an abridged title: *Tocqueville in America*.[46] What Johns Hopkins did, therefore, was to reprint a classic book in its entirety and bestow on it the same title as that text's abridged version. Beaumont was thus erased from the title. And just as egregiously, the press eliminated about two-thirds of Beaumont's sketches, which in their charm and specificity of observation had made a significant contribution to Pierson's 1938 volume—but also, evidently, to the publisher's overhead.[47]

Oxford University Press was perhaps more lazy than cynical in the 1940s, but the result of its Tocqueville publication effort was even worse. The press placed an abridgement contract for *Democracy in America* in the seemingly capable hands of Henry Steele Commager, probably in 1944 or 1945, "a time when interest in America was high [in Great Britain], but paper short and leisure fleeting," as Commager put it. The volume was prepared as a contribution to Oxford's World Classics series. Unfortunately for Oxford, the publication of Commager's abridgement nearly coincided with the appearance of Bradley's revised Reeve-Bowen translation. From the scant published record, it is not clear whether Commager and Oxford knew the Bradley edition was bearing down on them, but Commager's edition indicates that Bradley had taken the standard 1862 Reeve-Bowen text out of circulation, because for the Oxford version Commager stretched all the way back to the original Reeve translations of 1835 and 1840, without even the benefit of the revisions that Bowen had made in 1862. When the Oxford edition came out in America in 1947, Commager lamely defended his choice of the Reeve text ("it seems to me to catch more the spirit and style of the original") while managing a dig at Bradley ("some day, perhaps, the long-needed new translation will be given us").

Taken as a whole, Commager's World Classics edition—published in the United States as a Galaxy Edition—was the worst version of Tocqueville ever made available by a major publisher. One might say its deficiency was overdetermined. There was, first of all, Reeve's execrable translation. Whatever the shortcomings of Bowen's and Bradley's revisions, they did improve a sloppy and inaccurate rendition. For the Oxford Press and Commager to revert in 1946 to the 1835–1840 Reeve translation must have been a decision stimulated by more than a paper shortage. And there was, in the second place, the matter of the abridgement itself. Although abridgement always involves a risky set of choices, it is by no means to be avoided as a matter of principle. Yet the passages Commager chose for excision reflected an astonishing absence of sensitivity to both Tocqueville's themes and to postwar America's needs. "There is no need, now," he wrote for the British edition, "to preserve the rather tiresome account of the geography, native races, colonial history, local and state government of the United States, and we can, too, easily dispense with the numerous digressions on contemporary France and the speculations on the future of the three races in the United States."[48] Thus, Commager presented a Tocqueville in the unvarnished Reeve translation who had nothing to say on the subjects of race relations, the colonial origins of American culture, how local government served as the basis of political culture, or the immediate relevance of American political culture to the question of the maintenance of freedom in France. And finally, Commager included an introduction that is among the most slapdash examples of that difficult genre in all the Tocqueville literature. It contains misprints so serious that they reduce some passages to nonsense. One has to conclude that Commager did not read the proofs for the phrase "its restless frontier, sweeping across the continent like the tides at St. Michael" (viii)— presumably a copy editor's "correction" of Saint Michel, a reference to the mighty ocean tides at Mont-Saint-Michel. Tocqueville's cousin and confidant Louis de Kergorlay was rendered as "Kergolat" (xvii). But the Commager introduction is mainly of interest to the intellectual historian as a handy compendium of the most worm-eaten Tocqueville clichés. "By common consent his *Democracy in America* is the most illuminating commentary on American character and institutions ever penned by a foreigner, the one which, a century after its appearance, seems best assured of immortality" (xi).

Another shoddy piece of publishing and marketing was perpetrated by the University of Missouri Press when, in 1993, it published a volume whose only evident purpose was to link two eminent names in its title, which was *Commager on Tocqueville*. The volume consisted of a half-dozen brief, fluffy lectures that Commager had delivered at the University of Missouri some fifteen years before. The press fleshed out the slender volume with, of all pieces, the introduction that Commager had written for the World Classics edition of the *Democracy* half a century earlier, but with no indication as to its prove-nance. Moreover, that introduction appeared precisely as it had been printed in 1946, letter for letter—tides of St. Michael, Kergolat, and all. No one at the press bothered even to correct the typos; indeed, the press added several of its own howlers to the text of the lectures: "Stirfells" for Eugène Stoeffels, for instance.[49]

The marketing of the Tocqueville name was raised to a new level of refinement by the Oxford University Press in the 1990s. Edward T. Gargan had produced *De Tocqueville*, a short, balanced, comprehensive overview of Tocqueville's works in 1965; published by a small British firm, Hillary House, its circulation was limited. Other entries in the genre of brief but wide-ranging introductions sporting Tocqueville's name as their titles (such titles are assigned by the publisher) included those by Hugh Brogan, Matthew Mancini, and Larry Siedentop. The last named volume appeared in Oxford's Past Masters series in 1994 and was entitled *Tocqueville*. A few years later, however, Oxford published a second entry in the Tocqueville overview mar-ket, this one entitled *De Tocqueville*.[50] The author of this volume, Cheryl Welch, produced one of the most thoughtful and accessible works of this type. Setting aside the quality of the book, however, one wonders how a twenty-first-century publisher could publish a book under such a title. The most obvious explanation was that Oxford marketers could not offer two books on its list entitled *Tocqueville* so the press commissioned one *Tocque-ville* and one *De Tocqueville*.

The question of proper usage in referring to our French sage—of whether to say De Tocqueville or Tocqueville—is one that has a long history in American letters. In 1880, Wendell Phillips and Bowen carried on a good-natured exchange in *Harper's Magazine* on the issue. "If, in speaking, you adhere to the rule, and say 'Tocqueville,' you are sure, the next morning, to find that in the report of your speech the careful and judicious editor has inserted the inevitable 'De,' and made you, in spite of yourself, a French ignoramus," Phillips complained. Bowen, unmoved and sarcastic as ever, allowed that Phillips "is not too old to learn, and if he will prosecute his studies, I doubt not that he will become a good French critic."[51] But in the late twentieth century, the question had long been definitively settled. Here is how Pierson allowed his exasperation with the issue to show in "a mini-lecture":

Gentlemen, ladies, the name is Tocqueville. You may call him Monsieur de Tocque-ville, Alexis de Tocqueville, Comte de Tocqueville, but if you leave out the titles or the first name, it is plain Tocqueville; you don't put in the "de," just as we said Beaumont, not de Beaumont. This is the French rule. . . . It has one exception, one major exception. If, and I will finish my lecture in a moment, if it is a one-syllable name then you use the "de"—and you knew that: you speak of de Gaulle but you say Lafayette.[52]

Throughout her study, Welch always referred to her subject as Tocqueville.

Tocqueville played a role in several celebrated books of the mid to late 1950s that retrospectively came to be included in the spurious category known as consensus history. Prominent among them was Marvin Meyers's *The Jacksonian Persuasion: Politics and Belief* (1957), an effort to identify and analyze the elements that made up the shared ideology of Andrew Jackson's supporters between 1820 and 1841. Meyers's view of Jacksonian "false consciousness," as John William Ward called it in a review in the *American Quarterly*, was that the age of Jackson had solidified the ideal of the independent republican citizen bearing the hallmarks of republican virtue, while at the same time it ushered in the epoch of unbridled capitalism with its concomitant urges to consumption and display which were universally understood to undermine the very republican citizenship that had brought it into being. Meyers was one of the few historians actually to place Tocqueville near the center of his analysis. He distilled the essence of Tocqueville's discussion of American mores into a formula for understanding characteristic types of American behavior. Americans were "venturous conservatives" during the age of Jackson, he said. Meyers forthrightly defended the use of the *Democracy* as a form of ethnography. In his estimation, Tocqueville's masterpiece provided "a key" to understanding the Jacksonian era; consequently, "my study . . . attempts an extended development of Tocqueville's lead."[53]

The Jacksonian Persuasion garnered twenty scholarly reviews upon publication, making it one of the major works on American studies of the late 1950s. In general, the sociologists and political scientists liked Meyers's analysis better than the historians did. In the *American Political Science Review*, Cecelia M. Kenyon called it "a book of rare distinction," its analysis "sustained, perceptive, precise." Such distinguished social scientists as Sigmund Diamond and Irving Kristol concurred. Kristol invited readers to "a priceless initiation into what is most American in American politics." Historians, by contrast, were more restrained and skeptical, even though they generally remained favorable to the book. Arthur M. Schlesinger Jr., to whose *Age of Jackson* (1947) *The Jacksonian Persuasion* was in some measure a response, depicted a

Meyers myopically captivated by his own ideological creation—"so bemused by [his] theory of Jacksonian democracy . . . that he fails to see that it also cleared the path for government intervention in the economy." But it was Roy F. Nichols of the University of Pennsylvania, distinguished equally as teacher and writer, who pointed to the book's real flaw in the eyes of historians, namely that it "concentrat[ed] attention solely on a few spectacular national 'leaders' who were, in reality, often only the instruments of more potent but obscure local operators." Of the several prominent historians who reviewed the book, only Charles G. Sellers furnished an unequivocally positive opinion.[54]

A broader thematic net was cast by another Tocqueville-themed book of the period, David Riesman's *The Lonely Crowd* (1950), the social science bestseller of the 1950s. Riesman made no secret of his reliance on Tocqueville as he understood him, and he consulted with Bradley while he was writing the book.[55] The special quality of his use of Tocqueville was indicated in a 1958 lecture at the University of Chicago wherein Riesman spoke of the *Democracy* as a brilliant thought-experiment rather than a descriptive undertaking: "In envisaging what an 'ideal' (that is, complete) democracy would be like were it to go further in the American direction . . . [Tocqueville] imagined himself into the mind of a citizen of such a nonexistent land and pictured for himself how all aspects of life . . . would look to such a hypothetical person."[56] Whether that is really what Tocqueville was attempting to accomplish in the *Democracy* is, like so many such assertions by later scholars who made use of Tocqueville's insights, open to serious question, but it certainly was what drove Riesman's arguments in *The Lonely Crowd*, for thirty years later, he described Tocqueville's method as a "willingness to speculate about what the country might be like if it became even more egalitarian and democratic than the America into which he unevenly inquired in 183[1]."[57] Riesman, then, saw himself, in part, as having followed Tocqueville's lead in projecting ideal-typical character types and connecting those types to specific changes in economic and demographic trends.

Yet contemporary reviews of *The Lonely Crowd* ignored the Tocquevillean theme. Reviewers were instead struck by the sheer sweep of Riesman's claims and by the apparently cross-disciplinary links he had been able to forge between hard demographic analysis and soft descriptions of character development. Not a few social scientists, however, refused to be drawn in and sharply criticized the book for lacking adequate empirical support: for being too soft. "Before categoric statements are made about 'changes' in the treatment of children, accurate data for 1850 and 1950 must be compared scientifically," wrote Read Bain in the *American Sociological Review*. "Since there is not much accurate 1850 information, there can only be dubious guessing based largely on literary sources." Some of Riesman's efforts at cross-cultural comparison struck Bain as coming "close to scientific quackery." Bain's reservations were echoed in behavioral and social science journals like the *American Journal of Psychiatry* and *Social Forces*. Margaret Mead greeted the book with enthusiasm in the *American Journal of Sociology*, however, and the reaction of many readers, a combination that could be called skeptical openmindedness, was well captured by the *American Anthropologist* reviewer, who cautiously concluded, "His method of analysis is unique among the recent studies in character. . . . [I]t presents a number of hypotheses for testing, and certainly those who are concerned with American culture should not ignore it."[58]

Notable in the reviews was the fact that, although Riesman identified the method of thought-experiment as having come from Tocqueville, reviewers who noted it treated it as having been derived from Max Weber.[59] Weber had originated the formal construct of the "ideal type," but that is a concept that Riesman never alluded to in *The Lonely Crowd*; his very few references to Weber adverted directly to the relationship that Weber had hypothesized between Puritanism and capitalism. This example of information bypass provides further evidence that Tocqueville's supposed 1950s fame was a later creation. The seeming connection between Tocqueville and American intellectual culture that many scholars associate with the 1950s was actually a product of the 1960s that was retrojected by still later historians upon the preceding decade. In any case, none of the scholars who noted Riesman's use of ideal types connected such a method with Tocqueville. In other words, Riesman made use of a method that had resemblances to those used by both Tocqueville and Weber, and although he acknowledged his debt to the former, commentators ascribed it to the latter.

Not until 1963 was the Tocqueville theme in *The Lonely Crowd* fully illuminated, and then it was done by a historian, Carl Degler. Degler's simple and cogent argument was that, far from representing a new type of character formation profoundly different from nineteenth-century prototypes and caused by new developments in economic structures, Riesman's "other-directed" American character type was essentially unchanged from the "majority-dominated man of the nineteenth [century] of whom Tocqueville was so fearful." "What Riesman has called the central feature of the modern American character—other-direction—is, in fact, the dominant element in our national character through most of our history."[60]

Yet noting the evidence that Tocqueville's fame in the 1950s has come to be exaggerated should not lead to the error of ignoring his presence in the intellectual landscape of the decade. Pierson's *Tocqueville and Beaumont in America* was out of print by 1962, it is true; the Tocqueville centennial of 1959 was less noted than that of 1935 to 1938 had been, and the real surge in attention would occur in the late 1960s. But the late 1950s did see efforts to popularize Tocqueville. In their use of mass media and reliance on abridgement, some of these efforts foreshadowed the C-Span Tocqueville tour of 1997.[61]

Listeners who tuned in to NBC on January 17, 1962, at 8:30 P.M. could hear the first of fourteen broadcasts of dramatizations derived from *Democracy in America*. The scripts were written by a Canadian radio producer, Lister Sinclair, and George E. Probst of New York University. Harvard's Perry Miller and Alan Heimert were consultants to the project, but the records had been cut in Toronto in 1958 and 1959. Probst had been teaching the *Democracy* to adult students in Chicago throughout the 1950s and put great faith in the method of dramatization, much like the actor-historians who portray historical figures for Chautauqua programs did at the end of the century. One such actor, Dick Johnson, portrayed Tocqueville in many Chautauqua venues in the 1990s, including at the C-Span stop in Pittsburgh. Although he was deeply concerned to illuminate the relevance of Tocqueville to current American society, Johnson lacked the direct political agenda of Probst, who wrote, "To those who ask, 'What is the importance of Tocqueville in modern world politics?' it is enough to reply that he is the answer to Marx." Probst also put together a reader, *The Happy Republic*, to accompany the dramatizations.[62]

Richard D. Heffner's 1956 abridgement of the *Democracy* was also in the anti-Marx genre. Calling the *Democracy* "pre-eminently a tract for our times" and focusing on the ways in which, according to Heffner, Tocqueville's Americans could never accept the revolutionary or Marxian solutions to their social problems, Heffner complained about "an American historiography which, since Tocqueville's time, has long been dominated by determinists of one kind or another." He could not resist pointing out—"most prophetic of all"—Tocqueville's prediction about the United States and Russia, allotting the prediction the most space of any theme in his introduction.[63]

In 1992, Drescher correctly identified Tocqueville's views on revolution as the "most neglected" aspect of his thought: none of the previous major scholarly treatments of Tocqueville's prophetic insights had even addressed the issue.[64] Heffner was an exception, however: he was perhaps the first writer to draw attention to the chapter that Drescher, in a typical tour de force, explicated brilliantly, "Why Great Revolutions Will Become Rare" (Volume II, Part III, chapter 21). In that chapter Tocqueville had argued that "revolutions are made to destroy blatant inequalities," Heffner wrote. But because in the United States the very poor are few and "the American class structure—as the Marxist can never see or accept—is characterized by fluidity rather than by stratification," the citizenry hate violent upheaval. "Amidst the conservatism bred by well-being," he concluded on this point, "revolution must indeed be rare!"[65]

Heffner's abridgement diverged from earlier versions. In the nineteenth century especially, publishers focused on Volume I and ignored or minimized the 1840 volume. Heffner was the first to reverse the emphasis. Only 40 percent of his edition came from the first volume (in the unabridged book the Volume I to Volume II ratio is about 55 to 45). Unfortunately, most of the cuts from the first volume consisted of the last chapter on the three races, a mistake for an editor concerned in 1956 to show contemporary relevance. But this edition did contain a considerable allotment from what many scholars now consider the more important volume.

Notes

1. Nisbet, "Many Tocquevilles," 59–60.

2. A. V. Dicey, "De Tocqueville's Conversations," *Nation* 15 (November 28, 1872): 350, 351.

3. J. P. Mayer, "Tocqueville's *Democracy in America*: Reception and Reputation," introduction to the hardcover edition of *Democracy in America*, by Alexis de Tocqueville, ed. J. P. Mayer and Max Lerner, trans. George Lawrence (New York: Harper and Row, 1966), xx.

4. A. V. Dicey, "Alexis de Tocqueville," *The National Review* 21 (March–April 1893): 782. Subsequent references appear parenthetically in the text.

5. On the Dicey-Bryce American journey, see Ions, *James Bryce and American Democracy*, 39–80; quote on 79. Dicey and Bryce pursued separate itineraries for about ten days of their trip.

6. *John Graham Brooks, Helen Lawrence Brooks, 1846–1938: A Memorial* (Boston: Privately printed, 1940), 14, 30.

7. Barbara Miller Solomon, "John Graham Brooks," *Dictionary of American Biography* XXII, Supplement 2 (New York: Scribner's, 1958), 66–67; James T. Kloppenberg, *Uncertain Victory: Social Democracy and Progressivism in European and American Thought, 1870–1920* (New York: Oxford University Press, 1986). On the ASSA, see Thomas Haskell,

The Emergence of Professional Social Science: The American Social Science Association and the Nineteenth-Century Crisis of Authority (Urbana: University of Illinois Press, 1977).

8. John Graham Brooks, *As Others See Us: A Study of Progress in the United States* (New York: Macmillan, 1908), 231. Subsequent references appear parenthetically in the text.

9. James E. Mooney, *John Graham Brooks, Prophet of Social Justice: A Career Story* (Worcester, Mass: Privately printed, 1968), 43.

10. William Archibald Dunning, *A History of Political Theories from Rousseau to Spencer* (New York: Macmillan, 1920), 270.

11. For this contrast, see Bernard Edward Brown, *American Conservatives: The Political Thought of Francis Lieber and John W. Burgess* (New York: Columbia University Press, 1951).

12. McClay, *The Masterless*, 136–48, quote on 139; James Anthony Walsh, "Francis Lieber, His Life and Political Theory" (Master's thesis, Brown University, 1933), 63–80.

13. Philip R. Muller, "Look Back without Anger: A Reappraisal of William R. Dunning," *Journal of American History* 61, no. 2 (September 1974): 331.

14. Muller, "Look Back without Anger," 328.

15. Dunning, *Political Theories from Rousseau to Spencer*, 270, 274, 278.

16. George W. Pierson, "Tocqueville's Visions of Democracy," *Yale University Library Gazette* 51, no. 1 (July 1976): 8; "Paul Lambert White," *National Cyclopedia of American Biography* 6 (New York: James T. White Co., 1928), 32–33.

17. Paul Lambert White, "American Manners in 1830," *Yale Review* 12, no. 1 (October 1922): 116–29, quote on 116. Subsequent references appear parenthetically in the text.

18. George Wilson Pierson, "Two Frenchmen in America, 1831–1832: The Studies and Adventures of Alexis de Tocqueville and Gustave de Beaumont in the United States and Canada with the Story of the Origins and Development of Tocqueville's 'Democracy in America' from Their Letters, Diaries, and Sketches." Submitted in competition for the John Addison Porter Prize, 1933. Typescript, George Wilson Pierson Papers, Yale University Library; Diane E. Kaplan, Archivist, Yale University Library to the author, October 22, 2003; *Contemporary Authors*, New Revision Series, Vol. 3 (Detroit: Gale, 1981), 435–36.

19. Melvin Richter, "The Uses of Theory: Tocqueville's Adaptation of Montesquieu," in *Essays in Theory and History: An Approach to the Social Sciences*, ed. Melvin Richter (Cambridge, Mass.: Harvard University Press, 1970), 74–102.

20. William Henry George, "Montesquieu and de Tocqueville and Corporative Individualism," *American Political Science Review* 16, no. 1 (February 1922): 10–21, quotes on 10, 12, 21.

21. Katherine Harrison, "A French Forecast of American Literature," *South Atlantic Quarterly* 25 (1926): 357; Cushing Strout, "Tocqueville and American Literature," *New Literary History* 18, no. 1 (Autumn 1986): 125n6; Lionel Trilling, "The Revolving Bookstand: The Writer and His Responsibilities," *American Scholar* 14, no. 4 (Summer 1945): 503.

22. Richmond Laurin Hawkins, "Unpublished Letters of Alexis de Tocqueville," *Romanic Review* 19, no. 3 (July–September 1928): 195–217, and 20, no. 1 (January–March 1929): 351–56; quote on 195n1.

23. Thomas Perkins Abernethy, *Mississippi Valley Historical Review* 25, no. 3 (December 1938): 403–4; *The Atlantic* 162, no. 6 (December 1938): 75 (third quote); Phillips Bradley, *Annals of the American Academy of Political and Social Science* 201 (January 1939): 271–72; Phillips Bradley, *American Political Science Review* 33, no. 1 (February 1939): 107–8; Crane Brinton, "Two Frenchmen in Jackson's America," *Saturday Review of Literature*, July 30, 1938, 5–6; Gilbert Chinard, "Tocqueville on Democracy," *Yale Review* 28, no. 1 (Fall 1938): 205–6; A. C. Flick, *New York History* 20, no. 1 (January 1939): 69–70 (fourth quote); Albert Guerard, "Frenchmen in America," *New York Herald Tribune Books*, August 14, 1938, 2; William E. Lingelbach, *Pennsylvania Magazine of History and Biography* 63 (July 1939): 348–49; William MacDonald, "Tocqueville and Beaumont's Journey in Early America," *New York Times Book Review*, July 17, 1938, 8–9 (first quote); David S. Muzzey, *American Historical Review* 45, no. 1 (October 1939): 171–72; Albert Salomon, *Social Research* 5 (1938): 369–70; Robert E. Spiller, *New England Quarterly* 12, no. 1 (March 1939): 159–60 (second quote); *Time*, July 11, 1938, 63.

24. George Wilson Pierson, "On the Centenary of Tocqueville's *Democracy in America*," *Yale University Library Gazette* 10 (1935): 33–38; Albert Salomon, "Tocqueville, Moralist and Sociologist," *Social Research* 2, no. 4 (November 1935): 405–27; David S. Muzzey, "Alexis de Tocqueville: Pioneer Student of American Democracy," *Columbia University Quarterly* 30, no. 2 (June 1938): 85–90; William E. Lingelbach, "American Democracy and European Interpreters," *Pennsylvania Magazine of History and Biography* 41, no. 1 (January 1937): 1–25; Harold W. Stoke, "De Tocqueville's Appraisal of Democracy—Then and Now," *South Atlantic Quarterly* 36, no. 1 (January 1937): 14–22; Phillips Bradley, "A Century of Democracy in America," *Journal of Adult Education* 9, no. 1 (January 1937): 19–24; Matthew Josephson, "A Century After Tocqueville," *Virginia Quarterly Review* 14, no. 4 (Fall 1938): 479–95.

25. "Roosevelt Gets French Gifts," *New York Times*, June 28, 1935, 23.

26. Even Pierson's own centennial article in 1935, heralding the importance of the subject of his forthcoming book, stressed the familiarity of the *Democracy*: "Concerning the character and history of that oft-quoted treatise, neither Frenchmen nor Americans should need much instruction." Pierson, "On the Centenary," 33.

27. Daniel H. Thomas and Lynn M. Case, eds., *Guide to the Diplomatic Archives of Western Europe* (Philadelphia: University of Pennsylvania Press, 1959), v; Gerald Weales, "Hello, Dr. Chips," *Pennsylvania Gazette* 100, no. 4 (March–April 2002): 20–21.

28. Italics added to the book title.

29. Lingelbach, "American Democracy and European Interpreters," 12, 13; Weals, "Dr. Chips," 20.

30. Bradley, "A Century of Democracy in America," 19.

31. Irving Dilliard, "Three to Remember: Archibald Macleish, Stanley Kimmel, Phillips Bradley," *Journal of the Illinois State Historical Society* 77, no. 1 (Spring 1984): 45–59; *New York Times*, July 28, 1982, D20.

32. "A Note on the Text," in *Democracy in America*, by Alexis de Tocqueville, ed. Alan Ryan, Everyman's Library Edition (New York: Knopf, 1994), lix.

33. Bradley, "A Century of Democracy in America," 19, 20.

34. Donald Nielson, "Salomon's Ark: Experience, History, and the Life of the Mind," *International Journal of Politics, Culture and Society* 6, no. 4 (Summer 1993): 575; *New York Times*, December, 19, 1966, 37; Carl Mayer, "Albert Salomon, 1891–1966," *Social Research* 34, no. 2 (Summer 1967): 213–25.

35. Richard Grathoff, "Portrait: Albert Salomon (1891–1966)," *International Sociology* 10, no. 2 (June 1995): 235–42.

36. Albert Salomon, ed., *Autoritat und Freiheit* (Zurich, Switzerland: Rascher, 1936).

37. Salomon, "Tocqueville, Moralist and Sociologist," 424.

38. Albert Salomon, *In Praise of Enlightenment* (New York: Meridian, 1962), 372, quoted in Nielson, "Salomon's Ark," 576.

39. Albert Salomon, "Tocqueville 1959," *Social Research* 36, no. 4 (Winter 1959): 458, 470.

40. Charles S. Sydnor, *Political Science Quarterly* 60, no. 3 (September 1945): 459; Paul Kiniery, *Catholic Historical Review* 31 (1945): 345–46.

41. William Anderson, *Annals of the American Academy of Political and Social Science* 242 (1945): 182, 183.

42. Donald J. Pierce, *American Sociological Review* 10, no. 4 (August 1945): 569.

43. Thomas I. Cook, *American Historical Review* 51, no. 1 (October 1945): 131, 132, 133.

44. Drescher, "Appendix: Tocqueville and Beaumont: A Rationale for Collective Study," in *TBSR*, 201, 213; Schleifer, *Making*, 248.

45. Pierson, "Tocqueville's Visions of Democracy," 10.

46. George Wilson Pierson, *Tocqueville in America*, abridged by Dudley C. Lunt (Garden City, N.Y.: Doubleday Anchor, 1959).

47. Some of these criticisms were made by Hugh Brogan in the *Journal of American Studies* 32, no. 3 (1998): 553–54.

48. Henry Steele Commager, "Explanatory Note" in *Democracy in America*, by Alexis de Tocqueville (Oxford: World Classics, 1946), v. The American edition's "Explanatory Note" is substantially identical; see *Democracy in America*, by Alexis de Tocqueville (New York: Oxford University Press Galaxy Editions, 1947), v–vi.

49. Henry Steele Commager, *Commager on Tocqueville* (Columbia: University of Missouri Press, 1993), 34.

50. Edward T. Gargan, *De Tocqueville*, Studies in Modern European Literature and Thought (New York: Hillary House, 1965); Hugh Brogan, *Tocqueville*, Modern Masters Series (London: Fontana, 1973); Matthew Mancini, *Alexis de Tocqueville*, World Authors Series (New York: Twayne, 1994); Larry Siedentop, *Tocqueville*, Past Masters Series (New York: Oxford University Press, 1994); Cheryl Welch, *De Tocqueville*, Founders Series (New York: Oxford University Press, 2001).

51. *Harper's New Monthly Magazine* 62, no. 367 (December 1880): 149 (Phillips letter); *Harper's New Monthly Magazine* 62, no. 369 (February 1881): 469 (Bowen letter).

52. Pierson, "Tocqueville's Vision of Democracy," 5; see also Jacques Barzun, ed., *Fowler's Modern American Usage* (New York: Hill and Wang, 1966), 326.

53. John William Ward, *American Quarterly* 9, no. 4 (Winter 1957): 465; Marvin Meyers, *The Jacksonian Persuasion: Politics and Belief* (1957; repr. Stanford, Calif.: Stanford University Press, 1960), ch. 3 *passim*; 33, 35; for a defense of Tocqueville as a historical source, see 276–79 of the 1960 edition.

54. Cecelia M. Kenyon, *American Political Science Review* 53, no. 2 (June 1959): 539, 540; Sigmund Diamond, *American Sociological Review* 24, no. 2 (April 1959): 266–67; Irving Kristol, *Encounter* 10 (1958): 76; Arthur M. Schlesinger Jr., *The Historian* 20, no. 3 (May 1958): 367; Roy F. Nichols, *Pennsylvania Magazine of History and Biography* 82, no. 3 (July 1958): 360; Charles G. Sellers, *American Historical Review* 63, no. 3 (April 1958): 700–701.

55. David Riesman in collaboration with Reuel Denney and Nathan Glazer, *The Lonely Crowd: A Study of the Changing American Character* (New Haven, Conn.: Yale University Press, 1950), 20n9. A deeply informative and insightful discussion of the book's importance and significance, "rough synonyms [that] may be distinguished from each other," is Wilfred M. McClay, "The Strange Career of *The Lonely Crowd*," in *The Culture of the Market: Historical Essays*, ed. Thomas L. Haskell and Richard F. Teichgraeber III (Cambridge: Cambridge University Press, 1993), 397–440.

56. David Riesman, "Tocqueville as Ethnographer," *American Scholar* 30 (1960–1961): 176.

57. David Riesman, "Innocence of *The Lonely Crowd*," *Society* 27, no. 2 (January/February 1990): 79.

58. Read Bain, *American Sociological Review* 16, no. 2 (April 1951): 270; Fillmore H. Sanford, *American Journal of Psychiatry* 109 (December 1952): 471–72; Donald W. Calhoun, *Social Forces* 30, no. 1 (October 1951): 113–14; Margaret Mead, *American Journal of Sociology* 56, no. 5 (March 1951): 495–97; E. T. Hall Jr., *American Anthropologist* 54, no. 1 (January–March 1952): 97.

59. See the notices by Sanford and Bain, *supra* n. 58, and Joseph M. Goldsen, *Public Opinion Quarterly* 15, no. 1 (Spring 1951): 159: "Riesman's method is in the spirit of Max Weber: he employs a typology and a set of developmental constructs or 'models.'" That this typology came from Tocqueville rather than Weber was lost on Goldsen and every other reviewer.

60. Carl N. Degler, "The Sociologist as Historian: Riesman's *The Lonely Crowd*," *American Quarterly* 15, no. 4 (Winter 1963): 491, 497. Cushing Strout took issue with Degler's conclusions in "A Note on Degler, Riesman, and Tocqueville," *American Quarterly* 16, no. 1 (Spring 1964): 100–102. The point at issue in the present case is that Degler's 1963 essay, rather than any commentary of the 1950s, is when the Tocqueville connection began to be recognized.

61. C-Span's tour information: www.tocqueville.org. C-Span as teacher: "Symposium: Tocqueville and Democracy in America," *PS: Political Science and Politics* 32, no. 2 (June 1999): 194–226.

62. Lister Sinclair and George E. Probst, *Democracy in America Scripts* (New York: National Educational Television and Radio Center, 1962), 14; Dick Johnson interview; George E. Probst, ed., *The Happy Republic: A Reader in Tocqueville's America* (New York: Harper Torchbooks, 1962). Probst repeated his "Marx" statement verbatim in the foreword to *The Happy Republic*, xiii.

63. *Democracy in America*, by Alexis de Tocqueville, ed. Richard D. Heffner (New York: New American Library, 1956), 9, 19.

64. Seymour Drescher, "'Why Great Revolutions Will Become Rare': Tocqueville's Most Neglected Prognosis," *Journal of Modern History* 64, no. 4 (September 1992): 429–54, esp. 432n11.

65. Heffner edition, 17, 18.

CHAPTER SIX

✳

A Cottage Industry

Nineteen fifty-nine was a very satisfying year for the young Hungarian American historian John Lukacs of Chestnut Hill College outside Philadelphia. As soon as a new edition of the notes and sketches for Tocqueville's second volume on the French Revolution had been published in the *Oeuvres complètes* put out by Gallimard—the book that Tocqueville's death from tuberculosis at the age of fifty-three had until that moment prevented the world from seeing—Dr. Lukacs was contacted by Doubleday Anchor to produce a translation. Along with the notes on the Revolution, the Doubleday Anchor edition contained the letters exchanged between Tocqueville and the rather fawning aristocrat who had once served as his secretary and who became the first systematic racist theoretician in European history: Count Arthur de Gobineau. Lukacs set to work on the edition in the summer of 1955, and it finally left the printing presses in 1959. The result of Lukacs's labors was *"The European Revolution" and Correspondence with Gobineau*. It contained an introduction that was a model of explanatory context. In the spring semester of 1959, Lukacs organized a star-studded conference at his small Catholic college on the centenary of Tocqueville's death. Almost all the papers read at the meeting were soon published in excellent scholarly journal. And in the autumn, Lukacs published a discerning general-interest article on Tocqueville in *American Heritage*.[1]

Lukacs had read a great deal of Tocqueville since 1948, when he had first picked up the *Democracy* as a brand-new college teacher only two years after his arrival in the United States from a devastated Budapest. His extensive reading in French and English led him to be intrigued with the idea of pursuing Tocqueville studies as a historical specialty. But the idea did not fully take hold. "Then," he recalled many years later, "I went to a couple of con-

187

ventions of French Historical Studies. I found out . . . that Tocqueville was beginning to be a cottage industry. And I didn't want to get involved."[2] Although throughout his later career as a historian, theoretician, and essayist he continually referred to Tocqueville and echoed major themes of Tocqueville's philosophy of history, he wrote little about his French mentor after 1964, when his controversial article, "The Last Days of Alexis de Tocqueville," appeared in the *Catholic Historical Review.*

The year 1959, then, was indeed a milestone in the American reception of Tocqueville. There assembled in Philadelphia, thanks to Lukacs, a gathering of the leading Tocqueville scholars in the English-speaking world, which at that time, in fact, was where nearly all the Tocqueville scholars could be found. As illustrious as those writers were in retrospect, however, the conference and the event it commemorated did not attract a great deal of attention at the time, another indication that the surge in interest in Tocqueville during the 1950s was much less pronounced than later historians believed. Soon afterwards, David Riesman remarked on a comparative lack of interest in Tocqueville at the time. "Tocqueville founded no school and the centenary of his death in 1959 was little celebrated," Riesman wrote in 1960.[3]

The central figure at this conference was a German Jewish socialist refugee intellectual, Jacob Peter Mayer. Born at Frankenthal in 1903, Mayer was a precocious and politically active intellectual who, while still in his mid-twenties, became the archivist of the German Social Democratic Party (SPD). His first book was about Marx and Engels, and his second was an edition of Marx's early writings. Some months after Albert Salomon departed for the United States, Mayer, a prominent anti-Nazi, escaped as well, but to Great Britain. Mayer had taken part in the planning of an abortive SPD coup in 1934 that was called off because the Communists refused to take part. During the 1936 Olympic games, when restrictions on Jews were relaxed somewhat, Mayer and his wife and son traveled to Britain on a "holiday"—from which they did not plan to return.

Mayer, who died in 1992, was the most important single editor of Tocqueville's writings in the twentieth century. He played the pivotal role in establishing definitive texts of *Democracy in America*, the *Recollections*, and *The Old Regime and the Revolution*, as well as many minor works and much of Tocqueville's correspondence. In 1939, Mayer published *The Prophet of the Mass Age*, a biographical study of Tocqueville, which to this day is an excellent resource for any beginning student.

Mayer's biography drew the attention of the old Comte de Tocqueville, Alexis's great-nephew and heir (Tocqueville and his English wife, Mary Mottley, had no children). After the war, the comte asked Mayer to visit the Tocqueville château in Normandy in order to edit the immense family archive there. This invitation finally stirred the French government into action. A national commission was duly appointed to edit and publish all of Tocqueville's works, chaired originally by Mayer and later by Raymond Aron and including Gallimard as publisher; as a result, the definitive, still incomplete series of Tocqueville's *Oeuvres complètes* began to appear in the 1950s. Mayer was editor of the first volumes, which were of course the 1835 and 1840 volumes of the *Democracy*.[4]

In 1960, Harper Torchbooks brought out a reprint of Mayer's 1939 biography. In a foreword to this new printing, Mayer explained what brought about his desire to offer Harper's the reprint edition. The book, he wrote, was published "just a few days before Hitler began *his* war." Twenty years later came the centenary of Tocqueville's death, and Mayer participated in "a colloquy in America in which nearly all American Tocqueville scholars participated. . . . When, during our deliberations, America's most eminent Burke specialist referred to the present book as if no other authoritative general work on Tocqueville existed, I felt encouraged to republish it, for the English and American editions have been out of print for many years."[5] Several points are worth noting about this brief passage. First, almost all of the American Tocqueville scholars could easily gather for a single colloquium in 1959. There were only a handful. Second, the only general work about Tocqueville's life and writings was long out of print. And third, who was that scholar of Edmund Burke, and what was *he* doing there?

That scholar was a brilliant conservative convert to Catholicism named Ross J. S. Hoffman. By 1959, the workaholic Hoffman was an ailing and withdrawn figure, formal, professorial, and rather grave in manner.[6] A great teacher and formidable Catholic apologist, Hoffman was professor of history at Fordham University, the Jesuit university in New York City. He had been recruited there in 1938 from New York University, where he taught before his conversion. Hoffman was born in Harrisburg, Pennsylvania, in 1902, received his bachelor's from Lafayette College, and earned a Ph.D. in history from the University of Pennsylvania. His dissertation won the prestigious Henry Louis Beer Prize of the American Historical Association and was published by the University of Pennsylvania Press as *Great Britain and the German Trade Rivalry, 1875–1914* in 1933. The director of this dissertation was the Tocqueville scholar William E. Lingelbach. Lawrence Henry Gipson asserted in the 1960s, "Among American historians of standing there is probably no person more highly regarded as a spokesman for the faith of the Roman

Catholic church than Ross Hoffman."⁷ At Fordham, Hoffman did much to strengthen the graduate history program. One of his early students, John Olin, later a faculty member of that department, recalled in 1991, "The professor . . . that impressed me the most was Ross Hoffman. He was an impressive professor to say the least. I thought I would love to be a teacher like him. He was so dramatic and well ordered in class. . . . He did inspire me."⁸

By the time of the Philadelphia Tocqueville colloquium, Hoffman had been thinking for at least fifteen years about what he saw as certain parallels in the work of Tocqueville and Burke. He was a founder of a group at Fordham called the Burke Society, which held a series of annual symposia and lectures. The first such meeting, held in the spring of 1945, in specific response to the new publication by their friend and neighbor Phillips Bradley, who almost certainly attended, was entitled A Symposium on Alexis de Tocqueville's "Democracy in America."⁹ Hoffman wrote the introduction to the published proceedings and contributed an unremarkable paper on Tocqueville and religion. The symposium's director, Father William Schlaerth, clearly expressed the affinities the participants felt between Tocqueville and Burke. "There was little need to convince the participants that they had merely touched the surface and handled only a few of the kind of topics which Democracy in America will repeatedly raise when thoughtfully read. In the process of distillation it was felt that enough had been drawn off to support the end and object of the Burke Society, namely, a recall to the principles, values, and traditions which are the heritage of the political and international society of Christendom."¹⁰

Three years later, Alfred A. Knopf, publisher of the Bradley edition of Tocqueville, brought out Hoffman and Paul Levack's edition of the political writings of Burke, which would remain a standard reference in its special field for decades.¹¹ Perhaps Knopf was hoping for a second home run with Burke like the one Bradley had scored with his edition of Tocqueville.

By 1959, Hoffman had lost much of the contagious energy he had shown when he joined the faculty two decades earlier. Roger Wines, who joined the Fordham history department in 1959 and befriended Hoffman, recalled, "Sometime in the fifties, I was told, he had serious health problems, and toned down his activities considerably. He may also have been disappointed at how the postwar world turned out, or just a bit tired. When I met him he was a man of strong opinions but a limited range of activities."¹² Hoffman did, however, have enough energy to start a new publication, the Burke Newsletter, which lasted for only two or three issues. The first feature article in the first issue of the journal was a digest of Hoffman's opinions on the

Tocqueville connection, entitled "Tocqueville and Burke." In it Hoffman's fatigue is palpable. The piece does not attempt a systematic comparison of the two thinkers. Indeed, Hoffman admitted that he could find "no evidence of any acquaintance with Burke's philosophy of politics [in *Democracy in America*]," merely "many passages [in which] he showed a sensibility reminiscent of Burke," and he had to conclude rather weakly that the Frenchman showed only what he called "morphological resemblances" to Burke.[13]

The labors of Hoffman in this context illustrate the way in which many conservatives would turn to Tocqueville, or appropriate Tocqueville, depending on one's point of view, after the 1950s. I call it the tactic of assimilating Tocqueville to Burke. In this effort Hoffman was not alone, but his is the clearest, most consistent example of the phenomenon in the 1950s. Another writer, however, also made this identification, and perhaps to greater effect. Russell Kirk's *The Conservative Mind: From Burke to Santayana* was a magisterial survey of conservative thought. Granting that Santayana is uncategorizable either as to either politics or ethnicity, it is a remarkable fact about that book that the large cast of characters about which Kirk wrote was entirely Anglo-American, except for Tocqueville. The section on Tocqueville united him with an Englishman, Thomas Babington Macaulay, and an American, James Fenimore Cooper. It was a generally fair and judicious account of Tocqueville's concept of "democratic despotism," but at the end of his exposition, Kirk astonishingly referred to the Frenchman as "Burke's pupil." What united the two disparate thinkers, in Kirk's mind, was Tocqueville's fear of "social democracy," "a term," Kirk wrote, "coined to describe the centralized equalitarian state, which does not so much choke freedom as it simply ignores freedom. And, being Burke's pupil, Tocqueville never could submit to the delusion that 'the people' exist as an abstraction to be trusted or feared or hated or revered in place of Jehovah."[14]

The attempt to assimilate Tocqueville to Burke has both ancient and modern devotees. The conservative political theorist Bruce Frohnen tried it in the 1990s, and the redoubtable E. L. Godkin, the editor of the *Nation*, pointed out alleged affinities between the two in the 1860s.[15] But it was left to Hoffman and Kirk to make the connection between Burke and Tocqueville's aversion to social democracy during the 1950s.

How full of meaning in retrospect, then, was that encounter in Philadelphia in 1959 at the Tocqueville colloquium between Hoffman, the disciple of Burke, and Mayer, the former archivist of the Social Democratic Party of Germany. Between them, they mapped out two different paths to the understanding of Tocqueville, or, to change the metaphor, two different styles of portraiture that were brought to bear on both their ostensible subject and the underlying canvas on which they were fabricating their visions, that of the diverse and motley 1950s.

Other scholars of the late 1950s also, as it were, circled around Tocqueville without going ahead and embracing his work as a special field of study. Prominent among them were Salomon, Riesman, Marvin Meyers, Max Lerner, and Louis Hartz.

Salomon and Mayer, then, were by no means alone in their Central or Eastern European, Jewish, and socialist roots among those who helped to draw the portrait of Tocqueville in the 1950s and 1960s. Another was Lerner, a wide-ranging and energetic Russian immigrant who jointly edited the George Lawrence translation of the *Democracy* with Mayer. His one-time protégé, Martin Peretz, wrote, "Lerner's was a Jew's understanding of the meaning of America. Out of all diasporas, he believed, this was the one that allowed Jews to breathe free." Lerner and Mayer first met in Paris in 1957, and over the years, developed a friendly and collaborative relationship, something rare for Mayer. Lerner also wrote a long introduction for the hardcover edition of the Lawrence translation, which was several times reprinted as *Tocqueville & American Civilization*. The essay was like a stone dropped into a deep pool; it left no discernible effect on the course of subsequent scholarship. Indeed, in a scholarly biography of Lerner that appeared in 1998 written by Sanford Lakoff, a Straussian political scientist with a deep knowledge of Tocqueville, Tocqueville was almost entirely absent.[16]

But the scholar who made the boldest use of Tocqueville (in contrast to being a specialized scholar of Tocqueville's works) was the brilliant and troubled Hartz, author of one of those books everyone can have an opinion about without carefully reading, *The Liberal Tradition in America*, published in 1955. Hartz was the son of Russian Jewish immigrants and grew up in the Midwest—in Omaha, Nebraska. He received his bachelor's from Harvard in 1940 at the age of twenty-one, and his Ph.D. in 1946. *The Liberal Tradition in America* took as its own point of departure Tocqueville's flash of insight that in the United States equality had been established without revolution, that is, in the absence of a violent overthrow of the preceding social structure and its institutions. In Tocqueville's all-too-clever formula, adopted and then misquoted by Hartz, Americans had been "born equal."

Hartz suffered a mental breakdown in 1974 and resigned abruptly from his position at Harvard, left his family, and spent his remaining days wandering around the world. He died in Istanbul in 1986. In a sympathetic and insightful essay prompted by news of Hartz's death, John Patrick Diggins drew a parallel between Hartz and Henry Adams, seeing them both as intellectuals who were "haunted by a sense of failure." "What had disappointed them were two discrete traditions that each historian respectively had been brought up on, ideological traditions that had failed to take root in America," Diggins wrote. "For Adams, it was the eighteenth-century Enlightenment and the ideals of classical republicanism; for Hartz, nineteenth-century socialism and the promises of Marxism." Diggins stressed an obvious point about Hartz that resonates with Salomon's 1959 portrayal of an existentialist, Marxist Tocqueville, namely that "The Tocqueville-Hartz thesis could readily be endorsed by Marx, Engles [sic], Trotsky, and Gramsci, all of whom agreed that America had no feudal tradition, that the revolutionary potential of its working class was highly problematic, and that its ruling ethos or 'hegemony' was essentially bourgeois and liberal."[17] The importance of the fact that these nonrevolutionary and consensual characteristics of American political life were not admired, but deplored, by Hartz can hardly be overstated. For Hartz, American liberalism, far from being worthy of celebration, "was actually a nationalist ideology that was astonishingly parochial," one commentator wrote.[18]

Hartz's book seems to me to be impossible to categorize—and so, as one might expect, it has suffered the fate of being constantly thrown into categories. The most ironic, and certainly what would have been to Hartz the most baffling, example of misplaced taxonomy is its placement in the category of the so-called consensus historians. Diggins once again located the heart of the irony: "Even though Hartz expected to be dismissed as a scholar who could neither please nor be pleased, I don't think he expected to be classified as a defender and promoter of the 'consensus' school of thought and, by implication, an anthropologist [sic] for liberal capitalism who feared acknowledging class conflict in America because of McCarthyism and the Cold War." Then, he brought in a strange, frustratingly vague reference to the New Left of the 1960s: "Such was the charge [of fearing to acknowledge class conflict because of McCarthyism and the cold war] of young SDS historians who linked Hartz's book to Daniel J. Boorstin's *The Genius of American Politics*."[19]

Indeed, there is a Students for a Democratic Society pamphlet making such a bizarre link. Unidentified by Diggins in his article, this essay, written by University of Wisconsin graduate student James O'Brien, was called "America the Beautiful: An Essay on Daniel Boorstin and Louis Hartz," and its thesis was simply stated: Boorstin's *Genius* and Hartz's *Liberal Tradition* were "the twin monuments of the 'consensus' school"; therefore, "by examining the weaknesses of Boorstin and Hartz, it is possible to gain an appreciation of the failure of American historical scholarship to provide us with a coherent and meaningful picture of our past."[20] O'Brien simply posited Boorstin and Hartz as "twin[s]" of an alleged school and decided that only the weaknesses of their books needed to be addressed.

One egregious flaw in O'Brien's pamphlet was its total neglect of the fact that, far from being twins, Boorstin and Hartz were rather bitter opponents. Hartz, after all, emphasized the importance of ideology—albeit an ideology he despised—in American culture, while Boorstin denied its existence. That is, Boorstin identified as essential to and distinctive in American politics the absence of the very element that Hartz placed at the center of his own analysis. It was on just these grounds that Boorstin had savaged Hartz's book in the magazine *Commentary* when it appeared in 1955. That review made plain how starkly opposed their approaches to American political culture were. Hartz "confin[es] his thinking about America in a prison of European comparisons," Boorstin protested. "This is all like describing a horse by saying that it is an animal that lacks the trunk of the elephant, has not the neck of the giraffe, and also cannot jump like a kangaroo." Hartz suffered from a "prodigious bookishness," Boorstin believed. Indeed, his great weakness lay in "mistaking books for life": "Mr. Hartz writes as if the American past had been inhabited not by people but by books."[21]

But, more importantly, Diggins failed to note that SDSers were not the only observers to make a spurious connection between these two disparate historians. Indeed the argument of the SDS pamphlet had its origins in an impeccably establishment source, namely *Commentary* magazine itself, which was where, four years after Boorstin's attack on Hartz, John Higham completed the same operation on Boorstin that Boorstin had performed on Hartz, in one of the cleverest and most widely cited articles of the 1950s and 1960s.

Higham, the John Martin Vincent Professor of History at Johns Hopkins, was one of the nation's most respected historians for over forty years. His dissertation, published in 1955 as *Strangers in the Land: Patterns of American Nativism, 1860–1925*, is an indispensable, gripping study of anti-immigration ideas and movements, and it occupies a prominent place on all scholars' lists of what should be on even the smallest shelf of essential works on American history and culture. Author or editor of eleven books and scores of major articles, and president of several of the major professional associations for American historians, Higham spoke with a magisterial authority on the key issues in his fields of specialization, which were historiography, ethnic history, immigration history, and cultural conflict and consensus in the American past.[22]

So specialized has the practice of academic history become in the leading universities that some history departments joke about having a decade in which they are missing a specialist. Higham's work, by contrast, reveals a breadth of scope that is truly comprehensive. It is a matter of considerable irony, then, that one of the texts, if not the text, for which Higham was best known was, compared to the majority of his academic writings, written at the end of the 1950s in a general-interest rather than a scholarly publication, and that, in later years, Higham did not include it in the list of his major publications in his published résumé.[23] Yet it generated as much attention and controversy as any portion of his work, including *Strangers in the Land*, to which a complete issue of the journal *American Jewish History* was devoted.[24] The article bore the sweepingly provocative title "The Cult of the 'American Consensus': Homogenizing Our History."[25] It provided a convenient label with which to categorize a generation of historical scholarship, a label that would be slapped on scholars and books with less caution than Higham himself used in his essay.

Attacking Boorstin's 1953 *The Genius of American Politics* as a "celebration of the mindlessness of American life," Higham did not try to conceal his appalled disdain for the image that emerged from Boorstin's pages. "With sour, sidelong glances at Europe," Higham wrote, Boorstin "argued that Americans did not need basic theories. Having no deep antagonisms, they could dispense with metaphysical defenses." Rather than political theory, Boorstin's Americans "need only consult the wisdom imbedded in our historic institutions." Thus, Higham sardonically but accurately concluded, "in spite of [Boorstin's] contempt for European theory, a bit of Edmund Burke proved useful in the end" (96).

To be sure, Higham also discussed Hartz in conjunction with Boorstin as examples of historians presenting an image of a blandly consensual society—as did the SDS pamphlet—but he used Hartz chiefly as a foil to Boorstin, the latter representing a radicalization of a theme that Hartz had raised in a more nuanced way. More importantly, Boorstin celebrated the blandness that Hartz deplored, while denying the existence of even the Lockean ideology upon which Hartz thought America's political insipidity was based.

But the central importance of Higham's celebrated essay, for someone trying to understand how Tocqueville was viewed after the 1950s, is that, aside from his assessment of Hartz or Boorstin, he connected the allegedly pervasive placidity he detected in recent historical scholarship with the work of

Tocqueville. Here is what may be the most crucial passage in the postwar literature concerning Tocqueville (that was not written by a specialist):

> The new look of American history is strikingly conservative. More than at any time before, historians are discovering a bland, unexciting past. To an impressive degree, the dominant interpretations have recaptured the spirit of Alexis de Tocqueville, whose *Democracy in America* has emerged in recent years from a characteristic neglect during the early 20th century. As Tocqueville did more than a century ago, today's historians are exhibiting a happy land, adventurous in manner but conservative in substance, and—above all—remarkably homogeneous (94).

As a representation of the works of the historians under consideration this view is at least debatable, but as an interpretation of Tocqueville himself it borders on caricature. In an interview with me, Higham readily conceded that he was using Tocqueville as a symbol and was not speaking as a specialist, while regretting having missed the chance to note certain analogs to consensus history in sociology, political science, and literature at the time. What was "Tocquevillean" about the 1950s, Higham said, was "a certain tameness and amiability" in its intellectual life. But he knew he was talking about a narrow band of intellectual life and not about America as a whole, or even about Tocqueville's actual texts in any detailed manner.[26]

Higham almost immediately began to feel alarmed by the overwhelmingly positive reception that greeted his article. Scarcely one year after "The Cult of the 'American Consensus'" was published, he declared to a session at the 1960 American Historical Association: "Insofar as consensus gives an even simpler view of American history than we had before, it threatens critical judgment. Fortunately, the recognition of consensus in the past has not usually been unqualified. Nor has it always been presumed to sanction the status quo."[27] At a 1968 conference, Higham went on to make a stunning and courageous acknowledgment of his error of 1959, an admission that, however, was destined to be completely overshadowed by the notoriety of his *Commentary* article. "I was trying to pack the whole corpus of historiography into the interpretive framework my preconceptions had erected," he said. "As data accumulated, more and more of it would not fit. Distinctions between today's consensus historians and their progressive predecessors were not nearly as sharp as I had believed." He found that the consensual "trend," as he called it (for it had devolved greatly from having been a "cult"), had originated from within, not without, the progressive historiographical tradition, that it arose in the 1930s rather than the 1950s, and that there simply was no "identifiable group" of scholars to whom the label could justly be applied. To all intents and purposes, Higham's 1968 paper, "American Historiography in the 1960s," amounted to a repudiation of his position of 1959.[28]

Higham worked hard to fend off his identification as the man who had labeled the consensus school. "My early polemical outbursts against the 'consensus' school of historians," he said, "were received with widespread applause and very little criticism. . . . My own conclusion on being so widely praised was that the tendency I complained of must not be so far advanced or deeply entrenched as I had imagined."[29] Thirty years later, journalist Nicholas Lemann journeyed to Baltimore, while he was preparing a *New York Times Magazine* article on the idea of consensus in 1998 America, because, he wrote, Higham was the person who had "introduced [the word 'consensus'] into political discussion in quite a specific way." It should not be surprising, then, that Higham responded to Lemann's interview "mournfully," as Lemann put it; he had been trying to shed the identification for thirty-eight years.[30] (When I met with Higham one week later he was far more cheerful.)

From the moment his *Commentary* article was published until his death in the summer of 2003, then, Higham would best be known as the scholar of the idea of consensus. Indeed, as Lemann noted, the term itself—*consensus history* or *consensus historians*—was his own. It entered the discourse of American historiography in and through the *Commentary* article and then was given such extensive, nay pervasive, currency that it became one of the most common historiographical reifications of the second half of the twentieth century.

"The Cult of the 'American Consensus'" is thus in need of a scrupulous critique if we are to grasp with any precision the role it played in the shaping of Tocqueville's reception in the 1960s and beyond. For here in Higham's famous article we can find the same sort of lacunae that led to so much misunderstanding in the case of Robert Nisbet's "Many Tocquevilles," a much inferior yet, for specialists at least, equally influential text.

There is, to begin with, the title of Higham's essay, with its identification of a cult, and with those inverted commas around the term *American consensus*. The "American consensus," being in quotes, seems to refer to some phrase that someone else wrote; yet we know the term was Higham's own and was introduced into the cultural and historiographical discourse in the very article for which it provided the title. There was no such preexisting term, quotation, or designation that would justify placing the phrase in inverted commas. Taken together, the two portions of the title—that is, classification of cult status and the orientation of that cult toward an idea that, on the printed page, appears to be a preexisting entity—put forward an unmistakable sense of group coalescence or clustering. In short the title, like the essay, is an instance of reification par excellence. Within a few years, Higham would conclude that, on the contrary, the cult was actually a trend, the trend did not fit into the categories, and the categories had been based on his preconceptions—but his demurrals were destined to be utterly unheeded, while consensus grew into a bête noire of subsequent historiography. Mindful of the immense currency of an idea that he had come to see as a mistake, Higham finally removed from his résumé any reference to the most famous essay he ever wrote.

In the ensuing decades rivers of ink would be spilled trying to disavow the idea that one or another of the historians popularly linked with consensus could fairly be identified with the label. Nearly every study of Richard Hofstadter, for instance, takes pains to dissociate him from consensus.[31] Yet the idea of a "consensus school" persisted, even though in an ever more weakened state. Early in the twenty-first century, the whole notion of consensus history was finally demolished in a brilliant book by Ellen Fitzpatrick, in which she deconstructed "the myth of consensus history" by chapter and verse. Higham's work "helped breathe more life into the straw man of 'consensus history,'" wrote Fitzpatrick. "Higham's polemic . . . came to serve as a fixed description of historical reality. . . . The nuances of Higham's essay . . . receded. And in their place came a simplistic summation of postwar historical writing that made of the late 1940s, the 1950s, and the early 1960s a stolid, unimaginative, and deeply conservative moment in the intellectual history of the discipline." One scholar who would most enthusiastically have concurred with Fitzpatrick was Higham, who in 1995 asked, "Aren't we yet able to recognize that, however stunting the social constraints of the early Cold War years were, the intellectual life of the 1950s was far richer than what we now have or can anticipate?"[32]

Our immediate, narrower interest lies in the role Tocqueville played in the consensus story. The appearance of Tocqueville's ghost, as we saw, was simultaneous with the arrival of consensus itself. Higham's essay on "The 'American Consensus'" is essentially an extended critique of Boorstin's book, The Genius of American Politics (1953). Over one-half of Higham's essay is devoted to a discussion of Boorstin, with a few other books—most notably Hartz's The Liberal Tradition in America—referenced only in passing insofar as they seem to fit in with the thesis of Boorstin's book. Higham claimed that Boorstin (and some others), by virtue of having discovered "a placid, unexciting past," had "recaptured the spirit of Alexis de Tocqueville." This assertion raises an exceedingly simple and obvious question, albeit one that Higham completely ignored, namely, in what specific ways does the thought of Tocqueville figure in Boorstin's *The Genius of American Politics?* And the equally simple and obvious answer to that question is, in no way whatsoever. Tocqueville was not mentioned in Boorstin's book. He was wholly absent from *The Genius of American Politics* both in letter (with one very minor qualification to which I will return) and in spirit, for *Genius* does not reflect specifically Tocquevillean themes or preoccupations no matter how much one might stretch the meaning of the two men's texts.

Boorstin contended in this series of lectures that there had been no felt or perceived need for systematic political philosophy in America, that instead there was what he called a "givenness" that constituted a ground for thinking and action in American political life. It is surely uncontroversial to point out that this idea has no analog in any of the actual writings of Tocqueville. Indeed, in certain specific points, Boorstin took a position directly antithetical to Tocqueville's—for example, on the crucial issue of the role of the Puritans in developing this supposed sense of givenness.[33]

And yet it must be acknowledged that Tocqueville was not completely absent from every page of Boorstin's *Genius*, for Boorstin did include one slight mention at the very end of his volume. Concerning *Democracy in America*, Boorstin wrote, "Every student of American culture should read it. . . . To its many insights I am deeply indebted." However, this acknowledgement appeared not in the body of Boorstin's book, but rather in an appendix of "Suggestions for Further Reading." But in that section he also commended Vernon L. Parrington's *Main Currents in American Thought* ("a classic of our intellectual history"), Carl Becker's *Declaration of Independence* ("I especially recommend [it]"), William James's *Varieties of Religious Experience* ("a classic"), and Ralph Waldo Emerson's "American Scholar" (it "still speaks to us"), among many other works. Such a reference to Tocqueville in the further-readings section in no way made Boorstin's book a representation of "the spirit of Alexis de Tocqueville," any more than bibliographical references to those other American classics made his work an expression of the spirit of Becker, Emerson, or James.[34]

The concept of consensus history, then, was a construct that Higham erected at the very end of the 1950s to characterize the historical scholarship of a decade as it was passing away. Scholars did not use the term or the concept during the 1950s, and there is little evidence that they thought they were living in a consensual era. By 1960, Higham began to have doubts about the concept. He announced as much to the American Historical Association that year, and well before the end of the decade he came very close to renouncing his 1959 position altogether; certainly he revised it drastically. But the idea—that "straw man," as Fitzpatrick called it—had already obtained such a foothold that Higham could not shake it loose, even in the years and decades to come. Central to the illusion of 1950s consensus, principally because of Higham's having inserted him into the paradigm, was Tocqueville, or more precisely, Tocqueville's "spirit," as Higham put it. The archetypal consensus book, present at the creation of the idea and the real subject of Higham's attack, was Boorstin's *The Genius of American Politics*. But that text contains no discussion, and only the most marginal and fleeting mention, of Tocqueville. Therefore, Tocqueville's connection with consensus via Boorstin was as tenuous and unsubstantiated as the supposed reality of consensus history itself.

This assumed link between Tocqueville and consensus assumed in turn the emergence of a huge Tocqueville "boom," "explosion," "revival," or "vogue." To ascertain the validity of this claim, we might look to one important event in Tocqueville scholarship. George Lawrence's translation of the definitive Gallimard edition of the *Democracy*, published in 1966, provides us with a suitable moment in which a sort of snapshot of Tocqueville's postwar reputation might be taken and analyzed. This snapshot is useful because it furnishes evidence about Tocqueville's stature in the 1960s.

Throughout this book we have noted a recurring pattern in the history of Tocqueville's reception, that of highly respected authors passing along misleading and even erroneous assertions that reinforce the accepted version of events—that of Tocqueville's abrupt disappearance and celebrated return. We have observed it most clearly in works by such writers as A. V. Dicey and Robert Nisbet, both of whom were among the most eminent intellectuals of their times, and seen how it continued at the hands of scholars only slightly less renowned. This dubious tradition endures in the twenty-first century, and it is especially clear when one considers the significance of the Lawrence translation. In 2003, Penguin published a new translation of the *Democracy* by Gerald Bevan with an introduction by the distinguished eighteenth-century specialist Isaac Kramnick. Given the power of Penguin marketing, the book's reasonable price, and the fluid and accessible translation, the edition could be expected to enjoy a wide readership. Yet many of Kramnick's assertions in this introduction must be read with the utmost skepticism, a skepticism that ought to be triggered in a careful reader by the author's allusions to "George William Pearson" as the author of *Tocqueville and Beaumont in America*. Concerning the Lawrence edition, Kramnick represented it, first, as a great success that attracted a lot of attention and, second, as a confirmation of the existence of a "Tocqueville renaissance" during the 1950s and 1960s. In an "olé!" reference of the sort that has characterized this genre for over a century, Kramnick maintained that " 'consensus school' scholars never tired of quoting Tocqueville" in "their 1950s books" and that "the fuss generated by the 1966 edition is testimony to the explosion of interest in Tocqueville in the 1950s and 1960s." Indeed, to Kramnick, the success of the Lawrence volume furnished the proof of the existence of that renaissance. "The Tocqueville revival had succeeded so well," Kramnick claimed in circular fashion, "that the publication of this new translation was reviewed in the literary supplements of the *New York Times*, the *Washington Post* and the *Chicago Tribune*. *Book Week* devoted the entire front page and half an inside page of its Christmas issue to the new *Democracy in America*."[35]

Several difficult problems arise from this undocumented and tendentious assertion. My own careful search turned up no reviews in the *New York Times*, the *Washington Post*, or the *Chicago Tribune*. There was a review in *Book Week*—but if that title is unfamiliar to twenty-first century readers, it is for a good reason: *Book Week* was the Sunday book-review section of the *New York World Journal Tribune*, a daily newspaper that appeared between September 12, 1966, and May 5, 1967. December 25 happened to fall on a Sunday that year. As to the review itself, it was negative.[36]

Although many commentators have seen the Lawrence translation as a confirmation of Tocqueville's exalted stature, the demand for which sprang from the immense popularity of the author, lingering displeasure with the Bradley edition, and a sense that a new generation needed its own version, a 1966 snapshot reveals none of these features of Tocqueville's reception that have been retrojected upon it. Looking back at the contemporary evidence, one can only be mystified as to how anyone came to think that the Lawrence edition was any sort of publishing event. Far from causing a "fuss," the Lawrence translation received almost no serious notice, and most of what it did receive was negative. Only two scholarly journals reviewed it; one review was lukewarm, the other hostile. Such further attention as the book did attract at the time came mainly in the form not of reviews but of notices—fifty- to one-hundred-word announcements, usually anonymous, in trade publications like *Library Journal*, *Booklist*, and *Choice*.[37] Even these short announcements were seldom wholly favorable. Three years later, in 1969, Harper and Row produced its paperback version of the Lawrence edition, printed on paper one step above newsprint in quality. The publicity blurb on the book's back cover was supplied by the adult services coordinator of the Santa Rosa, California, public library.[38]

Lawrence's *Democracy*, then, caused barely a ripple in the academic or publishing worlds when it appeared. In the decade after Lawrence only slight attention was paid to the work, while the student even of recent literature on Tocqueville will be struck by the frequency with which the Bradley edition retains its familiar sway. And yet, in the case of the Lawrence edition as in so many instances before and since, the received version of the book's meaning came to take the form of a fable that is both directly at odds with the contemporary facts, and widely accepted, even by specialists. Post-1960s beliefs and opinions as to what that reaction had been reveal yet again the cloud of inaccuracies and distortions that continues to surround this subject in the twenty-first century.

Michael Kammen is one historian who has tried to take stock of Tocqueville's changing reputation in late-twentieth-century America. In 1997, Kammen noted an "anomalous asymmetry between liberals and conservatives" with respect to Tocqueville in the mid-1990s. Kammen was one of the few commentators to challenge the rather glib and, on the face of it, implausible orthodoxy that Tocqueville's "iconic" status had made him a paragon of political wisdom for both the Left and Right. Certainly, both liberals and conservatives scored points with Tocqueville citations in the 1990s. *Mother Jones*, for example, effectively brought "the prescient Frenchman" to bear against Newt Gingrich at about the same time that Gingrich was hawking the *Democracy* in its most cold war–friendly abridgement as "essential reading for his colleagues to understand their agenda."[39] Such left-right ironies are easy to adduce, but Kammen, with characteristic acumen and empirical support, pointed out the imbalance. Based on what he poetically referred to as "Alexis sightings and citations in Nexis," Kammen concluded that conservatives had "virtually appropriated *Democracy in America* as their favorite source of cerebral ammunition," while liberals, for their part, "by and large . . . simply do without Tocqueville."[40] Kammen did not directly address the possible causes of the "asymmetry," but in his own analysis, he, in a sense, performatively indicated one of them. By going on to argue that "Tocqueville is Not Our Contemporary," Kammen showed both why liberals tended to do without him (for partisan argument) and why some conservatives used him so much.

Much of late-twentieth-century scholarship has labored to historicize Tocqueville—historicize in the classic or Rankean sense of showing how inextricably tied to his own time and culture Tocqueville was, how he was "not our contemporary." Even in his disgust and disenchantment with the men and events of his era, Roger Boesche showed, Tocqueville exhibited a malaise of the spirit that was characteristic of his generation. According to Hugh Brogan, the chief task of Tocqueville scholarship—"the Tocqueville Problem"—is specifically to displace the Tocqueville who has answers to specific problems that we confront today with "attention for the real man," the particular historical figure.[41]

The most pervasive conservative influence on late-twentieth-century Tocqueville scholars was a man who abhorred the historicist direction of modern scholarship, the University of Chicago political philosopher Leo Strauss (1899–1973). Tocqueville commentators, scholars, and translators such as Marvin Zetterbaum, James Ceaser, Delba Winthrop, Harvey Mansfield, and Peter Augustine Lawler all acknowledged the deep impact that Strauss had made on their own approaches to Tocqueville.

Strauss and some of his followers were lightning rods for criticism at the time of the Iraq invasion in 2003. Largely because one of the architects of the George W. Bush administration's Middle East policy, Paul Wolfowitz, had been one of the last of Strauss's students, and a number of that administration's high-level staff and policy positions were occupied by people with expertise in Strauss's ideas, several journalists detected a Straussian clique active in Washington's corridors of power. So agitated did the controversy become that Strauss's daughter, Jenny Strauss Clay, felt she had to intervene. "My father was a teacher, not a right-wing guru," she wrote in a *New York Times* op-ed. "I do not recognize the Leo Strauss presented in these articles."[42]

Yet in the 1980s the picture of Strauss drawn by his numerous detractors was at least as unflattering as those of two decades later. In 1985, the *New York Review of Books* caricaturist David Levine portrayed Strauss as a creature endowed with two right hands. Two *New York Review* essays, in 1985 and 1988, contended that Strauss followers had effectively penetrated government, think tanks, and universities to such an extent that they were able to set the terms of discourse about key problems in American intellectual life, such as the "Founding" (as Straussians invariably referred to the generation that produced the Constitution). "Straussians are everywhere in government and academia, in both high and low places, in conferences, in symposiums, in books and journals," historian Gordon S. Wood lamented in 1988. Furthermore, Strauss had "influenced a large number of students, who in turn have passed on his teaching to their students. Now this third generation is conveying to its students the lessons of the master, thus continuing to widen the circle of the Straussian faith."[43]

In a vigorous 1988 interchange with Richard Rorty over Strauss's legacy,

Harvey Mansfield lodged a complaint that was a mirror image of Gordon Wood's impression that "Straussians are everywhere": Strauss, Mansfield maintained, "has been kept in obscurity by professors through the 'silent treatment' . . . to blight the academic prospects of his followers." Rorty's attack on Strauss was indeed "the first extended notice that a prominent American philosophy professor has taken of Strauss," Mansfield wrote.[44] To Mansfield, this great political philosopher was ignored, if not actively suppressed; to Wood, his followers formed a virtual cult whose influence extended throughout America's leading cultural institutions. Exactly how Straussians could be ubiquitous in a profession that systematically stymied their prospects for employment is a mystery to later readers, but the fact that these mutually canceling observations by distinguished scholars from Brown and Harvard were published within six weeks of each other in major journals indicates how contentious Strauss's ideas and influence had become by the late 1980s.

Strauss played his part in the Tocqueville story not because he had that much to say about the Frenchman but because the conservative commentary on Tocqueville's work came from scholars who candidly expressed an indebtedness to him: "I am a Straussian," Mansfield has said in several contexts; to Peter Augustine Lawler, Strauss was "the greatest political philosopher of the twentieth century."[45]

Influential political scientists like Martin Diamond and James Ceaser (a student of Mansfield) also linked Strauss with Tocqueville. Diamond like other conservative thinkers tried to ignore the amorality of Tocqueville's portrayal of America and to link virtue with Tocqueville's idea of self-interest properly understood. His larger, purely Straussian position was that in the development of human character, the "regime" or political order has an effect greater than all other material forces, such as mode of production or technology. Diamond was stricken by a heart attack immediately after testifying before the Constitutional Subcommittee of the Senate Judiciary Committee, opposing direct election of the president. Senators Orrin Hatch and Birch Bayh tried to revive him, but he died around noon on July 22, 1977, in Capitol Hill Hospital. He was 57. He had moved on that very day from Northern Illinois University to take up the Thomas and Dorothy Leavey Chair on the Foundation of American Freedom at Georgetown University.[46]

Ceaser is not a Tocqueville specialist per se but a thinker imbued with Tocqueville's spirit as he understands it. Lawler placed him in a direct line of descent stretching from Strauss through Mansfield. Echoing Tocqueville, Ceaser called for a new political science—one that would be, in one admirer's words, "an application of traditional political science to new (democratic) circumstances and in no way [entail] a definitive break with classical or Aristotelian political science." Yet his most important work was a fascinating study of European anti-American thought—the concept of America as degeneracy—from G. W. F. Hegel to Martin Heidegger, as well as of leading defenders such as Tocqueville and Strauss.[47]

It has been argued that no particular political position (in terms of the liberal-conservative divide in American politics) necessarily links Strauss to the political right. Gregory Bruce Smith maintained, for example: "While a significant number of prominent students of Strauss have been conservatives, or at least aligned with some causes customarily seen as conservative, I see no necessity for this in Strauss's work. [There is] no reason why he could not easily make cause against those who now have positioned themselves on the right." Smith also, perhaps more effectively, refuted the "cultist leader" charge that seemed always to dog Strauss's reputation. "Transcending historicism was for Strauss the highest task, but that could not be done by rhetoric, myth-making, or esoteric misdirection, as many of Strauss's detractors claim was his intention."[48]

Historicism as it developed in the nineteenth century originally embraced the idea, not particularly controversial now, that the separateness and foreignness of the past can never be fully comprehended by the tools and structures of interpretation that a later era necessarily employs for that purpose. The effort to know what really happened in the past inevitably carries with it a failure to understand that past. Historicism's corollary, which remained undeveloped until Strauss's adversary, Friedrich Nietzsche, threw a glaring light on it, was an unbending antifoundationalism. No truths can ever transcend the conditions of their production; no knowledge can be said to possess a foundation. For Strauss, not only were the consequences of this relentless relativism catastrophic, but the philosophy itself was specious. As the intellectual historian Ted V. McAllister explained the options, Strauss considered "the danger posed by the nihilism of the historicists to be much greater [than that of the ideological thinkers such as Auguste Comte and Karl Marx]. Strauss considered historicism to be the logical modern response to the limitations of ideology, and as such the final, bankrupt conclusion to the dialectic of modernity. The real challenge to the West, he believed, sprang from historicism."[49]

Historicism was a dangerous error because it led to a state of despair over the question of truth. The ancients in particular wrote about questions that are of eternal, not merely local or contemporary, significance, and their insights into the powers and limitations of man in society cannot be, as it were, just historicized away. Yet these ancient sages wrote in a manner and to an audience that assured that it would be impossible for all but a small elite of painstaking readers and scholars to ever understand their full meaning. On the one hand, then, truth could not be historicized into a mere reflection of a writer's social and historical position, such as Tocqueville's status as a white, European, aristocratic male of the nineteenth century; on the other, the wisdom that the great books do indeed contain is destined to be misappropriated by the majority of readers. Hence the charges of esotericism and elitism that Strauss's followers have faced. Theirs is a pessimism only one step less grim than Nietzsche's historicism. Nietzsche said that all truth claims are masks for a drive to dominate; Straussians believe that truth claims can be validated, but only by a few, and those few dedicated to truth, like Socrates, place themselves by structural necessity at odds with their societies, and especially with democratic society.

The meticulous concentration on the text and relegation of historical context to comparatively minor status, then, are the hallmarks of a Straussian approach to Tocqueville. The first Straussian to write about Tocqueville was Marvin Zetterbaum in 1967. Zetterbaum's careful study, *Tocqueville and the Problem of Democracy*, addressed the well-known theme of "Providence" in the *Democracy*. Tocqueville presented the advance of equality and the triumph of democracy over aristocracy as something that was fated, or inevitable. Zetterbaum called it the "inevitability thesis." But Tocqueville never explained *why* democracy was bound to triumph. The seeming paradox of the inevitability thesis—a fated advancement of freedom—lay, in Straussian fashion, in Tocqueville's using Providence as "a salutary myth."

Zetterbaum contended that Tocqueville's advocacy of freedom was instrumental. Tocqueville's hatred of the doctrine of necessity is indeed a universally recognized facet of his thought, but, for Zetterbaum, it was adequately explained by his fear that modern society had a fatal propensity toward lethargy and inaction. Tocqueville therefore promoted freedom as a strategy for countering the lassitude that opened the way to despotism. In similar fashion, with respect to religion, Zetterbaum held (with Doris Goldstein, who, however, was far from Straussian in her elucidation of the subject) that Tocqueville's interest in the question was purely practical: "one of unrelieved functionalism." Zetterbaum's interpretation of Tocqueville, based completely on close reading rather than historical context, was that "Tocqueville employs the tools and techniques of politics: enlightenment, persuasion, invention, and myth. Only if the art of politics can be brought to the aid of freedom can the problem of democracy be resolved. This, Tocqueville found, had been accomplished with consummate skill in America."[50]

Another exemplary case of the Straussian approach was evident in an important article by Delba Winthrop elucidating Tocqueville's chapters on women in the second *Democracy*. At the time her article appeared, "[Pierre] Manent's brief but incisive discussion of women is the only substantial one in the secondary literature of which I am aware," Winthrop wrote. This was in 1986, before essays were published on the topic by Gita May and Linda Kerber (both of whom ignored Winthrop). So Winthrop was in fact the first scholar to address this momentous issue.

Winthrop's stated aim was to place the "women" section in context in order to interpret it properly. But she did not understand "context" to mean the legal and social roles of women in the Jacksonian era, or the political and economic structures of an expanding, slaveholding republic as they impinged on white women's opportunities, or the new kinds of moral and religious roles that antebellum America set aside for female citizens, or the burgeoning scholarship on antebellum women's history; rather, "context" for Winthrop meant the particular location of those chapters on women within the inclusive text of *Democracy in America*. All but one of Winthrop's 101 notes were references to the *Democracy*. Her article was thus a work of pure explication. And as explication it was excellent. "Today it is supposed by virtually all advocates of women's liberation that active participation in the economic and political life of a democracy is needed for women's fulfillment," Winthrop argued. This, however, is precisely "the supposition that Tocqueville questions." Tocqueville was skeptical because he saw more deeply than superficial suppositions by current feminists about democracy's furnishing an adequate milieu for true emancipation. Instead, "Tocqueville intends to show that neither business nor political life is truly fulfilling or liberating; neither has an end that is both meaningful and attainable. Therefore, woman's lack of opportunities is no more a misfortune for her than for the men she benefits in abjuring worldliness." Again, in her focus on very close reading and attention to textual structure, her implicit and explicit critique of democracy's sunny mythology, her utter unconcern for historicizing Tocqueville's insights, and also, perhaps, her implicit reservations about a standard element of liberal orthodoxy, Winthrop's article was a worthy representative of the Straussian approach.[51]

The best, extended Straussian study of Tocqueville in the late twentieth century was Lawler's *The Restless Mind*. In this earnest book by a student of Winthrop one could encounter a careful, philosophically sophisticated, and at times profound meditation on Tocqueville's views of liberty. Readers must have had difficulty in putting aside their reaction to the very first sentences of the book, in which Lawler modestly described his effort by declaring, "This book will be of interest to Tocqueville scholars as the most comprehensive account of his extraordinary thought and life." Coming as it did well after the comprehensive accounts of André Jardin, J. P. Mayer, George Pierson, Edward Gargan, James T. Schleifer, and many others, Lawler's self-description was, at a minimum, not in the best of taste. But, in spite of, or even by virtue of, their very callowness, Lawler's words did offer an intimation of his book's contents and method. For in *The Restless Mind* none of the above scholars' major works were even mentioned, let alone addressed, save in a few cases and in the most glancing fashion. Schleifer's magisterial *The Making of Tocqueville's "Democracy in America,"* for example, was glaringly absent. Moreover, despite his claim of furnishing a "comprehensive account" of Tocqueville's life, Lawler mentioned Jardin's definitive biography but once. Lawler was clearly in pursuit of something very different from what those scholars had been after. He wished to tease out the meanings of liberty in Tocqueville's work as it is given to us in the printed text. "Tocqueville's liberalism, with Strauss's help, can be viewed as remarkably similar in some respects to that of the ancient or classical thinkers," Lawler contended.[52] In this endeavor, he succeeded admirably. Students of Tocqueville who wish to see what the result of very close and philosophically informed readings on this most crucial of Tocquevillean themes can produce could do no better than to read, with a similar kind of care, *The Restless Mind*. However, in its lack of concern with the historical scholarship, this work also starkly revealed the limitations of Straussian scholarship on Tocqueville. *The Restless Mind* exhibited an insularity of reference that left it outside the stream of Tocqueville scholarship. If Straussians sometimes complained of marginalization by the academy, they must also have recognized that the very nature of their philosophy led them to withdraw from current scholarly trends and issues. Their marginalization was to a degree self-imposed. Straussian writers like Lawler and most of the writers included in a deeply disappointing sesquicentennial anthology entitled *Interpreting Tocqueville's "Democracy in America"* referred mainly to each other's works without significantly engaging the historical scholarship.[53]

Interpreting Tocqueville's "Democracy in America" was the product of a large conference held in California under the auspices of the conservative, Strauss-influenced Claremont Institute. At the other end of the continent, at about the same time, a quite different conference convened at the City University

of New York. It was very much an East Coast affair. The westernmost contributor was Seymour Drescher of the University of Pittsburgh; everyone else
was from the greater New York area. That meeting also produced a volume,
Reconsidering Tocqueville's "Democracy in America," consisting of eleven sparkling essays, something far better than the usual run of conference-generated
anthologies. The two books' titles indicated the approaches taken at the two
conferences, for the New York meeting rendered a series of critical reapprais-
als—a "reconsidering"—while the California symposium concentrated in
Straussian fashion on explication—"interpreting." What was striking about
the New Yorkers was the sense they conveyed that, while Tocqueville's greatness must be acknowledged, he had to be understood as a man of his time
and place; and, concomitantly, perhaps the time was approaching when his
usefulness to contemporary thinkers was reaching a stage of diminishing
returns. Daniel T. Rogers, for example, roundly criticized the clichéd image
of Tocqueville as a prophet. "It is time to stop reading *Democracy in America*
as a book of prophecy," he concluded. Tocqueville "got a great deal wrong
. . . To think he had his eye on us has been for too long our private, oddly
egocentric folly." Sean Wilentz was more critical still, condemning much of
the then-recent scholarship for its superficiality, its reverential attitude
toward Tocqueville, its "gloss[ing] over *Democracy*'s bad hunches, misinformed reporting, and ideological biases . . . its slighting of so much important recent work about the past."[54]

The remark by Michael Kammen about the conservative-liberal asymmetry with respect to uses of Tocqueville might be profitably considered in light
of these two antithetical sets of conferences and books. While the California
scholars, who were mostly political philosophers, were presenting readings of
the *Democracy* and using Tocqueville to make specific points about current
affairs—the conference was replete with complaints against "the intellectuals of the 1960s" who brought America to "the edge of despotism," the congressional hearings to confirm Robert Bork for the Supreme Court, the policy
of affirmative action, the evils of big government, the Tocquevillean prediction about Russia and America dividing the globe, and "the bureaucratiza-
tion of women and children"—the group in New York, mostly historians,
were not only showing the limitations of applying Tocqueville to specific
contemporary problems but even suggesting that his day of dominion might
be drawing toward its evening hours.[55] In such stark contrasts, these two conferences anticipated Kammen's observation by a dozen years.

Perhaps the leading Straussian at the end of the twentieth century was
Harvey C. Mansfield. In 2000, Mansfield and Delba Winthrop produced the

first full translation of the *Democracy* since the 1966 Lawrence version. *Harvard Magazine* designated Mansfield the "Prince of the Conservatives" in 1999, although the moniker alluded as much to Mansfield's stature as the foremost scholar of Niccolò Machiavelli as to his position in some royal line of succession.[56] Mansfield's first encounter with Tocqueville came in 1952 when he attended a course at Harvard given by Louis Hartz. While he did not concentrate on Tocqueville for years to come, the tension between liberty and equality that he found in Tocqueville resonated in his mind—much as it did for Schleifer and Drescher—to be brought out later. For a period during the 1970s, J. P. Mayer was ensconced in Harvard's Center for European Studies, and "for some reason he took a shine to me," Mansfield recalled. The two became close; this was a second encounter with Tocqueville. It was, however, Leo Strauss who made the deepest impression on Mansfield's thinking, although the two did not work together as colleagues. Strauss was a "friend but not an *enthusiast*" of democracy, Mansfield has said; and it is Tocqueville's comprehensiveness, his seeing that all of America is permeated by a kind of moderate democracy, which, by being very close to a Straussian concept of "regime," is what attracted Strauss to the Frenchman and led him to "recommend him to his students."[57]

For Winthrop, Mansfield's partner in translation, as for almost all of the leading scholars in the field, Tocqueville was a scholarly direction that came late. Her serious interest in political philosophy began at Cornell where she was an undergraduate; she then moved to Harvard for a Ph.D. Her dissertation was on Aristotle, and, she explained, it seemed logical to move from the leading philosopher of ancient liberty to his modern counterpart.[58]

In an interview, both Mansfield and Winthrop communicated a useful sense of the affinities between Strauss and Tocqueville, namely that they were not interested in the merely social but rather in a true political sociology; that they concerned themselves with regimes comprehensively; that they were "friends but not *enthusiasts*" for democracy; that, for them, politics itself is a realm of imperfection, and they did not see simple political solutions to human problems; and finally that the study of regimes entailed the examination of mores. To this list, Cheryl Welch added another element, the concern with religion.[59] Taken together, these preoccupations at least partially explained the elective affinities of late-twentieth-century Straussians for the works of Tocqueville—but only partly. Of at least equal importance was Straussians' contempt for poststructuralist and postmodern trends in the humanities, a disdain for which they found inspiration in Strauss's rejection of historicism.

When, in 2000, Straussians Mansfield and Winthrop produced the first new translation of the *Democracy* since 1966, then, it was the most literal, careful translation that had been done to date. Mansfield and Winthrop contended that Henry Reeve and George Lawrence, the previous translators, "do not believe Tocqueville was a deep thinker; we do." Consequently, they devoted themselves to "the intrinsic subordination of translator to author." Some of the response supported Mansfield's earlier contention that Straussians faced marginalization; for example, they were subjected to pointless and mean criticism in the *New York Times* for having used an "archconservative style" and looked on with suspicion because foundations that were "widely known for their support of the intellectual right wing" supported the project. Yet, the self-segregating tendency was pointed out as well, notably by Drescher. Drescher's review also raised a pointed question that echoed those asked by many reviewers of Tocqueville translations from the time of Francis Bowen to that of Phillips Bradley, namely why they had not undertaken to translate the most complete scholarly French edition.[60]

Neoconservative and Straussian Tocqueville scholars may have showed disdain for the late twentieth century's fashionable theoretical approaches to history and literature, but by no means did it follow that structuralist and poststructuralist theories departed the field in consequence. Tocqueville was of interest to postmodern theorists too. Although Kammen's observation about conservatives' using the *Democracy* as a dump of "cerebral ammunition" was correct as to a specific partisan political deployment, several major efforts were made to apply structuralist and poststructuralist insights and methods of interpretation to Tocqueville's works. None of these efforts (perhaps symptomatically) was addressed to the *Democracy*, however, but instead were directed toward what were, from a narcissistically American viewpoint, the more "marginal" classics, such as *The Old Regime* and the *Recollections*.

Hayden White's hugely influential *Metahistory* (1973)[61] attempted to establish a taxonomy of nineteenth-century European historical writing and, in a move that was at least as bold, to show how the development of such writing occurred in tandem with the philosophy of history itself. A classic—or perhaps a museum piece—of structuralism with numerous debts, as Dominick La Capra noted,[62] to the New Critics, *Metahistory* comprised a highly ramified theoretical introduction, plus chapters on the giants of nineteenth-century European historical writing from Jules Michelet to Benedetto Croce, including Tocqueville. In White's taxonomy, reminiscent of Northrop Frye's beautiful structural–New Critical *Anatomy of Criticism*, Tocqueville was presented as a tragical-realist historian, in contrast to his great peers who were variously romantic, satirical, or comic in their modes of argument.[63] To Kammen, White's attempt was little more than another example of the decorative tendency that I have discussed in chapter 1 of the present work: he called White one of the writers "who want ornamentation to decorate pronouncements that Alexis de Tocqueville might not understand, recognize, or accept" and argued that "Tocqueville would be quite surprised (if not astonished) by the chapter devoted to his work in" *Metahistory*.[64] Yet, when read in conjunction with his discussion of the other historians, White's bold and almost hubristic study did convey the context of history as it was being developed in nineteenth-century Europe, even if his specific treatment of Tocqueville or any of the other historians and philosophers taken in isolation was deficient.

White's book represented the splendid autumn of structuralist analysis of history and its practitioners. He had characterized his book as "an analysis of the deep structure of the historical imagination" at the height of the prestige of structuralism in the mid-1970s. By the end of that decade, however, all "meta" claims were subjected to a new kind of attack as Jean-François Lyotard pointed to an "incredulity toward metanarratives" as the sine qua non of the condition of postmodernity at the moment when White's *Metahistory* enjoyed widespread prestige.[65]

Rather than rejecting, willfully misreading, or simply ignoring Tocqueville, as conservative commentators strongly implied would be Tocqueville's fate at the hands of poststructural critics, Tocqueville was served quite well in several studies by such scholars. Indeed, the openness toward this French theorist by his twentieth- and twenty-first–century descendants was a more reliable indicator of his continuing broad-gauge relevance in American intellectual life than Kammen's search for liberal versus conservative references to the *Democracy* in Nexis. In *History and Reading*, Kammen's Cornell colleague Dominick La Capra placed Tocqueville in dialog with Michel Foucault in order to explore the ways that various reading strategies and approaches to history itself could enrich our understanding of the Enlightenment and its legacy. Most scholars interested in either Tocqueville or Foucault, La Capra found, tended to share the assumptions—liberal or transgressive—of the object of their attention and failed adequately to subject those assumptions to critical scrutiny. La Capra thought this failure might have been more pronounced among scholars who worked on Tocqueville, which is arguable, but he saw the possibilities for illumination that could be actualized by setting up an exchange between these nineteenth- and twentieth-century critics. He believed moreover that "scholars working in the traditions of one of these important figures rarely read either the works of or commentary on the other." While repulsing the temptation to minimize or level out the gulf separating the two analysts, La Capra pointed out an impressive list of similarities. La Capra's elegant book validated Tocqueville in another way, as well, namely in its use of the comparative method.[66]

But the most impressive deployment of poststructural reading strategies for interpreting Tocqueville came in a provocative study of the *Recollections* by L. E. Shiner. The most rewarding way of approaching that tragicomic memoir is to bring to it an interpretive tool-kit consisting of an excellent history of 1848, such as Georges Duveau's *1848*, and Shiner's book, *The Secret Mirror*.[67] Tocqueville began his *Recollections* by designating it as a private, hermetic text rather than a book written for the public gaze: "a mirror, in which I can enjoy seeing my contemporaries and myself, not a painting for the public to view" (*R* 3–4). Shiner focused on this stated intention in order to undermine it. "Tocqueville's explicit nonliterary intention offers the reader an excellent occasion for exploring the unconscious working of literary and rhetorical devices in a text that disclaims them" (6). Shiner made most effective use of reader-response criticism—the "reverse side" of rhetorical criticism, he called it (7)—to illuminate Tocqueville's rhetorical devices. He found Tocqueville to construct his narrative on such devices as the portrait, the aphorism, and the tableau, and concluded from this discovery that "the *Recollections* belongs in the general tradition of the French *moralistes*" (33).

Having identified such devices and captured two sets of binary oppositions that permeate Tocqueville's tableaux and portraits, Shiner constructed a "thematic code" of the *Recollections* (90). The opposed pairings he identified were liberty and equality, and grandeur and greed. "From these two moral poles," he explained, "one can work outward toward all the other leading substantive terms and concepts of the text. Thus, *grandeur* leads through *désintéressement* to 'aristocracy' in general and to Tocqueville and his friends in particular, whereas *cupidité* leads through *égoïsme* and *bassesse* to 'bourgeoisie' in general and to Havin and Thiers in particular" (89). The *Recollections* reads like a different book after one has encountered Shiner.

Although the *Democracy* faded in the scholarly literature toward the end of the twentieth century, it was not the *Recollections* or the "Memoir on Pauperism" that supplanted it, but *The Old Regime and the Revolution*. After languishing in the American academy for a century, Tocqueville's "other" masterpiece began to gather tremendous momentum as the bicentennial of the French Revolution drew near. Much of the force behind the new American attention derived from the writing and teaching of the great French historian François Furet. Furet's 1978 masterwork, *Penser la Révolution française*, was the culmination of a protracted swing in historical interpretation that one of its architects, Keith Michael Baker, called "a shift from Marx to Tocqueville."[68]

Furet died in 1997 from a head injury suffered—tragically yet somehow fittingly for a historian of the French Revolution—while playing tennis. His loss was mourned by the scholarly world of two continents. In Chicago, the loss was especially severe, because in 1985 Furet had crossed the Atlantic to accept a position at the University of Chicago, while maintaining his old position at the Institut Raymond Aron in Paris. Furet spent every autumn term at Chicago, returning, as would any man of sense and sensibility, to Paris for the spring. While he was in Chicago, he worked with the British-born Baker, who had studied with Furet during the 1970s at the Institut Raymond Aron (known then as the Ecole des Hautes Etudes en Sciences Sociales), and together they trained a gifted band of graduate students that included Daniel Gordon and—especially known to Tocqueville scholars—Alan S. Kahan, the author of *Aristocratic Liberalism* and translator of *The Old Regime*, published by the University of Chicago Press. *Aristocratic Liberalism* began as Kahan's doctoral dissertation, completed under the direction of Baker, with Furet a member of the committee.

"The first task of the historiography of the French Revolution must be to rediscover the analysis of its political dimension," Furet boldly announced.[69] The focus on the political represented a drastic shift in interpretation because, for a century, the dominant paradigm for understanding the Revolution had been derived from Marx's conviction that the event had constituted a social upheaval first and foremost, that it was indeed a paradigm of modern class struggle. Not only did the purely social interpretation of 1789 collapse of its own weight toward the end of the twentieth century, however,[70] but Furet showed that there was a robust, superior alternative to it. In other words, the failure of the *marxisant* approach need not result in an interpretive vacuum. Instead it was time to turn to the study of politics and ideas. Furet "wrenched the study of political culture away from those who endeavored to embed it in economic or social history," one admirer wrote. "His work gave ideas a new dignity and power by demonstrating the circumstances under which ideas were autonomous agents, operating more or less independently of any of the many apotheosized notions of 'society' or of 'social context' that had captured mainstream historiography and the social sciences."[71]

The turn to the political was not, nor could it be, simply a restatement of

Tocqueville's themes. Rather, in the hands of Furet and others, the subject matter of this new approach to the Revolution was political culture. This concern was itself transformed by new theoretical approaches that became au courant in and after the 1970s. In this case, the political turn in history gained momentum from the linguistic turn in philosophy. During the 1980s, Baker published a series of essays in which he addressed the question of how the ideas of 1788–1789 became so thoroughly radicalized as to culminate in the Terror of 1793. In this project Baker was hardly alone, but he adopted a method that was at odds with the social historians and in harmony (though not uncritically) with the political and intellectual history epitomized by Furet's work. To be precise, he understood the concept of political culture to be a *linguistic* concept. Politics is "about making claims," he wrote. It is "the activity through which individuals and groups in any society articulate, negotiate, implement, and enforce the competing claims they make upon one another and upon the whole. Political culture is, in this sense, the set of discourses or symbolic practices by which these claims are made."[72]

The specific arguments that Baker made concerning the discourses of revolution, nationhood, democracy, representation, constitution, and history in the era of the Revolution were complex, subtle, and erudite; and because of those very qualities, they gave the reader a feeling of being "in on" the great arguments as they unfolded. Several factors linked this approach to American scholarly opinion about Tocqueville. First, there was the institutional connection with American higher education via the University of Chicago and the mentorship of Furet. Second, and more directly, the attempts to elucidate the manner in which a culture's modes of framing discourses shape actual structures of political institutions and affect desperate political struggles both drew from and advanced the reigning linguistic approaches to texts and events in current humanities scholarship. Finally, the subtext of anti-Marxism in the historiography of the French Revolution coincided with the collapse of Central and East European Communist regimes, while the belated, but fervent, repudiation of prior Communist commitments by French intellectuals, Furet most prominent among them,[73] echoed the somber perspective of Tocqueville's views about 1789 and 1848 a century and a quarter earlier: the first time as tragedy, and the second time, too.

Notes

1. John Lukacs, "Introduction" and "A Note on Gobineau," in Alexis de Tocqueville, *"The European Revolution" and Correspondence with Gobineau*, ed. and trans. John

Lukacs (Garden City, N.Y.: Doubleday Anchor, 1959), 1–28 and 179–87; "Tocqueville Centenary. Commemorating the One Hundredth Anniversary of the Death of Alexis de Tocqueville, Philadelphia, 13 and 14 April 1959," Archives, Chestnut Hill College; John Lukacs, "Reading, Writing, and History"; Edward T. Gargan, "The Formation of Tocqueville's Historical Thought," *Review of Politics* 24, no. 1 (January 1962): 48–61; Fritz Stern, "The Liberalism of Tocqueville," *Columbia University Forum* 2, no. 4 (Fall 1959): 33–36; Hoffman, "Tocqueville and Burke"; Salomon, "Tocqueville 1959."

2. Lukacs interview.

3. Riesman, "Tocqueville as Ethnographer," 175.

4. M. R. D. Foot, "Professor J.-P. Mayer," *The Independent*, December 21, 1992, Gazette, 11; *The Daily Telegraph*, January 1, 1993, 19.

5. J. P. Mayer, *Alexis de Tocqueville: A Biographical Study in Political Science* (New York: Harper Torchbooks, 1960), ix, xi.

6. Roger C. Wines to the author, February 26, 2003.

7. Lawrence Henry Gipson, "An Appreciation," in *Crisis in the "Great Republic": Essays Presented to Ross J. S. Hoffman*, ed. Gaetano L. Vincitorio (New York: Fordham University Press, 1969), xii–xix.

8. John C. Olin interview, in *As I Remember Fordham: Selections from the Sesquicentennial Oral History Project* (New York: Office of the Sesquicentennial, Fordham University, 1991), 152. Concerning his conversion, see Ross J. S. Hoffman, "The Verdict of History," in *The Road to Damascus: The Spiritual Pilgrimage of Fifteen Converts to Catholicism* (Garden City, N.Y.: Doubleday, 1950), 72–97; Ross J. S. Hoffman, *Restoration* (New York: Sheed & Ward, 1934), *passim*; and Allitt, *Catholic Converts*, 222–23.

9. William J. Schlaerth, S.J., ed., *A Symposium on Alexis de Tocqueville's "Democracy in America,"* Burke Society Series No. 1 (New York: Fordham University Press, 1945).

10. Schlaerth, "Editor's Preface," in *Symposium on Tocqueville*, 7.

11. Ross J. S. Hoffman and Paul Levack, eds., *Burke's Politics: Selected Writings and Speeches on Reform, Revolution and War* (New York: Alfred A. Knopf, 1948).

12. Roger C. Wines to the author, February 26, 2003.

13. Ross J. S. Hoffman, "Tocqueville and Burke," *The Burke Newsletter* 2 (1961): 44.

14. Russell Kirk, *The Conservative Mind: From Burke to Santayana* (Chicago: Henry Regenery Company, 1953), 194–95.

15. Bruce Frohnen, *Virtue and the Promise of Conservatism: The Legacy of Burke and Tocqueville* (Lawrence: University Press of Kansas, 1993); E. L. Godkin, "De Tocqueville on the French Revolution."

16. Martin Peretz, "The Making of a Patriot," *Wall Street Journal*, November 10, 1998, A20; J. P. Mayer, foreword to *Democracy in America*, by Alexis de Tocqueville, ed. J. P. Mayer and Max Lerner, trans. George Lawrence (New York: Harper and Row, 1966), vii; Max Lerner, *Tocqueville and American Civilization* (New Brunswick, N.J.: Transaction, 1994); Sanford Lakoff, *Max Lerner: Pilgrim in the Promised Land* (Chicago: University of Chicago Press, 1998).

17. John Patrick Diggins, "Knowledge and Sorrow: Louis Hartz's Quarrel with American History," *Political Theory* 16, no. 3 (August 1988): 356, 361.

18. "Louis Hartz," in *Scribner Encyclopedia of American Lives, Vol. 2, 1986–1990*, ed. Kenneth T. Jackson (New York: Scribner's, 1999), 388.

19. Diggins, "Hartz," 370.

20. James O'Brien, "America the Beautiful: An Essay on Daniel Boorstin and Louis Hartz" (Ann Arbor, Mich.: Radical Education Project, n.d.), 2–3.

21. Daniel J. Boorstin, "American Liberalism," *Commentary* 20 (July–December 1955): 99, 100.

22. See the appreciations by George M. Fredrickson, "Hanging Together," *New York Review of Books* 49, no. 3 (2002): 37–40, and Michael Kammen, "John Higham and the Nourishment of Memory," *Reviews in American History* 32, no. 2 (June 2004): 293–304.

23. "John Higham, C. V., " at www.jhu.edu/~history/html/John_Higham_CV.html (accessed September 6, 2002).

24. *American Jewish History* 75, no. 2 (December 1986).

25. John Higham, "The Cult of the 'American Consensus': Homogenizing Our History," *Commentary* 27 (February 1959): 93–100. Subsequent references appear parenthetically in the text.

26. Higham interview. Higham was quoting himself; see John Higham, "Beyond Consensus: The Historian as Moral Critic," in *Writing American History: Essays on Modern Scholarship* (Bloomington: Indiana University Press, 1970), 146; originally published 1962.

27. Higham, "Beyond Consensus," 146.

28. Higham, "American Historiography in the 1960s," *Writing American History*, 159–60.

29. Higham, "American Historiography in the 1960s," 159.

30. Nicholas Lemann, "The New American Consensus," *New York Times Magazine*, November 1, 1998, 70.

31. The most cogent study is Daniel Joseph Singal, "Beyond Consensus: Richard Hofstadter and American Historiography," *American Historical Review* 89, no. 4 (October 1984): 976–1004. Susan Stout Baker, *Radical Beginnings: Richard Hofstadter and the 1930s* (Westport, Conn.: Greenwood Press, 1985), provides much confirmatory evidence on this point during the early career. See also Stanley Elkins and Eric McKitrick, "Richard Hofstadter: A Progress," in *The Hofstadter Aegis: A Memorial*, ed. Stanley Elkins and Eric McKitrick (New York: Knopf, 1974), 300–67, esp. 309–12; Arthur M. Schlesinger Jr., "Richard Hofstadter," in *Pastmasters: Some Essays on American Historians*, ed. Marcus Cunliffe and Robin W. Winks (New York: Harper and Row, 1969), 278–315. In one of his last scholarly contributions, a paper on Hofstadter that he read at the Chesapeake Branch of the Historical Society on February 28, 1999, Higham said, "This is not to say, however, that Hofstadter ever was, as many have contended, a part of the Consensus school of historians that flourished in the 1950s and early sixties." John Higham, "The Comic Genius of Richard Hofstadter: A Personal View with Special Reference to *The American Political Tradition and the Men Who Made It*," typescript in the possession of the author, 6.

32. Ellen Fitzpatrick, *History's Memory: Writing America's Past, 1880–1980* (Cambridge, Mass.: Harvard University Press, 2002), 190, 191; John Higham, "The Limits of Relativism: Restatement and Remembrance," *Journal of the History of Ideas* 56, no. 4 (October 1995): 673.

33. Daniel J. Boorstin, *The Genius of American Politics* (Chicago: University of Chicago Press, 1953). On "givenness," see esp. 8–10; on the Puritans, see 36–65.

34. Boorstin, *Genius of American Politics*, 191, 192, 193, 194.

35. Kramnick, "Introduction," xlii–xliii.

36. John William Ward, "The Democratic Animal," *Book Week* 4, no. 16 (December 25, 1966), 1, 10.

37. Kramnick, "Introduction," xlii; Durand Echeverria, *William and Mary Quarterly*, 3rd. ser., 24, no. 4 (October 1967): 637–40 (favorable); Lynn L. Marshall, *Journal of American History* 54, no. 2 (September 1967): 378–80 (hostile); anonymous, *New York History* 51, no. 1 (January 1970): 117–18; anonymous, *Booklist* 63, no. 14 (March 15, 1967), 747; anonymous, *Choice* 4, no. 4 (June 1967): 474; John Lustig, *Library Journal* 91, no. 1 (January 1, 1966), 108.

38. John Lustig in *Library Journal*.

39. Kammen, *Alexis de Tocqueville*, 38; "Editor's Note: The American Way," *Mother Jones* 24, no. 1 (January/February 1999): 7; Tocqueville, *Democracy in America*, specially edited and abridged for the modern reader by Richard D. Heffner (New York: New American Library, 1956). The *Democracy*, Heffner wrote in this Gingrich-endorsed edition, is "pre-eminently a tract for our times" (9); Michael Kammen, "Wrecked on the Fourth of July," *New York Times Book Review*, July 6, 1997, 23.

40. Kammen, *Alexis de Tocqueville*, 34, 36.

41. Boesche, *Strange Liberalism*, esp. 34–40; Boesche interview; Brogan, *Tocqueville*, 11. As Alan S. Kahan wrote, instead of asking Tocqueville what his questions were, we ask him our own questions, "and as a result get an answer that is distorted or misunderstood." Alan S. Kahan, *Aristocratic Liberalism: The Social and Political Thought of Jacob Burckhardt, John Stuart Mill, and Alexis de Tocqueville* (Ithaca, N.Y.: Cornell University Press, 1992), 164.

42. Seymour M. Hersh, "Annals of National Security: Selective Intelligence," *New Yorker* 79, no. 11 (May 12, 2003), 44–51; Lexington, "Philosophers and Kings," *Economist*, June 21, 2003, 629; James Atlas, "Leo-Cons," *New York Times*, May 4, 2003, Section 4, 1, 4; Jenny Strauss Clay, "The Real Leo Strauss," *New York Times*, June 7, 2003, A29.

43. Gordon S. Wood, "The Fundamentalists and the Constitution," *New York Review of Books*, February 18, 1988, 30; see also M. F. Burnyeat, "Sphinx without a Secret," *New York Review of Books*, May 30, 1985, 30–36; Levine drawing 30.

44. Harvey C. Mansfield, "Democracy and the Great Books," *New Republic*, April 4, 1988, 33, 34.

45. Mansfield, "Democracy and the Great Books," 34; Mansfield interview; Peter Augustine Lawler, "Ceaser's American Political Science," *Perspectives on Political Science* 29, no. 3 (Summer 2000): 135.

46. Martin Diamond, "Ethics and Politics," in *The Moral Foundations of the American Republic*, ed. Robert H. Horwitz, 3rd ed. (Charlottesville: University Press of Virginia), 75–108, see esp. 82–85 and 101–7; *New York Times*, July 23, 1977, 22.

47. Lawler, "Ceaser's American Political Science," 135–41; Daniel J. Mahoney, "Renewing the Political Perspective: Reflections on James Ceaser, Political Science, and Liberal Democracy," *Perspectives on Political Science* 29, no. 3 (Summer 2000): 153; James W. Ceaser, *Reconstructing America: The Symbol of America in Modern Thought* (New Haven, Conn.: Yale University Press, 1997); see also Richard Wolin, *The Seduction of Unreason: The Intellectual Romance with Fascism from Nietzsche to Postmodernism* (Princeton, N.J.: Princeton University Press, 2004), 278–314, for an excellent further meditation on the same subject that began as a review of Ceaser.

48. Gregory Bruce Smith, "Leo Strauss and the Straussians: An Anti-Democratic Cult?" *PS: Political Science and Politics* 30, no. 2 (January 1997): 189n12, 185.

49. Ted V. McAllister, *Revolt against Modernity: Leo Strauss, Eric Voegelin, and the Search for a Postliberal Order* (Lawrence: University Press of Kansas, 1996), 135; on Strauss and historicism, see 132–53.

50. Marvin Zetterbaum, *Tocqueville and the Problem of Democracy* (Stanford, Cal.: Stanford University Press, 1967), 3, 18, 19, 116, 88.

51. Delba Winthrop, "Tocqueville's American Woman and 'The True Conception of Democratic Progress,'" *Political Theory* 14 (May 1986): 239–61, quote on 256n5; on this subject, see also Gita May, "Tocqueville on the Role of Women in a Democracy," in *Voltaire, the Enlightenment and the Comic Mode: Essays in Honor of Jean Sareil*, ed. Maxine G. Cutler (New York: Peter Lang, 1990), 159–70, and Kerber, "Separate Spheres." Winthrop's Straussian approach to Tocqueville as a commentator on key social problems of her own time is also evident in Delba Winthrop, "Race and Freedom in Tocqueville," in *The Revival of Constitutionalism*, ed. James W. Muller (Lincoln: University of Nebraska Press, 1988), 151–71.

52. Peter Augustine Lawler, *The Restless Mind: Alexis de Tocqueville on the Origin and Perpetuation of Human Liberty* (Lanham, Md.: Rowman & Littlefield, 1993), 101.

53. Ken Masugi, ed., *Interpreting Tocqueville's "Democracy in America"* (Savage, Md.: Rowman & Littlefield, 1991).

54. Daniel T. Rodgers, "Of Prophets and Prophecy," *Reconsidering*, 206; Sean Wilentz, "Many Democracies: On Tocqueville and Jacksonian America," *Reconsidering*, 208.

55. Masugi, *Interpreting*, 171, 169, 232.

56. Janet Tassel, "The 30 Years' War: Cultural Conservatives Struggle with the Harvard They Love," *Harvard Magazine* 102, no. 1 (September–October 1999): 56–66, 99. The soubriquet appeared on the magazine cover.

57. Mansfield interview.

58. Winthrop interview.

59. Cheryl Welch, *De Tocqueville* (Oxford: Oxford University Press, 2001), 245–47.

60. Mansfield and Winthrop, "Translating Tocqueville's *Democracy in America*," 154, 155; Crain, "Tocqueville for the Neocons"; James Q. Wilson to the editor, *New York*

Times Book Review, February 4, 2001, 2; Seymour Drescher, *Journal of American History* 88, no. 2 (September 2001): 612–14. A balanced survey of the issues raised by the translation is John Gould, "Translations: Stealing Tocqueville?" *American Prospect* 12, no. 17 (September 24–October 8, 2001): 37.

61. Hayden White, *Metahistory: The Historical Imagination in Nineteenth-Century Europe* (Baltimore, Md.: Johns Hopkins University Press, 1973).

62. Dominick La Capra, *History and Reading: Tocqueville, Foucault, French Studies* (Toronto: University of Toronto Press, 2000), 28.

63. White, *Metahistory*, 42.

64. Kammen, *Alexis de Tocqueville*, 57, 64n96.

65. White, *Metahistory*, ix; Jean-François Lyotard, *La condition postmoderne: rapport sur le savoir* (Paris: Éditions de minuit, 1979); *The Postmodern Condition: A Report on Knowledge*, trans. Geoff Bennington and Brian Massumi (Minneapolis: University of Minnesota Press, 1984).

66. La Capra, *History and Reading*, 5.

67. Georges Duveau, *1848: The Making of a Revolution*, trans. Anne Carter (Cambridge, Mass.: Harvard University Press, 1984); L. E. Shiner, *The Secret Mirror: Literary Form and History in Tocqueville's Recollections* (Ithaca, N.Y.: Cornell University Press, 1988). Subsequent references appear parenthetically in the text.

68. François Furet, *Penser la Révolution française* (Paris: Gallimard, 1978); François Furet, *Interpreting the French Revolution*, trans. Elborg Forster (New York: Cambridge University Press, 1981); Keith Michael Baker, *Inventing the French Revolution* (Cambridge: Cambridge University Press, 1990), 1.

69. Furet, *Interpreting the French Revolution*, 29.

70. A process summarized in Baker, *Inventing the French Revolution*, 1–4.

71. Michael Mosher, "On the Originality of François Furet: A Commemorative Note," *Political Theory* 26, no. 3 (June 1998): 392.

72. Baker, *Inventing the French Revolution*, 4.

73. François Furet, *The Passing of an Illusion: The Idea of Communism in the Twentieth Century*, trans. Deborah Furet (Chicago: University of Chicago Press, 1999).

CHAPTER SEVEN

Lumpers and Splitters

At the time that the two *Democracy in America* sesquicentennial conferences were held in New York and Los Angeles, only one scholar was invited to both coasts to present his views. Understandably, it was James T. Schleifer, the world's leading authority on *Democracy in America*. Schleifer is both the author of the most important study of the *Democracy* ever published and the representative of the great Yale University tradition (it has even been referred to as a "Yale School"[1]) of Tocqueville scholarship. Schleifer's journey to the field was marked by adventure and happenstance. Along the way, he got to know the "formidable" George Wilson Pierson well. It was not always, it seems, a pleasant experience. Despite (or some might say because of) his profound engagement with democracy's greatest explicator, Pierson was far from enthusiastic about many forms of social equality. When he was the chairman of Yale's History Department, he fretted about the low social standing of the department's majors. "Apparently the subject of English still draws to a degree from the cultivated, professional, and well-to-do classes, hence more young men and women from able backgrounds," he candidly reported to the president. "By contrast, the subject of history seems to appeal on the whole to a lower social stratum. . . . Far too few of our history candidates are sons of professional men; far too many list their parent's occupation as janitor, watchman, salesman, grocer, pocketbook cutter, bookkeeper, railroad clerk, pharmacist, clothing cutter, cable tester, mechanic, general clerk, butter-and-egg jobber, and the like."[2]

Pierson directed Schleifer's dissertation, which Schleifer expanded into *The Making of Tocqueville's "Democracy in America"* and published in 1980. Pierson's mentorship was his last service to Tocqueville scholarship. Indeed, after Pierson had published his own *Tocqueville and Beaumont in America* in

1938, he turned his back on Tocqueville almost completely. Pierson's subsequent projects were a two-volume history of Yale College and a much anticipated and poorly received study of American mobility.[3] His voluminous papers in Yale's Sterling Memorial Library are devoid of Tocqueville materials, save for a copy of his dissertation. As I noted earlier, Pierson delivered a public lecture on Tocqueville on the occasion of the American bicentennial, but aside from that occasion, what is evident is how completely he let Tocqueville go. Fortunately, the French travelers remained welcome in his classroom, and in time Schleifer appeared to pick up the reins and move the scholarship to a further destination.

Schleifer offered a fascinating account of the genesis of his dissertation in an interview with me in his office at the Gill Library at the College of New Rochelle in 1998.

MATTHEW MANCINI: Speaking of Yale, tell me a little bit about Pierson.

JAMES T. SCHLEIFER: Well, the great irony is that when I went to Yale to do graduate work in the history department, I really didn't know anything about George Pierson, and his work on Tocqueville. I did know something about Tocqueville, but not very much at that point.

MM: You went to Hamilton.

JTS: I went to Hamilton College. My initial introduction to Tocqueville was junior year abroad, in France. I took a course at "Sciences Po"—Sciences Politiques—and Jean-Jacques Chevallier was giving his course on the history of political ideas, and one of his favorite political theorists was Tocqueville. So of course there's a chapter in his book which is essentially the text of his course,[4] and he also lectured on Tocqueville in the course. So that was really my introduction. And for some reason I was just interested—who knows exactly why, but something about his ideas interested me. So, I went out and bought a copy of the Gallimard *Democracy in America*, and I'm not sure I really read it fully at that point but I felt compelled to go buy it. . . .

And then I came back for my senior year at Hamilton, and we took a course in American intellectual history. And curiously enough—I mean, in one sense it's logical but in another sense if you're taking a course in American intellectual history, you wouldn't necessarily be reading Tocqueville. But we did. . . . So that was another introduction. . . .

But then I went to Yale for work in American intellectual history, and my thought really was, the reason I went to Yale, largely, was to work with Sidney Ahlstrom. I didn't really know very much about Sidney Ahlstrom except that he was one of the important figures in American intellectual history. I wasn't even interested particularly in religious history. . . .

So I went off to do that. And I arrived in the fall and discovered that he was off on sabbatical in Scotland. And so they simply—I had asked for him as my advisor so of course people who arrive in that situation with their requested advisor gone— they simply assign them to other people in the department, so I was assigned to George Pierson.

And he was a very formidable character, very formidable. Over the long run as I worked with him I got to know him and we got along very well. But initially he was formidable.

He was teaching a course in . . . really a course in the American character . . . a unique sort of course. But I signed up for it, and the first time I met him as he was to be my advisor he said, "Well, I'd think more of you if you weren't taking my course." And I guess what he meant by that was that most people had the good sense not to take the course of their advisor because if they didn't do well in the course they were in double trouble. So, I guess that's what he meant; I don't know. And I don't know whether he was serious in his remark or just being sarcastic.

But in any case I did take the course and I did a couple of reports on Tocqueville. And toward the end of the year he was talking about possible dissertation topics, and he said, "By the way, there are these wonderful papers of Tocqueville that have been accumulated over the last decades, and there's a lot of work to be done in those papers, particularly relating to the development of the *Democracy*, because we have the working manuscript, and we have the drafts and all of the letters and so on. So really it's a wonderful opportunity for some young scholar to do that."

And for some reason I had the feeling in the class that he was talking to me— you know, that was, again, who knows? but in any case I had that feeling. So . . . the next time that I went to see him, I said, "You know, I am kind of interested in Tocqueville. I'm interested in the French American connection; that's always been something that's fascinated me ever since junior year abroad." So I expressed an interest, and he said, "Well, that's a possibility but if you do that, it's a very important topic. It's a difficult topic. You're not going to be able to finish your dissertation in four or five years and then you're out of here. It's going to take you longer. It's going to be slower. And if you're going to do it you must do it well because you don't want to waste this opportunity for somebody else." And so, he said, "it's going to take time, and you don't want to rush into this."

So he said, "Why don't you write up . . . a little proposal, some comments, analysis . . . think about it some more, and we'll talk some more." So, his initial response was not, you know, throw him in your arms, and there you go. He cautioned me. . . .[5]

We talked about it some more, and finally after we had talked about it a bit, he said, "Well, let's go over . . . and see the Tocqueville papers." And, so, we went over to the Beinecke [Library]. And I went into the vault with him. I mean, you know, we actually went into the book vault. Which they don't let people do. I mean, they bring the papers to you. But in the case of George Pierson, because he had been so important in assembling these papers, obviously he was allowed to do that. . . .

So, we went down to the, whatever level underground it is, to the book vault, and he just stood there, and he pulled the papers off the shelf, box by box. [Smiling] And showed me. "This is the manuscript, and these are drafts, and this is this, this is that." And that ended up being my dissertation. . . . Essentially, I doubled the size of it. I wrote the last two sections or three sections for the book. . . .

MM: More than twenty years ago, Pierson called you "my successor."

JTS: Well.

MM: Was that a help? Or does it make you nervous, or . . .?

JTS: Well, it made me nervous in some ways. The thing is that I am his successor in one sense because what I did with *The Making of "Democracy"* was . . . we both understood it as the next step. Obviously, you do the physical journey; then, you do the mental journey, once the book [*Democracy in America*] is being written. So, I mean, that's how I thought of it; that's how I still think of it. . . . It's the second voyage, as George Pierson called it.[6]

The second voyage, but one life, one work: this was the thrust of Schleifer's argument concerning the key scholarly controversy surrounding Tocqueville in the late twentieth century, that of the continuity and unity of his work. Not all disputes among scholars are bloody, give-no-quarter affairs, despite the attention bestowed on the more melodramatic cases. Indeed, this most conspicuous controversy in the scholarship on Tocqueville was conducted with notable decorum and mutual respect. "There are no absolutists in this debate," wrote Schleifer, one of the key participants.[7] Yet, the debate took place over an issue that is crucial to our understanding of *Democracy in America*. The politeness of the discussion was partly due to the respect paid to its instigator, Seymour Drescher.

The specific point at issue was the relationship between the two volumes that constitute *Democracy in America*. They were published five years apart, in 1835 and 1840. The question was, Do the two volumes cohere into a unified whole, or are they really two different books that only seem to make up one unit because they are yoked together by a single title? In 1985 Drescher dubbed the proponents of these two positions the "lumpers" and the "splitters."[8] The question had first been raised in an article that Drescher published in 1964; it is one of the two or three most important articles on Tocqueville ever published.[9] In it, Drescher contended that certain key clusters of ideas—centralization, individualism, association, revolution— underwent changes between 1835 and 1840 so drastic that they cannot really be reconciled. These changes arose out of the altered political and industrial climate in France by 1840 compared to what had been the case only five years earlier. Other scholars—notably Pierson and Schleifer, later joined by Mansfield and Winthrop—emphasized the continuities in Tocqueville's experiences and the slow evolution of his thinking from the time he was a teenager and viewed the differences between 1835 and 1840 as variations in tone. Schleifer, captain of the lumper force, explained in a survey of the debate why it was important: it "involves answers to when and how some of [Tocqueville's] fundamental ideas emerged and developed."[10]

Drescher's article appeared in the same year as his first book, *Tocqueville and England*, a monograph that literally provided a new perspective on Tocqueville. That Tocqueville was a comparative thinker almost by nature everyone knew. By his travels in America, he intended to comprehend France's present and future condition. Drescher showed that England furnished Tocqueville with "a third society against which he could triangulate the other two."[11] In 1968, he published the most important compilation of Tocqueville texts in English, translated and annotated, that had appeared in one hundred years. *Tocqueville and Beaumont on Social Reform* contained both Beaumont's and Tocqueville's chief writings on slave emancipation, industrialism, pauperism, and prison reform. In an accompanying volume, he provided a study of Tocqueville's reactions to those problems viewed synoptically under the rubric of "modernization."[12] Among them, Drescher's 1964 to 1968 contributions constituted the most important body of Tocqueville scholarship in the 1960s or 1970s.

To some degree, Drescher extends the heritage of the mostly Jewish, Central European, refugee intellectuals who came to their studies of Tocqueville out of a concern to elucidate the nature of liberty. While refugee Central European Tocqueville scholars like Francis Lieber, Michael Heilprin, J. P. Mayer, Albert Salomon, Hannah Arendt, and John Lukacs turned to Tocqueville because he stood in contrast to the would-be slavemasters of Europe, Drescher moved in the opposite direction in his research, from freedom to unfreedom, that is, from studies of Tocqueville as a thinker who was concerned to preserve liberty in modern political regimes predicated on equality to highly sophisticated comparative studies of slavery and slave emancipation in the eighteenth and nineteenth centuries.[13]

Drescher is the son of immigrant Polish Jews: his father, a hatter, was an orphan from a shtetl near Lvov (now Lviv in the Ukraine), and his mother was raised near Warsaw. Drescher recalled how "enthusiastic" his parents always were about the simple fact that they enjoyed basic human freedoms in America rather than the oppression, war, and anti-Semitism that remained the lot of those they had left behind. He was raised on 180th Street in the Bronx and attended City College of New York. Immediately upon graduating in 1955, he married Ruth Lieberman. He received his master's in 1956 with a thesis on French romanticism and the July Monarchy and a Ph.D. in 1960, both from the University of Wisconsin. His director, whom Drescher holds in the highest regard and to whom he dedicated *Dilemmas of Democracy*, was George Mosse. His first teaching job was at Harvard, where he became close to Raymond Aron, the great French sociologist and early French champion of Tocqueville. Aron read and criticized Drescher's dissertation as it was being prepared for publication as *Tocqueville and England*.[14]

Like Schleifer, Drescher also did not intend to devote a scholarly career to Tocqueville when he began graduate school. Yet, when the opportunity arrived, he heard echoes of Tocqueville from his undergraduate years. Drescher's introduction to Tocqueville came in 1954.

SEYMOUR DRESCHER: I was in an honors program at City College in New York, and we had a Great Books series, and one of them was Tocqueville's *Democracy in America*; and I read it and some of the passages struck me as, not just wisdom but poetry. And I remember writing a poem of my own. I think of all the great books I read that year, Tocqueville was the only one about whom I wrote a small poem.

MATTHEW MANCINI: Is the poem still extant?

SD: It probably is somewhere in the bowels of my notes, but I don't have it. It was about . . . Tocqueville starts one of the chapters in the second *Democracy* saying there are certain corners of the world, in which, and he's talking about the Old World, in which you seem to be able to travel back into the past. In America, nothing is like that. Everybody is connected to the present. . . . America is a totally modern society. And it was about that that I wrote this little poem about past and present.

MM: You were a graduate student at Wisconsin. Were you pretty much working on Tocqueville from the start?

SD: No. I went out to Wisconsin without a clear idea of exactly what I wanted to do. I knew I wanted to do something in transnational history, international history, and probably something having to do with intellectuals. And my idea was to do a study of the image of America in France. And I got a Fulbright based on that project. . . . I went to France, and there I discovered that my advisor [René Rémond] had written one of these great French theses on that very project.[15] So what I did was I returned to that earlier poetic moment and decided that, in fact, bubbling at the back of my head, having read both the *Democracy* and the *Ancien Régime*, was that there was a connecting thread—that throughout Tocqueville's life he had had a third society against which he could triangulate the other two. So it fit into my initial interest in transoceanic, transatlantic ideas and the movement of ideas and concepts, but also it referred back to a person who had fascinated me from my undergraduate days.

MM: Who was your advisor?

SD: George Mosse. . . . At that time he was doing things in the Reformation, and he later started to come into twentieth-century Germany. He always felt that I was . . . he said, "How can you study a man like Tocqueville? He's so sane, so liberal." George was interested of course in studying Nazism and the irrational and the exotic sources of irrational thought in the twentieth century. . . .

I certainly was not looking at Jacksonian America. I was not interested in that aspect, except insofar as it told me something about Tocqueville. And I was really not interested in his grasping at the essence of America. What I wanted, what I became interested in, was how did he construct his view of the world, and this is one of the reasons I became interested in England. I felt that Tocqueville was this intensely comparative person, who comes to the United States precisely because he wants both to synthesize the future and to get at what's happening and what is possible through comparative analysis. To literally put his central focus, France, in perspective by stepping outside that focus, that in fact he had done more than one step, he had made two steps. He had stepped to England, which gave him a double vantage point. . . . And I found very early, I said there is a connection between what he says about democracy in America and what he says about aristocracy *and* democracy in England and they just seemed to fit together; they're almost seamless. . . . I could see it almost immediately on reading the two [*Democracy* and *The Old Regime*], and I thought, "Gee, nobody has picked up on this. Nobody has actually . . . people treat the *Democracy* and the *Ancien Régime* as two different books about two different things rather than one book about Tocqueville's thought.

MM: Do you feel a temperamental affinity with Tocqueville?

SD: Yes. I mean, there's a quality about the man. There's a search for clarity, a sense of not wanting to give into the irrationality at almost any point. Not that he didn't have powerful emotions, but that he wanted to make sure that those emotions were simply driving motives to see the world more clearly, not a place to end up in, to have big experiences, that was not what he was about. He had them— *Fortnight in the Wilderness*—he wrote them down beautifully, but they don't, they're not the central, they're not what he really wants to do. He wants to understand how societies work. Nor does he want to internalize things and say, "This is the way I feel, this is the way the universe is." He wants other people from the outside to see what he has to write and say, "That's the way *things* are"; not "that's the way he is." . . . So, yes, he is more of a scientist than he is a romantic. . . .

It's a message that I transmitted to my students as well.

MM: Is there anything in Tocqueville's method that is reflected in your method?

SD: Oh, absolutely. First of all, the comparative method. I have been comparing endlessly. . . . I ask a question, and I look for a comparative dimension which gives me an alternate possible outcome or an alternate past. How do you get these variations upon a central theme? Tocqueville had equality as his central theme, liberty and nonliberty as his variables, and I do the same thing with all of my work on slavery and abolition.

MM: What did happen for you to make the switch over to being a scholar of emancipation?

SD: Well, you study liberty at the beginning. I mean, basically, I'm tracing Tocqueville's ideas through his desire to save and secure freedom. Then you look at the fact that he's operating in a context and a time in which unfreedom presents itself starkly, in a major way, and he tries to do something about it. And so I started to look at what was his involvement; I mean, what was the French antislavery society like? That was my initial feeler. And then all of a sudden I had my contrast. And it feeds back to the original contrast: mobilized Anglo-America—unmobilized France. All of a sudden, it looks quite clear that there is a Tocquevillean question here: why here and not here? Why does Britain constitute the first mass mobilized [antislavery] society in the world, whereas France not only abolishes but restores slavery with no involvement whatsoever of national opinion?[16]

Drescher's employment of the comparative method and approach to Tocqueville, as I indicated earlier, is hardly unique to him. Indeed, Tocqueville studies virtually demand the comparative approach. It takes a talent and training that only a "comparatively" few scholars can muster, however, which is one reason why good scholarship on Tocqueville in the late twentieth century was so good. Perhaps, too, the one-dimensional approach of looking at Tocqueville as an American commentator accounts for some of the weaknesses in Tocqueville studies.

Certainly there was one influential philosopher whose engagement with Tocqueville could not be considered one-dimensional. Indeed of all the examples we have of leading twentieth-century intellectuals whose works bear Tocqueville's imprint, that of Hannah Arendt is the most mysterious. She herself maintained an almost complete silence concerning Tocqueville's impact on the development of her own distinctive political categories, and although Tocqueville does appear at crucial moments in her works and is duly cited, the references are more or less in passing and oblique.

Hanna Fenichel Pitkin's assertion in 1998 that Arendt never "discussed Tocqueville's ideas systematically," however, was inaccurate, for Arendt gave several lectures on Tocqueville during a course on the history of political theory at Pitkin's own institution, the University of California, Berkeley, in 1955. But Pitkin came close to the essence of the matter when she wrote of

Tocqueville as one of Arendt's two "hidden intellectual debts" (the other being Karl Marx). "Hidden" expresses the matter well: Arendt never paid special tribute to Tocqueville or acknowledged his influence on her. Only in one instance did she make any disclosure on the matter, and then only in response to a direct query from an enterprising graduate student. Even that single acknowledgment was couched in the most abstract terms possible: Tocqueville had exercised a "great influence" on her, she told Drescher in a letter of March 12, 1959—and then she declined to elaborate.[17]

No wonder, then, that Tocqueville hardly figured prominently in earlier efforts to explicate Arendt's work. This silence has been especially regrettable because understanding Arendt properly is an enterprise that depends on reliable interpreters even more than is the case for most other serious thinkers. This need for careful interpretation is due chiefly to the fact that, as the leading Arendt scholar Margaret Canovan stressed, Arendt simply "did not make great efforts to communicate her ideas." In a 1965 interview, Arendt maintained that her motive for writing had always been "her own desire to understand, and writing was a part of the process of understanding."[18] While there is certainly reason for skepticism about this remark—it could function as a stratagem of concealment as effectively as of revelation—it is nevertheless true that Arendt's work is often maddeningly imprecise in terminology and confusing in organization, hence more dependent on careful explicators who proceed with their labors armed with a full awareness of context and subtext. Certainly, as the furor over Arendt's love affair with Martin Heidegger revealed, where such careful contextualization was lacking, the commentary obscured far more than it clarified about Arendt's place in the history of political thought.[19]

It was only at the end of the twentieth century, then, that much attention was directed to the affinities between Tocqueville and Arendt. As late as 1996, Roger Boesche, a scholar who had written about Tocqueville as insightfully as anyone in recent decades, wrote an entire book on the subject of tyranny that included excellent separate analyses of both Tocqueville and Arendt but did not investigate the direct lines of influence between the two that such analyses would seem to demand. And in 1997, Mark Reinhardt perceptively surmised that "Tocqueville's absence from this debate [on Arendt's influences] has, I suspect, more to do with his having less cachet among those now interested in continental philosophy than with the degree of his actual importance to Arendt."[20]

But this situation was subjected to a sudden reversal at the end of the century. Articles on the Tocquevillean themes in Arendt appeared in 1991 and 1995, and by the end of the decade, one distinguished scholar, Pitkin, had gone so far as to posit a triad of Arendt's deepest sources of indebtedness: Heidegger, Marx, and Tocqueville. The last two of these master thinkers were unacknowledged or "absent authorities," Pitkin called them.[21]

Yet if Tocqueville's shadowy presence in Arendt's work was underappreciated until the 1990s, surely the contention that Tocqueville was one of the three most profound influences on Arendt went too far in attempting to state the opposite case. There are several reasons why such privileging of Tocqueville is an overstatement. To begin with, the flimsiness of the documentary record should lead us to proceed with great caution in ascribing such links, even as we concede the logical and spiritual discernment behind the conjectures of Pitkin. Then, there is the matter of just who gets relegated to the margins of Arendt's circle of alleged major authorities by this account. Among the more marginal thinkers in this portrayal would have to be Karl Jaspers, Søren Kierkegaard, and Montesquieu, all of whom are acknowledged major sources of Arendt's ideas. And finally, one has to reckon with the sheer capaciousness of Arendt's mind; as Canovan noted, Arendt's preparatory work for *The Origins of Totalitarianism* during the 1940s consisted of systematically achieving a mastery of the entire tradition of Western political thought—in five languages.[22] "The forms of government under which men live have been very few," Arendt observed in *Origins*; "they were discovered early, classified by the Greeks and have proved extraordinarily long-lived. . . . The fundamental idea [of these findings] did not change in the two and a half thousand years that separate Plato from Kant."[23] Although they can only welcome the careful work that identifies the specific strands of thought linking Tocqueville and Arendt, then, scholars should take care to limit their imputations of direct influence to cases where there is clear documentary evidence, or very strong circumstantial evidence, or unmistakable parallels in thought.

Yet, if we err in making Tocqueville central to Arendt's thinking, we must at the same time recognize how numerous are those thought-parallels, how convincing that circumstantial evidence often is. It is fair to say that the Arendt of *The Origins of Totalitarianism* and Arendt the theorist of evil, were inconceivable without Tocqueville. And, indeed, those two defining themes in Arendt's work showed especially striking family resemblances to Tocqueville's treatment of the same problems. The achievement of Arendt, the political philosopher Jerome Kohn wrote in 2001, was to have "discerned a radically different meaning of politics, whose source was the original clearing, in the midst of a plurality of human beings living, speaking and interacting with one another, of a public space that was brought into existence not for utility but for the sake of human freedom."[24] For such a quest the thought of Tocqueville could provide a positive starting point, as well as a negative one—an example of how to recognize and how to avoid despotism.

Throughout his life, Tocqueville struggled to understand modernity and its greatest peril, a kind of despotism that was utterly new, something mankind had not encountered in all its previous experience, and consequently something prior analysts "in the two and a half thousand years that separate Plato and Kant" had not been afforded the chance to describe or analyze.

The sheer literary power of Tocqueville's hallucinatory vision of despotism makes it one of the greatest set pieces in all political philosophy, comparable in its psychological penetration to the terrifying opening chapter of Thomas Hobbes's *Leviathan*. Tocqueville opened the passage by radically shifting focus from the great mass to the lone individual and then making another reversal back to the mass. He imagined "an innumerable host of men, all alike and equal, endlessly hastening after petty and vulgar pleasures. . . . Each . . . is virtually a stranger to the fate of all the others. . . . He exists in himself and for himself."

> Over these men stands an immense tutelary power, which assumes sole responsibility for securing their pleasure and watching their fate. It is absolute, meticulous, regular, provident, and mild. . . . It likes to see the citizens enjoy themselves, provided that they think of nothing but enjoyment. It gladly works for their happiness but wants to be the sole agent and judge of it. It provides for their security, foresees and takes care of their needs, facilitates their pleasures, manages their most important affairs, directs their industry, regulates their successions, and divides their inheritances. Why not relieve them entirely of the trouble of thinking and the difficulty of living? (*DIA* 818)

As is so often the case in Tocqueville's work, context is of vital importance here. What is so striking at this exact place in *Democracy in America* is the way language fails Tocqueville. Here, one of the great prose stylists of his century, at the precise moment when he attempted to explain modern unfreedom, not only faltered in his use of language but did so openly, almost ostentatiously. In fact, as he took pains to point out, he resorted to the technique of describing a scene or pageant specifically because *theoretical* language had failed him. It is not simply that the dystopian spectacle Tocqueville depicts is one of oppression but that it is oppressive in an unforeseen way—a modern way.

In the tradition of nineteenth-century political discourse, the noun "despotism" was often conventionally linked with the adjective "Oriental." The latter term signified not so much a place or a direction as a time, the time prior to the rise of the Greek polis. The lexicon spoke not of places but of epochs in human history. The Persians had practiced despotism, the Greeks tyranny, and the Romans dictatorship. These regimes had been described and classified in the great tradition of Western political thought. But now, Tocqueville feared he had run out of words to name modernity's unique form of unfreedom. Now there is a new kind of domination "unlike any the world has seen before" (*DIA* 818).

"I search in vain for an expression that exactly reproduces my idea," Tocqueville wrote. "The old words 'despotism' and 'tyranny' will not do. The thing is new, hence I must try to define it, since I cannot give it a name" (*DIA* 818).

In the end, Tocqueville was forced to invent an awkward neologism for the phenomenon, one that he admitted left him quite unsatisfied. He called it "democratic despotism."

Nearly two decades later, toward the end of his life, Tocqueville used the same terms to describe the same kind of eerie spiritual exhaustion that overcame him when he tried to give a name to the uniquely violent character of the French Revolution. "My mind is worn out with forming a clear notion of this object and with looking for ways of painting it well. Independent of everything that is accounted for in the French Revolution, there is something unaccounted for in its spirit and its acts. I sense where the unknown object is, but try as I may, I cannot raise the veil that covers it. I feel this object as if through a strange body preventing me from either touching it well or seeing it."[25]

It is in this conviction—that linguistic failure is the counterpart of the political novelty, that despotism has been made utterly new and cannot be named—that a link between Tocqueville and Arendt can be discovered. Some scholars have argued that Tocqueville's famous vision of soft despotism is so unlike Arendt's theory of totalitarianism or hard despotism that he could not have provided a model for her. Others, especially Margie Lloyd, contended that Tocqueville's incisive censures of slavery, of the treatment of Indians, and of Europe's blood-soaked revolutions, as well as his summons for a new political science, together were so compelling that they did afford a model for Arendt's totalitarianism. Indeed, Lloyd saw Arendt as being so deeply indebted to Tocqueville that she stood "in Tocqueville's shadow."[26]

I would maintain that, contrary to Lloyd's well-argued position, Arendt did not derive her analysis of totalitarianism from Tocqueville's views or arguments but that she was deeply indebted to him nevertheless. That indebtedness originated in Tocqueville's picture of soft despotism, and it consisted of her recognition that despotism's essence had been utterly transformed in the twentieth century.

Tocqueville's greatest contribution to Arendt's enterprise was to have *historicized modern despotism*. He showed that you could not just paste a convenient old label on the new model and remain satisfied that it was but a recent manifestation of an enduring political form.

We might therefore draw this rough analogy between Tocqueville and Arendt: Arendt's concept of totalitarianism was to the twentieth century what Tocqueville's democratic despotism was to the nineteenth. Specifically, the isolated, indifferent, passive citizen with only a semblance of free will formed the basis of the modern "masses" that, in her theory, were the indispensable precondition to the rise of totalitarian movements. Although it was completely novel in Tocqueville's day, the new kind of despotism was to be superseded in our own.

Arendt signaled this point of departure at key points in *The Origins of Totalitarianism*. For example, in stressing the role of ideology in totalitarianism, she characterized Tocqueville's harsh judgment of Arthur de Gobineau's race thinking as a distinctively nineteenth-century form of thought. Nineteenth-century racial opinions, she maintained, "by themselves would hardly have been able to create or, for that matter, to degenerate into racism as a *Weltanschauung* or an ideology. In the middle of the last century, race opinions were still judged by the yardstick of political reason. Tocqueville wrote to Gobineau about the latter's doctrines, 'They are probably wrong and certainly pernicious'" (158).

But the most fruitful text for assessing both the congruence and divergence of Arendt's and Tocqueville's conceptions is the brilliant final chapter that Arendt composed for the revised edition of *Origins of Totalitarianism* in 1967, seventeen years after the first edition, entitled "Ideology and Terror: A Novel Form of Government." Ironically, it is only by going beyond anything Tocqueville ever claimed about modern unfreedom that Arendt allows us to perceive the true nature of her indebtedness to him.

First, the divergence: "In the preceding chapters," she insisted, "we emphasized *repeatedly* that the means of total domination are not only more drastic but that totalitarianism *differs essentially* from the other forms of political oppression known to us as despotism, tyranny and dictatorship" (460). In light of such an adamant and well-supported assertion, it is difficult to see how Lloyd can place Arendt "in Tocqueville's shadow."

Arendt then sought to understand whether totalitarianism "has its own essence and can be compared with and defined like other forms of government such as Western thought has known and recognized since the times of ancient philosophy" (461). Her answer was an emphatic Yes. Totalitarianism's essential qualities are ideology and terror.

Totalitarianism, in a strange sense, is not lawless. Indeed, it claims to implement and advance certain laws, but they are putative laws of nature and of history, not of man. Totalitarianism "def[ies] legality" and, instead, "executes the laws of History or of nature without translating them into standards of right and wrong for individual behavior of men" (462).

In contrast, human legality, true lawfulness, erects fences, establishes zones of peace where men can act creatively and in freedom. Arendt continually contrasts the stability and quietude of these lawful spaces with the turbulence and violent, ceaseless movement of totalitarian societies: "Positive laws . . . are primarily designed to function as stabilizing factors for the ever changing movements of men. [But in totalitarianism] all laws have become laws of movement" (463). Or again: "In these ideologies, the term 'law' itself changed its meaning: from expressing the framework of stability within which human actions and motions can take place, it became the expression of the motion itself" (464). Positive law is what terror deposes. "Terror is the realization of the law of movement" (465).

Like Arendt, Tocqueville contrasted fixity and mobility; it was one of the constant dichotomies informing his work from *Democracy in America* through *The Old Regime and the Revolution.* But the movement he was concerned with was a constant, yet gentle, agitation. In the *Democracy,* he described American society as agitated and monotonous. Here is the other great difference between democracy, even democratic despotism, and totalitarianism: it lies the violence and extremity of the swirling movement of totalitarian society.

Here is Arendt's full statement of the antithesis:

Positive laws in constitutional government are designed to erect boundaries and establish channels of communication between men whose community is continually endangered by the new men born into it. With each new birth, a new beginning is born into the world, a new world has potentially come into being. The stability of the laws corresponds to the constant motion of all human affairs, a motion which can never end as long as men are born and die. The laws hedge in each new beginning and at the same time assure its freedom of movement, the potentiality of something entirely new and unpredictable; the boundaries of positive laws are for the political existence of man what memory is for his historical existence: they guarantee the pre-existence of a common world, the reality of some continuity which transcends the individual life span of each generation, absorbs all new origins and is nourished by them. (465)

Then she proceeded not only to describe tyranny using the metaphor of the desert but also to show how the desert of tyranny is itself superseded by that new thing in totalitarianism, ceaseless, violent flux, so that the desert is tormented by a continual sandstorm. These are absolutely crucial issues for Arendt. "To abolish the fences of laws between men—as tyranny does—means to take away man's liberties and destroy freedom as a living political reality; for the space between men as it is hedged in by laws, is the living space of freedom. Total terror uses this old instrument of tyranny but destroys at the same time also the lawless, fenceless wilderness of fear and suspicion which tyranny leaves behind. This desert, to be sure, is no longer a living space of freedom, but it still provides some room for the fear-guided movements and suspicion-ridden actions of its inhabitants" (466).

The influence of Tocqueville reveals itself at this moment of her divergence from him. The old, truly Tocquevillean unfreedom has been blown apart by the new century's new sandstorm.

In her bringing together Tocqueville with great figures in Western political thought, Arendt exemplified another recent trend in the literature, that of comparative studies of Tocqueville and other founders of modern political theory. Tocqueville could truly be said to be a touchstone late in the twentieth century not only because of his high reputation but also because, when comparative studies in the history of political thought were published, it seemed it was invariably Tocqueville to whom other thinkers were likened. Outstanding examples of such studies in comparative political theory in the 1990s were Dominick La Capra's *History and Reading* (2000); Irena Grudzinska Gross's *The Scar of Revolution* (1991), on Tocqueville and the Marquis de Custine, sojourner in backward Russia; and George Armstrong Kelley's *The Humane Comedy* (1992), a study of French liberalism that contrasted Tocqueville and Benjamin Constant.[27] Kelley, a distinguished intellectual historian at Johns Hopkins who died in 1987 before *The Humane Comedy* was completed, illuminated the intellectual context of French liberalism and argued by means of a comparison of Tocqueville, Joseph Renan, and Gustave Flaubert that it ascended during the course of the nineteenth century to a position of a detached, or "Parnassian," liberalism. Parnassian liberalism "is the resort of a doctrine in retreat from political competition to spheres of culture and criticism, where it stands its ground," Kelley wrote (222). By that process of retreat, "true political liberalism was more or less lost to the French as a way of conceiving and carrying out public business for more than a century" (224). While Tocqueville never succumbed to such disillusion, Kelley argued, Renan "refused to be politicized" (224), and Flaubert fled from politics in disgust.

La Capra, Kelley, and Gross limited their extended direct comparisons to two figures. In analyses that must have been geometrically rather than arithmetically more difficult, Bruce James Smith (1985) and Alan Kahan (1992) wrote very provocative studies comparing Tocqueville to not one but two major figures in the history of political thought. Smith delicately orchestrated a dance among Niccolò Machiavelli, Edmund Burke, and Tocqueville in order to examine the interplay between memory and politics in the development of republican politics and culture.[28] Yet Kahan's study was even bolder and more rewarding because the three figures he brought together came from the same historical "moment" in the Hegelian sense: Jacob Burckhardt, John Stuart Mill, and Tocqueville. Among Kahan's objectives was to establish a framework for understanding the history of European liberalism between the reign of Louis Philippe and the Franco-Prussian War. For him, Burckhardt, Mill, and Tocqueville shared the same fears that had always plagued Western humanism, and such anxieties provided a justification for viewing the three great thinkers in terms of their affinities, indeed as classic exemplars of a peculiar kind of liberalism that Kahan labeled "aristocratic liberalism." Kahan made creative use of Pierre Bourdieu's concept of bohemia and Karl Mannheim's notion of the "socially unattached intelligentsia" to suggest the reasons for the aristocratic liberals' sense of intellectual isolation, as well as the failure of their liberalism to become attached to concrete political organizations.[29] In their common pursuit of this theme of understanding European liberalism, Kelley's and Kahan's books make good companion pieces, but a rushed reader would be well advised to pick up the latter volume first.

La Capra's *History and Reading* also fit into this comparative-study category, and its practice of setting Tocqueville and Michel Foucault into dialog, without minimizing the differences in objectives, methods, or historical vision between the two, contrasted sharply with a one-dimensional comparative study—such an oxymoron is needed to describe the work—by Bruce Frohnen, *Virtue and the Promise of Conservatism* (1993), in which Tocqueville's thought was simply assimilated into the conservatism of Burke. Frohnen's method was to explain key elements of Burke's conservatism, then to contend that Tocqueville was a Burkean à la Frohnen's description. Central to this strategy was his insistence that Tocqueville abhorred theory or abstract thought of any sort ("general ideas are tyrannical by nature"), a characteristic he was supposed to share with Burke and all subsequent conservatives.[30] But such a position distorts Tocqueville's thought massively, a problem, as we have seen, endemic in attempts to assimilate Tocqueville to Burke since the days of E. L. Godkin during the Civil War. Tocqueville's distrust of abstract theory was, like nearly every idea he held, subtle, ambiguous, and predicated on particular, but changeable, circumstances. Abstractions were indeed not what the Cartesian French needed in the nineteenth century, Tocqueville thought. But the down-to-earth Americans were in fact sorely in need of such general concepts because in democratic societies mores, education, and desires combine to drag the hearts and minds of citizens to earth. Indeed Tocqueville explicitly argued that "men who live in democratic times cannot fail to perfect the industrial [practical] aspects of science, and . . . henceforth the social power should direct all its efforts to supporting advanced studies and fostering great scientific passions. Nowadays the human mind needs to be *forced to concentrate on theory*" (DIA 527–28, emphasis added). Historian Susan Dunn expressed the issue with precise good sense. Tocqueville, she argued, "wrote a prescription for the healthy partnership of Burke's two antagonists, abstract theory and political experience, ideas and power."[31]

Among the characteristics that set La Capra, Kelley, and especially Kahan apart from Frohnen was the former trio's use of the comparative method in a search for a better understanding of something outside the immediate object of their analysis; for Kelley and Kahan, it was European liberalism, for La Capra, the state of scholarship in French studies. While for Frohnen the greater goal was to describe a certain conservative ideal, his deployment of Tocqueville was wholly subordinated to the political project of establishing Burke as the patriarch of conservative thought.

I hope readers might find it appropriate, rather than merely disheartening, that I conclude this book with an example of a misreading of Tocqueville that sports a pedigree nearly a century and a half old. Not only Tocqueville's works, but also Americans' beliefs about how Tocqueville has been received in the past, are subjects that have been vulnerable to that "loss and decay, neglect, and iconoclasm" that Frank Kermode observed was the fate of many great books.

In these pages I have argued that Tocqueville never did sink below the chilling waters of oblivion after the Civil War but remained, rather, a continuous presence in American intellectual life. Scholars who adopted the oblivion narrative were eager to position themselves on the cutting edge of their very competitive fields, or they rushed to unsustainable conclusions about prior generations when they noticed how Tocqueville's visibility increased after World War II, or they simply took earlier historians' (often undocumented) assertions as established fact. There is nothing particularly shocking or mendacious about these approaches. As Tocqueville put it in Volume II of the *Democracy*, a strictly Cartesian approach to all life's problems would present impossible burdens. Descartes had exalted the ability of each individual's unaided powers of reasoning to allow him or her to reach clear and distinct conclusions. Americans were the most Cartesian of all peoples, Tocqueville argued with considerable wit and irony, because "The American relies solely on the unaided effort of his own individual reason," and Cartesianism means that one seeks "on one's own and in oneself alone the reasons for things" (*DIA* 483). Yet the ordinary actions and decisions of everyday life would be rendered impossible if each person really did "rely on individual judgment" for every such decision. Therefore people require certain dogmas, ideas that become accepted without critical judgment: "It is . . . impossible to eliminate the existence of dogmatic beliefs, by which I mean opinions that men accept on faith and without discussion" (*DIA* 489). Opinions passed on by good scholars are taken up and accepted by those who come after them because it is neither possible nor beneficial to the advancement of knowledge to verify every assertion by returning to original sources and applying one's individual judgment to every scrap of evidence. Applying this insight to the scholarship about Tocqueville's stature for American intellectuals, we can say that Tocqueville's eclipse became, in Tocqueville's definition, a dogma.

If there is something to be said in extenuation of historians who thought Tocqueville had been visiting the Underworld following the Civil War, however, there was one aspect of the portrayal that was more susceptible to criticism. Especially obvious is the fact that these oblivion claims were wholly anachronistic. If Tocqueville was not, as Robert Nisbet put it, very much "footnoted" after 1870, that was because, outside of the natural sciences, people did not write footnote citations in the 1870s. Indeed, the entire line of reasoning about Tocqueville's reception that is based on the number of articles presumes the existence of a scholarly infrastructure and apparatus that did not come into existence in anything like the form that would be required to support such oblivion arguments until after World War II. Ironically, Drescher's claim that 44 percent of the scholarship on Tocqueville appeared from 1950 to 1969 might be applied to almost any subject or writer of the nineteenth century. As to quantifying scholarly publications, then, one might plausibly contend that the increase in the number of articles on Tocqueville was due as much to the GI Bill, the massive expansion of higher education, the emergence of an academic army of Ph.D.'s, the explosion in the number of scholarly journals in the social sciences and humanities, and the intensification of the expectation that professors must publish in those journals or face losing their jobs, as to any purported deep resonance that Tocqueville established with postwar America. If quantitative measures are to be deployed, perhaps the more pertinent statistic would be that, while the population of the United States doubled between 1947 and 2000, the number of college students rose from 2.3 million to 15.3 million persons.[32]

Moreover, all of the publications on Tocqueville that appeared in the late nineteenth century were occasional; that is, they were brought on by a particular event, or occasion. In almost all cases, the occasion was the appearance of a new book or a new edition. Such was simply the nature of intellectual journalism in the late nineteenth century. There were no scholarly journals of the modern type to which professors or other intellectual workers sent in their essays for peer review and publication; there were only reviews or, in some cases, essays on broader topics for which the publication of a new book or article served as a pre-text.[33]

So if articles on Tocqueville appeared less frequently in and after the 1870s, it was for an exceedingly mundane reason: Tocqueville died. His voice was silenced and his pen laid down. As I have discussed in the preceding pages, editions, translations, and previously unpublished writings such as correspondence appeared quite regularly between 1861 and 1868; but after the final volume in a nine-volume set of *oeuvres complètes* landed on the desks of literary editors in 1868, there was, in a sense, little more to say. There would be no more occasions or events to which a Michael Heilprin or E. L. Godkin might respond.

If Tocqueville had fallen off the cliff of public memory in 1870 or so, then his absence should have been more noticeable to later historians by virtue of its contrast with the presence of other important thinkers. But Tocqueville's treatment accords with that given to other, comparable figures. One example is Mill. The case of Mill publications, in fact, furnishes an interesting control group for testing this issue. Two events of great significance for Mill scholarship occurred in 1873. The first was the publication of Mill's great *Autobiography*, and the second was Mill's demise. An examination of *Poole's Index* reveals that a small number of articles about Mill and his ideas appeared in

American publications during the 1860s and early 1870s. Not surprisingly, 1873 and 1874 saw an increase in such articles, but in the years after 1874, Mill articles drop almost completely from the tables of contents of America's periodical literature. In 1882, a British article was reprinted here in several venues, but before and after that time the silence about the greatest philosopher of liberty in the British tradition is deafening. Was Mill, then, consigned to oblivion, erased, utterly neglected? Did signs of interest in his greatest works in the twentieth century constitute a revolution in tastes and intellectual fashions? Did Mill, in short, have to be presented anew to an intellectual community who had completely forgotten about him? Few would argue such a case; yet in the case of Tocqueville that is precisely the received story of his post–Civil War reputation.

In summary, then, late-nineteenth-century articles in periodicals were occasional. Almost without exception they were review essays. When a particular writer died his output ceased and so did articles about it. The modern apparatus of scholarly citation also did not exist. The population of active scholars was tiny after the Civil War, and not until the 1890s did a market for the Ph.D. in the social sciences begin to emerge.[34] There were only eleven professors of history in the United States in 1880.[35] Some journals in the social sciences originated in that and the following decade, most notably the *American Political Science Review* (1886) and the *American Historical Review* (1895). Their second-generation counterparts were the *Political Science Quarterly*, founded in 1906, and the *Mississippi Valley Historical Review*, later the *Journal of American History*, which first appeared in 1914. The decline in the number of articles about Tocqueville is roughly comparable to the attention received by other political philosophers. Most important, the methodology used to measure Tocqueville's presence in American intellectual life in the fifty years after the Civil War was not appropriate to the subject matter. Besides being anachronistic, quantitative measurements in this case failed to register effects that appear when the articles themselves are carefully read and construed in context.

In the same manner, a search for the roots of the notion that Tocqueville was considered passé as the twentieth century opened reveals those roots' shallow penetration and circumscribed extent. The success of James Bryce's *American Commonwealth* was to some degree predicated on his successful displacement of Tocqueville as chronicler of American institutions. His intimate and influential friend A. V. Dicey reinforced these images of Tocqueville's obsolescence and Bryce's timeliness, and many years later Dicey's animadversions were literally torn out of context and added to the stack of phony evidence concerning the deepening obscurity that had purportedly enveloped the figure of Tocqueville.

The evidence is also indisputable that Pierson's *Tocqueville and Beaumont in America* did not, as so much of the literature on Tocqueville maintains, simply make an entrance onto a bare and empty stage, but rather onto a stage covered with well-wrought scenery and populated by costumed actors—some of whom were luminaries—in front of a full house. What is striking to the twenty-first–century observer about these "pre-Pierson" commentators on Tocqueville is not merely the sense of their comfort and familiarity with the texts and ideas in question but also the degree to which their work assumes a like familiarity on the part of their readers. Nowhere among these works do we encounter a scholar presenting his or her findings as a far-reaching rediscovery or a bold foray into obscure recesses of American intellectual history. Tocqueville was a given. His works, like those of any other master thinker, demanded rethinking and refashioning as a matter of course, as social conditions and intellectual preoccupations were altered by a continuously evolving society and culture. But that his work was familiar, even renowned, that he was canonical, and that he constituted an indispensable guide to modern political formations: these facts are abundantly evident from the scholarly literature.

As we have also seen, so pervasive was the conventional wisdom on this matter that writers continually, if unconsciously, resorted to question-begging arguments. We have noted, for instance, how some eminent historians disputed about the reasons for Tocqueville's disappearance without checking first to see if the disappearance was real; or brought antithetical arguments to bear to explain that same alleged absence; or argued in circular fashion that the success of the George Lawrence translation of the *Democracy* grew out of an "explosion" in the attention Tocqueville received in the 1950s and 1960s, and also that the success of the Lawrence translation demonstrated the Tocqueville explosion, while neglecting to provide independent evidence of the existence either of the explosion or of the success. A search for evidence of those putative events came up, if not quite empty, at best with only meager results.

Consensus history, and Tocqueville's link to it, suffer likewise from a deficit of compelling evidence. Consensus history was a hypothesis that John Higham put forward in a nonscholarly magazine article. It was a hypothesis that he quickly and drastically modified—indeed fled from—after he considered the question in a more sober fashion. Higham also linked Tocqueville with that abandoned hypothesis. His principal source for positing consensus and connecting it, in a purely rhetorical fashion, to Tocqueville was a series of lectures by Daniel Boorstin in which Tocqueville was never mentioned. If the disappearance of Tocqueville had become a widely accepted "fact" that turned out to be, as Mark Twain said in another context, greatly exaggerated, so was the revival, resurrection, or boom of interest in Tocqueville in the quarter of a century after World War II.

In almost two centuries of attention to his life and work, Americans have made a great many things out of Alexis de Tocqueville. He has been an impartial observer and a partisan French nationalist; a defender of liberty and a supporter of colonial domination. Some commentators thought he was quite British, for a Frenchman; and others insisted on Americanizing him. Cultural conservatives thought his ideas fit in just fine with Burke's; while others deployed poststructuralist reading strategies to reveal new meanings in his many ambivalences. John Graham Brooks thought he was a Progressive reformer; Francis Lieber believed Tocqueville was so important a thinker as to be on a par with Lieber himself. Some writers used him in ornamental fashion, even though his specific ideas were not particularly germane to their analyses. To Central European refugee scholars like Albert Salomon, Hannah Arendt, and John Lukacs, he furnished an indispensable frame of reference for understanding the modern, that is postaristocratic, world. Meanwhile, scholars of great talent and accomplishment have gone about their business, producing work that met the highest standards of evidence and argument, as well as reader interest. The American academy has been enormously enriched by Tocqueville's presence in and through these scholars' contributions. What should be obvious, however, is that, conceding the natural ebbs and flows that accompany any thinker's interpretation history, the American focus on Tocqueville never really faltered since the day he stepped aboard the *Le Havre* in the spring of 1831 with Beaumont at his side.

Notes

1. Lamberti, *Tocqueville and the Two Democracies*, 1.

2. George W. Pierson to A. Whitney Griswold, July 15, 1957, quoted in Peter Novick, *That Noble Dream: The 'Objectivity Question' and the American Historical Profession* (Cambridge: Cambridge University Press, 1988), 366.

3. George Wilson Pierson, *Yale College: An Educational History 1871–1921* (New Haven, Conn.: Yale University Press, 1952), *Yale: The University College 1921–1937* (New Haven, Conn.: Yale University Press, 1955), and *The Moving American* (New York: Knopf, 1973).

4. Jean-Jacques Chevallier, *Les grandes œuvres politiques de Machiavel à nos jours* (Paris: A. Colin, 1949).

5. This approach replicated that taken by Pierson's own mentor, John M. S. Allison, many years before. See Pierson, "Tocqueville's Visions of Democracy," 9.

6. Schleifer interview.

7. James T. Schleifer, "How Many Democracies?" in *Liberty, Equality, Democracy*, ed. Eduardo Nolla (New York: New York University Press, 1992), 354.

8. Seymour Drescher, "More Than America: Comparison and Synthesis in *Democracy in America*," in *Reconsidering*, 77–93.

9. Seymour Drescher, "Tocqueville's Two *Démocraties*," *Journal of the History of Ideas* 25, no. 2 (April–June 1964): 201–16.

10. Schleifer, "How Many Democracies?" 354. A persuasive lumper argument is Kloppenberg's "Life Everlasting," esp. 25–31, while a splitter rebuttal is in Kammen's *Alexis de Tocqueville and "Democracy in America,"* esp. 31–34.

11. Drescher interview.

12. Drescher, *Tocqueville and Beaumont on Social Reform* (New York: Harper Torchbooks, 1968); Drescher, *Dilemmas of Democracy: Tocqueville and Modernization* (Pittsburgh: University of Pittsburgh Press, 1968).

13. See, especially, Seymour Drescher, *Econocide: British Slavery in the Era of Abolition* (Pittsburgh: University of Pittsburgh Press, 1977), *Capitalism and Antislavery: British Mobilization in Comparative Perspective* (New York: Oxford University Press, 1987), *From Slavery to Freedom: Comparative Studies in the Rise and Fall of Atlantic Slavery* (New York: New York University Press, 1999), *A Historical Guide to World Slavery*, ed. with Stanley L. Engerman (New York: Oxford University Press, 1998), and *The Mighty Experiment: Free Labor versus Slavery in British Emancipation* (New York: Oxford University Press, 2002).

14. Drescher interview; Drescher, telephone conversation with the author, February 19, 2003; *Contemporary Authors*, vol. 94 (Detroit: Gale, 2001); an article derived from Drescher's master's thesis is "America and French Romanticism during the July Monarchy," *American Quarterly* 11, no. 1 (Spring 1959): 3–20.

15. René Rémond, *Les Etats-Unis devant l'opinion Française, 1815–1852*, 2 vols. (Paris: Colin, 1962).

16. Drescher interview.

17. Hanna Fenichel Pitkin, *The Attack of the Blob: Hannah Arendt's Concept of the Social* (Chicago: University of Chicago Press, 1998), 116; "History of Political Theory," Subject file, Hannah Arendt Papers, Manuscript Division, Library of Congress, Washington, D.C.; Suzanne D. Jacobitti, "Individualism and Political Community: Arendt and Tocqueville on the Current Debate in Liberalism," *Polity* 23, no. 4 (Summer 1991): 586n3; Seymour Drescher, telephone conversation with author, October 1998.

18. Margaret Canovan, *Hannah Arendt: A Reinterpretation of Her Political Thought* (Cambridge: Cambridge University Press, 1992), 2.

19. Mark Lilla convincingly demonstrated both of these points by the cogency of his attack on Elzbieta Ettinger's *Hannah Arendt/Martin Heidegger* and with his own reflections

on the love affair between Arendt and her teacher: "Ménage à Trois," *New York Review of Books* 46, no. 18 (November 18, 1999), 35–38, and "The Perils of Friendship," *New York Review of Books* 46, no. 19 (December 2, 1999), 25–29.

20. See, in addition to Pitkin, *Attack of the Blob*, and Jacobitti, "Individualism and Political Community," Margie Lloyd, "In Tocqueville's Shadow: Hannah Arendt's Liberal Republicanism," *Review of Politics* 57, no. 1 (Winter 1995): 31–58; Roger Boesche, *Theories of Tyranny from Plato to Arendt* (University Park: Pennsylvania State University Press, 1996); Mark Reinhardt, *The Art of Being Free: Taking Liberties with Tocqueville, Marx, and Arendt* (Ithaca, N.Y.: Cornell University Press, 1997), 217–18n8.

21. Pitkin, *Attack of the Blob*, 115–44.

22. Canovan, *Hannah Arendt*, 67.

23. Hannah Arendt, *The Origins of Totalitarianism*, new edition with added prefaces (New York: Harcourt Brace Jovanovich, 1968). Subsequent references appear parenthetically in the text.

24. Jerome Kohn, "The World of Hannah Arendt," *Library of Congress Information Bulletin* 60, no. 3 (March 2001): 60.

25. Tocqueville, *Selected Letters*, 373.

26. Lloyd, "In Tocqueville's Shadow."

27. Irena Grudzinska Gross, *The Scar of Revolution: Custine, Tocqueville and the Romantic Imagination* (Berkeley: University of California Press, 1991); George Armstrong Kelley, *The Humane Comedy: Constant, Tocqueville, and French Liberalism* (Cambridge: Cambridge University Press, 1992). Subsequent references appear parenthetically in the text. The discussion here is based on my review in *Nineteenth-Century French Studies* 21, nos. 3 and 4 (Spring–Summer 1993): 532–34.

28. Bruce James Smith, *Politics and Remembrance: Republican Themes in Machiavelli, Burke, and Tocqueville* (Princeton, N.J.: Princeton University Press, 1985).

29. Kahan, *Aristocratic Liberalism*, 159–65.

30. Frohnen, *Virtue*, 105; this discussion follows my review in *Journal of American History* 81, no. 1 (June 1994): 272–73.

31. Susan Dunn, "Revolutionary Men of Letters and the Pursuit of Radical Change: The Views of Burke, Tocqueville, Adams, Madison, and Jefferson," *William and Mary Quarterly* 53, no. 4 (October 1996): 733–34.

32. U.S. Bureau of the Census, School Enrollment, Historical Table 6-A, at www.census.gov/population/www/socdemo/school.html (accessed February 5, 2005).

33. See Larzer Ziff, "Upon What Pretext? The Book and Literary History," *Proceedings of the American Antiquarian Society* 95, no. 2 (October 1985): 297–315.

34. Bender, *Intellect and Public Life*, 131.

35. Holt, *Historical Scholarship*, 8.

Index

In this index, T stands for Alexis de Tocqueville

About the Author

MATTHEW MANCINI is professor and chair of the Department of American Studies at Saint Louis University. He is the author of *Alexis de Toqueville* and *One Dies, Get Another: Convict Leasing in the American South, 1866–1928*.